J. C. NICHOLS AND THE SHAPING OF KANSAS CITY

J. C. NICHOLS
AND THE SHAPING OF
KANSAS CITY

———

Innovation in Planned Residential Communities

WILLIAM S. WORLEY

UNIVERSITY OF MISSOURI PRESS
COLUMBIA AND LONDON

University of Missouri Press, Columbia, Missouri 65201
Printed and bound in the United States of America

5 4 3 2 1   94 93 92 91 90

Library of Congress Cataloging-in-Publication Data
Worley, William S.
    J. C. Nichols and the shaping of Kansas City : innovation in
planned residential communities / William S. Worley.
        p.   cm.
    Includes bibliographical references.
    ISBN 0-8262-0744-8 (alk. paper)
    1. Urbanization—Missouri—Kansas City—History—20th century.
2. Nichols, Jesse Clyde.   3. Real estate developers—Missouri—Kansas
City—Biography.   4. Real estate development—Missouri—Kansas City—
History—20th century.   I. Title.
HT384.U52K368   1990
333.77'15'092—dc20
    [B]   90-35052
                                                                  CIP

⊚™ This paper meets the requirements of the
American National Standard for Permanence of Paper
for Printed Library Materials, Z39.48, 1984.

Designer: Darin M. Powell

Typesetter: Connell-Zeko Type & Graphics

Printer: Thomson-Shore, Inc.

Binder: Thomson-Shore, Inc.

Type face: Galliard

For Kathryn

CONTENTS

PREFACE

This study of J. C. Nichols and the beginnings of planned residential development in the United States is based on original research using available company records from the J. C. Nichols Company, the Roland Park Company records at Cornell University, and the verbatim *Proceedings* of a series of annual conferences held in 1917–1919 on expensive subdivisions and chaired by Nichols. The author was not able to utilize the business records of the J. C. Nichols Company. According to J. Clyde Nichols, Jr., most of the personal correspondence of Nichols for the period under study was destroyed after his death in 1950 by his secretary. A small portion of Nichols's personal correspondence with his children during the 1940s is available at the Western Historical Manuscript Collection at the University of Missouri–Kansas City.

The Western Historical Manuscript Collection has done a significant work in microfilming the company scrapbooks and obtaining the existing personal records of Nichols from the Nichols Company. The scrapbooks contain newspaper clippings, some copies of legal documents on land development, personal recollections of the compiler, Mrs. Faye Littleton (a long-time company employee), and many examples of company brochures and promotional materials.

It must be noted that the available sources tend to portray Nichols in a favorable light. The scrapbooks, advertisements, and newspaper clippings all fall into that category. This study focuses on Nichols's role in urban development and therefore uses these mostly positive assessments for their contributions to understanding development sequence and city growth patterns. Other sources, such as the Grantor List and Plat Book records, are neutral with regard to Nichols. The *Proceedings* of the annual conferences of the Developers of High Class Residential Property for the years 1917, 1918, and 1919 are actually more neutral than might be initially apparent. These documents were distributed only to the men actually present, with the provision that the documents were not to be shown to anyone but their most important employees. The Cornell Library acquired them directly from one of the participants, Robert Jemison of Birmingham, Alabama, more than two decades after Nichols's death. If the Nichols Company retains its copies of these documents, they were not made available. As a result of the anticipated restrictions on the use of the *Proceedings,* the participants were quite candid in their comments.

Using so much material from sources favorably disposed toward Nichols could conceivably create an aura of sainthood around the principal actor. The focus here, however, is on viewing Nichols's work in the context of his own time and in comparison with similar developments during the pre–World War I period. What follows is not presented as biography, although biographical components necessarily form part of the analysis; rather, it is presented as a study of a firm that was a pioneer and synthetic catalyst in developing a method of homebuilding and land subdivision that came to dominate the North American urban scene in the late 1940s and 1950s.

Other sources utilized include the *National Real Estate Journal* and additional resources available in the Library of the National Association of Realtors in Chicago, along with an extensive survey of the company advertisements in the *Kansas City Star* between 1903 and 1950. This time frame was chosen to commence with Nichols's first residential construction and to conclude with the developer's death in February 1950. These company advertisements were almost always placed in the Sunday issue of the paper after 1908, as were articles of relevance to real estate activity in the Kansas City area. The newspaper search focused on these Sunday listings. After 1940, the company did less specific advertising for individual subdivisions on the Kansas side.

This book is a revision of the author's dissertation (cited in the bibliography), which was defended at the University of Kansas in May 1986. Serious students of the city building process and Nichols's place in that process will want to consult the dissertation for its more complete explanatory notes on certain subjects.

The author wishes to acknowledge the assistance of the staff of the Western Historical Manuscript Collection, the National Board of Realtors Library, the Manuscripts and Archives Section of the Olin Research Library at Cornell University, the support staff of the Llano Estacado Center for Research and Advanced Professional Studies (LECAPSR) at Eastern New Mexico University, and the public relations staff of the J. C. Nichols Company. Their help and direction are most appreciated.

All of the illustrations in this book are reproduced courtesy of the Western Historical Manuscript Collection at the University of Missouri–Kansas City, which is a joint collection of the University of Missouri and the State Historical Society of Missouri. The negative number used by that organization to identify the individual photograph is given at the end of the caption. The original photographs were furnished for reproduction by the J. C. Nichols Company. Their support of the reproduction costs is hereby acknowledged, and particular thanks go to Lee M. Fowler and his staff in the Public Relations department of the Nichols Company.

Three people are most responsible for the development of these ideas into manuscript form. First, Dr. Lloyd Sponholtz of the University of Kansas helped the author pick up this project at a critical point and see the dissertation phase through to completion. Second, David Boutros worked at the Missouri Valley Room of the Kansas City Public Library when I first met him. After moving to the Western Historical Manuscript Collection in Kansas City, he tirelessly suggested sources and assisted in the formulation of concepts. In the final stages, David also guided the process of reproducing the photographs, which greatly enhance the usefulness of the text. From that position he also suggested the manuscript to Dr. Louis Potts, the third important person in this process. Dr. Potts suggested the manuscript to the staff of the University of Missouri Press and invited the author to present a Henry Haskell Lecture at UMKC on Nichols in April 1989. Thanks go to all three of these helpful gentlemen.

One other gentleman was quite helpful at an early stage of this research. Dr. Richard Coleman, now Professor of Marketing at Kansas State University, employed the author as a research assistant in 1979–1980. Many of his insights are reflected in the text and notes.

Most recently, the author has had the pleasure of working closely with editor Rick Boland of the University of Missouri Press. Rick's thoroughly professional editing, timely advice, and occasional brilliant company over lunch have made the final preparation of this manuscript most enjoyable and satisfying.

The help, love, and support of the author's parents, Olan and the

late Roberta Smith Worley, were essential. The patience and understanding of three young men, Jon, Matthew, and Aaron Worley, as
they put up with long absences and increased chores because "Daddy's working on his book," have been a continual inspiration.

To my wife, Kathryn, who did not type the manuscript and was
only occasionally able to do a little editing, but who literally gave up
ten years of her own goals, ambitions, hopes, and dreams so that the
dissertation on which this book is based might be completed, this
work is gratefully dedicated.

CHRONOLOGY

The Life of Jesse Clyde Nichols and the Development Sequence of the Country Club District

1880
Nichols is born in Olathe, Kansas, to middle-class farmer-merchant parents.

1887
Plat of Bismark Place is filed.

1902
Nichols graduates at the top of class at the University of Kansas and receives a one-year scholarship to attend Harvard University.

1903
Nichols receives a second bachelor of arts degree from Harvard and returns to the Midwest to look at land development possibilities.

1903–1904
Nichols and his fraternity-brother partners, the Reeds, operating as Reed, Nichols & Company, sell land and some completed houses in Kansas City, Kansas, just northwest of Thirteenth Street and Quindaro Boulevard.

1905
The first advertisements for Bismark Place in Kansas City, Missouri, appear in the *Star*.

Plat for portion of Rockhill subdivision filed by W. R. Nelson's Rockhill Realty and Improvement Company.

Nichols marries Jessie Miller of Olathe. They move into one of the first houses completed in the Bismark Place subdivision.

1906
Nichols forms financial alliances with Frank Crowell, Herbert F. Hall, and E. W. Shields (all grain merchants at the Kansas City

Board of Trade), as well as a land development and sales agency agreement with Hugh Ward for the Sunset Hill section.

Plat of Rockhill Annex is filed by the Brush Creek Park Land Company, which lists E. W. Shields as president and J. C. Nichols as secretary. This is the first newly platted area laid out by Nichols.

1907

Beginning with the Rockhill Place plat filed in this year, Nichols files deed restrictions on land use with the plat or on a separate but binding document.

Rockhill Park is platted as the first Nichols subdivision with some streets following the topography rather than right-angle gridiron layouts.

Rockhill Park Extension plat is filed.

First section of conversion of Dodson "dummy" streetcar line from steam to electricity is completed.

First shopping center is built at 55th and Brookside next to the newly completed streetcar stop.

Nichols sells a five-acre tract to the architectural firm of Wilder & Wight. This marks the beginning of the trend toward architect-designed home construction in his areas.

1908

Announcement made of control of 1,000 acres for residential development.

Land sold to St. Theresa's so that the exclusive Catholic girls' school will relocate in the Country Club District, the name first applied to Nichols's developments in this year.

Purchase of 229 acres from the Armour family in Johnson County, Kansas, which will become Mission Hills.

Nichols sets up his own real estate company, which henceforth bears his name in the title.

Nichols named as a director of Commerce Trust Company, thus establishing a long-held local financing and political connection.

Country Side and Country Side Extension subdivisions (owned by Kate Yeomans and sold by Nichols) plats are filed and sales begin.

Sunset Hill is announced as an exclusive subdivision although official plat filing is not done until 1909.

1909

Founding of the Country Club Improvement Association, the first homeowners' association. Membership in the CCIA is voluntary.

Southwood Extension plat is filed by Hall and Shields. They build large homes on this land, which is now the site of the Linda Hall Scientific Library.

Rockhill Heights plat is filed.

Southwood Annex plat is filed.

Nichols's Missouri developments and holdings are included in a successful annexation drive to bring them into the Kansas City, Missouri, incorporated limits. Election is challenged in court. Actual annexation postponed until 1911.

First lot sold in what will become Mission Hills.

Restrictions amended for Rockhill Place subdivision to allow landowners the right to extend restrictions beyond the stated life of the restrictions by majority vote.

1910

Sunset Hill streetcar line commences service up what will become Ward Parkway.

Construction approved for Mill Creek Parkway (now J. C. Nichols Parkway) as far as Brush Creek.

Country Day School organized as a private school for boys. Originally housed in the old Wornall mansion on Wornall Road, Country Day later moved to a campus next to State Line at Ward Parkway, where it combined with Pembroke School to become Pembroke Country Day school.

Wornall Homestead plat is filed by J. C. Nichols Land Company.

First Country Club Ridge plat is filed by J. C. Nichols Realty Company.

Cockin's Addition plat is filed by W. W. Cockins. This land is sold by Nichols on an agency contract.

E. C. White School is established at 51st and Oak streets. In 1913 it will be moved to 49th and Main, on land provided by Nichols. It is now the site of the Plaza Public Library.

1911

Annexation completed by court action. City installs sewage system for Country Club District using Special Benefit District bonds, ultimately paid off by the company or subsequent homeowners.

First plat of Country Club Plaza filed by Grampion Land Company, George F. Law, president. An additional plat is filed in 1912.

First Country Club Heights plat is filed by J. C. Nichols Land Company.

Bowling Green subdivision plat is filed by L. R. Wright with limited deed restrictions. In the 1920s this subdivision petitions and is allowed to be governed by Rockhill Park deed restrictions.

1912

Mansion-building is underway along Santa Fe Road (55th Street) with the Louis Curtiss–designed Corrigan house at the northwest corner of Santa Fe and Ward Parkway nearing completion while the C. S. Keith house (purchased in 1920 by Nichols and occupied by him and his family until his death in 1950) is under construction.

Second Presbyterian Church announces it is purchasing land at 55th and Oak streets to build a new sanctuary for their congregation, which had formerly worshiped on Quality Hill next to what is now the site of H. Roe Bartle Hall.

Nichols begins his "bird campaign" by bringing naturalists to talk to residents about the desirability of attracting birds to the district. Nichols will sell residents birdhouse kits at cost and sponsor essay contests in order to bring attention to the bird population in his areas.

The first Country Club District Lawn and Garden Contest is held to call attention to well-kept lawns and gardens ("backyards" to Nichols).

Nichols gives his first nationally recognized speech to the National Association of Real Estate Boards meeting in Louisville, Kentucky. He becomes involved with Horace McFarland's American Civic Association, which, in turn, involves him in formation of the National Conference of City Planners.

Nichols establishes personal contact with E. H. Bouton, the developer of Roland Park near Baltimore. This initiates a friendship and idea exchange that ends only with Bouton's death in 1940.

Randall and Wheelock's subdivision plat is filed with similar restrictions to those applied in surrounding Nichols property. Like the Bowling Green subdivision (see 1911, above), these residents later petition to come under Nichols's restrictions and protection in the 1920s.

Morningside Park plat is filed by Cowherd Land Company. This adjacent development never came under Nichols restrictions or protection but included quite similar clauses in the Cowherd-written restrictions.

First section of Country Club District subdivision plat is filed by J. C. Nichols Land Company.

Initial section of Mission Hills plat is filed by J. C. Nichols Realty Company and A. C. Jobes (the first lot owner).

1913

First tract in Mission Hills offered for sale.

Westwood Park plat is filed by L. R. Wright with limited deed restrictions. In 1920 Nichols will buy the remainder of this partially developed subdivision from Wright.

Wornall Manor subdivision is platted by the C. H. Wornall Realty Company. Restrictions are similar to Nichols's examples. The plat was notarized in Nichols's offices by his company treasurer, Frank Grant.

Hare & Hare, landscape architects, begin a long association with the Nichols companies in planning residential neighborhoods. First Hare & Hare project is Hampstead Gardens subdivision (not platted until 1917).

Mill Creek Boulevard completed to connections with the beginnings of Nichols-constructed (later donated to the city) Brookside Boulevard and Ward Parkway.

Mission Hills Country Club is organized by Nichols to provide a club for his purchasers who are not able to be members of the Kansas City Country Club.

Sunset Hill School for girls is organized in Mrs. Hugh Ward's home. Campus is later established across Wornall Road from the Walnuts site. Sunset Hill and Pembroke Country Day combined in the mid–1980s to form one coeducational private school with two campuses.

1914

Mission Hills subdivision plat is filed with deed restrictions that will automatically renew unless a majority of landowners vote to disapprove the extension within a stated time limit. Enforcement of restrictions is delegated to the landowners, which usually include the Nichols Company in the early years.

The Mission Hills restrictions establish the first automatic home-owners' association in Nichols' developments, the Mission Hills Homes Company (so named to comply with Kansas law at the time).

Nichols constructs the first "artistically designed" gasoline service stations for automobiles in carefully chosen locations around his developments.

Westwood Park Annex plat is filed by a Kolney B. Wright. This may have been L. R. Wright's son; at any rate, the Annex was bought by Nichols in 1920 as well.

South Country Side is platted by Kate and Edwin Yeomans with the same restrictions as Nichols-controlled land. Nichols had an agency contract on this subdivision as well.

1914–1915

With the outbreak of World War I, Nichols reorganizes his building department under J. C. Taylor and again commences more speculative building, which the company had deemphasized since 1912.

1915

Land is acquired by the Kansas City School Board for the William Cullen Bryant School at 57th and Wornall Road.

1916

Visitation Catholic Church and School opens as the first Catholic church and coeducational parochial school in the district.

The Episcopalian Church purchases land on Wornall Road at Meyer Boulevard to construct St. Andrews Church.

The portion of Rockhill subdivision that in 1990 comprises the site of Midwest Research Institute and the University of Missouri–Kansas City is platted by the widow of W. R. Nelson and his daughter.

1917

First plat of Hampstead Gardens is filed by J. C. Nichols Land Company. Outside the Sunset Hill section, this subdivision shows the mark of a landscape architect (Hare & Hare) in the drives, which conform to topography to a much greater extent than earlier Nichols subdivisions.

Greenway Fields initial plat is filed by J. C. Nichols Land Company with similar design features to those in Hampstead Gardens.

1917–1920
Conferences of the Developers of High Class Residential Property meet annually with Nichols as chairman.

1918
Community Golf Club opens on land purchased by Nichols for future use by the Kansas City Country Club. Located in Mission Hills, the Community Golf Links is a forerunner of the Indian Hills Country Club.

Nichols is elected to serve on the Kansas City Board of Education as a Democrat (Kansas City then had partisan elections for everything). He will serve for eight-and-a-half years, until he is appointed to the National Capital Park and Planning Board in Washington and to the trustees of the proposed Nelson Art Gallery in Kansas City.

1919
Country Club District Bulletin is inaugurated as a communications vehicle between the Nichols Company and the homeowners.

Nichols forms Women's Community Council to help plan community-wide events.

Construction of the Brookside Shopping Center is underway.

The Nichols companies open a horseback riding stable on the future site of the Country Club Plaza in the Brush Creek valley. Riding trails are laid out through the southern and as-yet-undeveloped sections of Mission Hills. The riders gain access to this trail system by directing their mounts southwestward from the stable area along Brush Creek to the state line.

At Christmastime, Nichols personally organizes a caroling party that goes on wagons throughout the district singing Christmas carols to residents.

Initial Crestwood subdivision plat is filed by Isla Derr, Nichols's personal secretary.

1920

Nichols announces to homeowners at an annual banquet that he has decided to remain in Kansas City and to make the development of the Country Club District his life's work. He had previously been toying with the idea of pulling up stakes to develop land elsewhere or to get into another line of work.

Crestwood subdivision is offered for sale.

The Nichols building department wins the contract to build the mansion of oilman A. R. Jones in Mission Hills. The contract is for construction costs well in excess of $100,000 and comprises the largest single-home construction project of the company to date.

Nichols gains a court order requiring the Lyle Brickyard to cease and desist from making brick at their site, which overlooks Brush Creek and is adjacent to his developments.

The construction department tears down an existing structure at the future Plaza site and builds a new Spanish-style headquarters building for Chandler Florists. This indicates the choice of Spanish architectural style for the Plaza had already been made two years prior to the public announcement of the planned shopping area.

Country Club Christian Church is organized in the Community Hall of the Brookside Shopping Center. It will acquire land on Ward Parkway to build a cathedral-style sanctuary.

Wornall Road Baptist Church purchases land for its sanctuary.

1921

Westwood Park is bought as an established subdivision. Nichols upgrades the deed restrictions, and lots sell quickly.

Crestwood shops open the first section for retailing activities.

The first Country Club District Flower Show is held in the Community Hall on the second floor of the Brookside Shopping Center.

Nichols begins the Community Field Day competitions among district schoolchildren in May.

Both Tom Pendergast and future Kansas City city manager H. F. McElroy own homes by this time in the Country Club District. Opposing Republican mayor A. I. Beach also lives in the Country Club District at this time.

Additional lots in Westwood Park (acquired in 1920 from L. R. Wright) are platted by Isla Derr.

Country Club District Homes Association agreement is filed. This is the first "automatic membership" (for future purchasers) homes association on the Missouri side and the first Nichols association to use the title "Homes Association." The dates homes association agreements are filed indicates when Nichols decided there were enough residents in the affected area to set up self-government.

1922

Nichols and the Lyle Brick Company agree to terms so that development of the Country Club Plaza site can move forward.

Crestwood Homes Association agreement is filed.

Armour Hills subdivision is announced as a moderately priced subdivision for bungalows and small, growing families. Armour Hills Homes Association agreement and deed restrictions are filed.

Suncrest subdivision plat is filed by Harry E. Clark. This subdivision fronting on Ward Parkway, surrounded by Nichols' areas, will later choose to come under the same restrictions as the Nichols-developed properties.

First plat of Stratford Gardens is filed by J. C. Nichols Investment Company.

Westwood Homes Association agreement is filed.

Country Club Plaza plans are announced.

1923

First retail building opens in Country Club Plaza at 47th and Mill Creek Parkway.

Armour Fields first plat is filed by the J. C. Nichols Investment Company.

Initial plat of Armour Lawn subdivision is filed by J. C. Nichols Investment Company. This small subdivision will be the site of the Romanelli shops.

Westwood Hills initial plat is filed.

Westwood Hills Homes Association agreement is filed.

Armour Fields Homes Association agreement is filed.

1924

Several additions to Armour Hills are platted and filed by J. C. Nichols Investment Company.

Country Club Homes Association agreement is filed, including Country Club Heights, Country Club District, and Country Club

Ridge subdivisions. This homes association is a successor to the first Missouri association, filed in 1921.

Wornall Homestead Homes Association agreement is filed.

Country Side Homes Association agreement is filed. This group includes residents from the following subdivisions: Country Side, Country Side Extension, Rockhill Place, Rockhill Park, Rockhill Extension, Southwood Extension, Southwood Annex, Bowling Green, and South Country Side.

1925

Kansas City reaches it peak building year for single-family homes with 3,645 new homes begun during the year. Housing starts fall by more than 1,000 in 1926 and trend downward from there toward the Great Depression.

Planning begins for Romanelli shops at Gregory (71st Street) and Wornall Road.

Plaza Christmas lighting tradition commences with thousands of colored lights strung along rooflines in December 1925.

First unit of Southwest High School on Wornall Road south of the Bryant School location.

The Sixth Church of Christ Scientist purchases land at Sixty-sixth Street Terrace and Wornall Road for its sanctuary.

First plat of Romanelli Gardens is filed by J. C. Nichols Investment Company.

Initial plat of Indian Hills subdivision on the Kansas side is filed.

1926

Kansas City Country Club prepares to move to its previously purchased (in 1921) Kansas site within Mission Hills. Nichols later persuades Mrs. Jacob Loose to buy most of the old Country Club site in order to donate it to the city for use as a park.

Meyer Circle subdivision first plat is filed by the J. C. Nichols Land Company and specified individual lot owners.

La Solana subdivision plat is filed by Charles E. McCoy with Nichols Company lawyer Frank Guy serving as notary. This subdivision will become the site of low-rise apartments built facing the Country Club Plaza area.

First plat for Fieldston subdivision on the Kansas side is filed.

Stratford Gardens Homes Association agreement is filed.

1927

The 63rd and Troost Shopping Center opens. It is now known as the Landing Shopping Center. It is the only Nichols center not located contiguous to his housing developments.

Nichols moves the district model boat regatta from the reflecting pool on Ward Parkway to Lake Hiwassee in Mission Hills to accommodate the large number of sailboats entered by district boys and their fathers.

Loma Linda subdivision is platted by the J. C. Nichols Investment Company. This will become the site of high-rise apartment buildings constructed on the south bank of Brush Creek and the bluff behind.

Oak-Meyer Gardens is first platted by the J. C. Nichols Investment Company.

Oak-Meyer Gardens Homes Association agreement is filed.

Fieldston (in Kansas) Homes Association agreement is filed.

1928

Additional Country Club Plaza land is subdivided and platted by the J. C. Nichols Development Company.

Additions to Oak-Meyer Gardens subdivision are platted by the J. C. Nichols Investment Company.

1928–1930

High-rise apartment building reaches its zenith during Nichols's lifetime in this period. All five of the ten-story units lining Ward Parkway just south of Brush Creek, as well as most of the early high-rises built west of the Plaza, open in this span. The Walnuts, Kansas City's most exclusive address then and now, opens in the Sunset Hill area two blocks south of the Plaza on Wornall in 1930.

1930

Armour Hills Gardens plat is filed by the J. C. Nichols Investment Company, as are additions to Romanelli Gardens and Meyer Circle. These are all filed on July 8–9.

Nichols ceases publication in October of the *Country Club District Bulletin* as an economy measure brought on by the onset of the Great Depression.

1931
The Nichols Company opens a rental department for the first time in order to assist landlords and tenants in the apartments ringing the Country Club Plaza.

A small five-block addition to Romanelli Gardens plat is filed.

1932
A small section is added to the Westwood Hills subdivision on the Kansas side by plat filed in September.

1933
The Ten-Year Plan bond issue is passed just as the Depression hits bottom. Designed as a work-relief program, it also serves as a subsidy for the Pendergast Concrete Company, which paves Brush Creek against Nichols's wishes. Nichols had served on the planning committee but opposed the Brush Creek part of the proposal.

Plats are filed for small additions to Armour Hills Gardens and Oak-Meyer Gardens in the latter half of the year after the banking crisis has passed.

1934
A small addition is platted for Armour Hills Gardens.

1935
The northeast corner of Sagamore Hills is platted as a part of Mission Hills subdivision on the Kansas side.

1936
Plats for small additions to Meyer Circle and Oak-Meyer Gardens are filed. Several blocks in Armour Hills Gardens are added by new plats.

1937
Labor unrest that gains the support of the declining Pendergast political machine brings about a break between City Manager McElroy and Nichols.

A few blocks in Armour Hills Gardens are added by new plat filings.

The smallest complete subdivision planned by Nichols is platted and filed. Mission Woods was carved out of a corner of land left over from the Mission Hills Country Club fairways.

A larger section of Sagamore Hills is added to the area platted in 1935.

1938

The initial plat is filed for Fairway subdivision on the Kansas side west of Mission Hills Country Club.

1939

The *National Real Estate Journal* devotes an entire issue to a description of the history and workings of the J. C. Nichols companies. This is the first (and only) time the trade magazine has done such a thing. It is not an advertisement, but rather an informative series of articles designed to serve as a mini-textbook on the real estate and land development business.

1940

Fairway subdivision opens for sale with lots moving briskly.

Fieldston Hill subdivision is platted between Fairway and Fieldston on the Kansas side.

1941

First plat filed for Prairie Village subdivision.

1946

Initial plat filings for Romanelli West subdivision are made by the J. C. Nichols Company.

1948

Shelley v. Kraemer decision by Supreme Court outlaws racial references in deed restrictions.

Prairie Village Shopping Center opens first section of buildings.

1950

Over one thousand homes have been built in Prairie Village, with the vast majority being constructed since the cessation of World War II.

J. C. Nichols dies of cancer at age 69.

J. C. NICHOLS AND THE SHAPING OF KANSAS CITY

———

INTRODUCTION

The availability of land for ever more intensive and economically productive use was a central feature of United States history from the beginnings of European exploration. The lure of land ownership served as the single most important magnet for English and European immigrants from the sixteenth century until well into the nineteenth. In the last third of the nineteenth century, this hunger for land was transformed into desire for ownership of city and town lots in or quite near population concentrations rather than out in the countryside. The rural native-born population began to be the dominant group in acquiring such land. Despite the American myth that portrayed the nation as a confederation of agriculturalists, the United States moved toward larger and more numerous urban centers as industrialization quickly transformed the lives of native-born and immigrant alike.

What has come to be called "the city-building process," which is essentially the physical expansion of land holdings and building improvements within and near city boundaries, proceeded at an increasing pace throughout nineteenth-century United States history. Supported by "the freest land system in the world" and a tradition of handyman construction unparalleled elsewhere in the world, United States villages became towns, towns became cities, and cities grew into metropolises.[1]

The central feature of this growth, which has been but lightly studied, was the acquisition and holding of land in urban areas for present and future gain. While both the Land Preemption Act of 1841 and the Homestead Act of 1862 were intended to spur rural development, the fact that they eased the difficulty of buying land resulted in urban expansion as well as rural population growth. People wanted land that would increase in value over time. Land near population centers, no matter how small they were, tended to

1. The term *city-building process* has been used by urban historians to describe the physical expansion of urban areas. Lubove, "The Urbanization Process: An Approach to Historical Research"; Sam Bass Warner, Jr., *The Urban Wilderness: A History of the American City,* 18.

advance in value more rapidly than did land lying further away. One urban historian has stated that these cheap land policies resulted in land speculation far more often than they created more diversified land-holding practices. Speculators, who had the greatest interest in escalating land values, could afford to borrow more money with which to buy inexpensive land or to buy out the first claimants. North America's cities were built largely on borrowed money.[2]

By as early as 1830, North American cities were growing rapidly. Suburbs, or population clusters located outside formal urban boundaries, appeared in that era. In an extreme example, almost as many people lived outside the city limits of Pittsburgh, Pennsylvania, in 1830 as lived inside its borders. Outlying areas also supplemented the population of growing urban centers such as Cincinnati and Louisville by that same year. Ferry suburbs and then railroad suburbs appeared in pre–Civil War America. People wanted to live on land of their own, if they could afford it.[3]

Indeed, the history of United States growth is replete with examples of urban and suburban expansion at relatively rapid rates, dating almost from the end of the American Revolution. Just as surely as people moved to the cities in growing numbers, suburbs either spun out or expanded from the urban centers. Architect and historian Robert A. M. Stern argued that American suburbs date from the opening of the industrial age in the first two decades of the nineteenth century. Stern explained four ways in which the industrialization process contributed to suburban development: industrial growth brought increased prosperity to a wider segment of the population; its requirements for moving goods resulted in improved forms of transportation for people as well as goods; the sheer unhealthiness of the industrial environment encouraged those who could to move beyond the reach of the noisome and noxious factories and rail yards; and this negative view of the immediate environment surrounding industrial enterprises came rather quickly to

2. Warner, *The Urban Wilderness*, 18–19.

3. Population figures are from Richard C. Wade, "Urban Life in Western America, 1790–1830." Kenneth T. Jackson, *Crabgrass Frontier: The Suburbanization of the United States*, 25–39.

include the entire city as a poor place to raise children or to achieve domestic harmony.[4]

Regardless of whether the cities grew inside their borders or externally through suburbs that were then absorbed in the annexation process, the physical expansion of the urban centers required land as the basic building block. Land subdivision for residential sites was one of the basic economic activities in any North American urban center. A major factor that distinguished rural areas from urban areas was the population density as measured by the number of people living within the legal limits of the specified area. As the population center increased (or, quite often, was merely expected to increase), the land subdivision activity extended beyond the formal limits of the municipality into previously open country. Usually after a period of time the government of the original population center annexed the extensions of subdivided, but as yet unincorporated, land. In the twentieth century, outlying residential sections frequently organized themselves as a new municipality.[5]

The construction of houses, stores, and service buildings on these subdivided lots was the next logical step in the process of changing unimproved land into city territory. The construction phase did not always happen immediately or in any necessarily rational pattern. Some lots or subdivisions might be built upon soon after subdivision; others lay dormant for months, years, or even decades before physical development transformed them into building sites. This disparity in development rates between land acquisition and building construction was caused primarily by the fact that in most cases the two processes were done by different people. The land transactions were usually handled by real estate dealers or brokers, while building construction was normally done by members of the building trades. This pattern has changed significantly in the last half of the twentieth century; a pattern of vertical integration has become common, with the same company

4. Stern, *Pride of Place: Building the American Dream*, 126.
5. The best summary of the annexation process and the trend toward outlying self-incorporation to resist annexation is in Jackson, *Crabgrass Frontier*, 138–56.

subdividing the land, improving the site for residential use, and erecting the building(s).[6]

The two activities in question—land subdivision into lots and blocks as well as building construction by professional builders—are uniquely urban in thrust. In rural areas farms were laid out according to section and quarter-section areas according to the rectilinear survey methods and coordinates that date from the Land Ordinance of 1785 and the Northwest Ordinance of 1787. The rural landowner usually erected the needed houses (again until the post–World War II era) and other farm buildings with help from friends. Urban land subdividers took acreages and divided them into building lots. The very word *subdivision* implies that an initial division (by square mile sections or townships) had already taken place. To subdivide was to take a divided area and divide it again. This was done to prepare the land legally for sale to small landowners in towns and cities.

Building tradesmen conducted most of the construction activities in nineteenth-century and early twentieth-century North American urban spaces. The predominant method was for a small builder to put up a single building or house at a time. He would hire other tradesmen and laborers as needed to help him do what he could not do himself. Occasionally the small builder would be so successful that he could organize himself and his men into construction teams to put up several buildings at one time. As the nineteenth century drew to a close, a growing number of such construction companies began to emerge. In Kansas City, Missouri, for example, two companies began as real estate companies engaged in the brokerage of land sales and the sales of existing structures. During the land boom of the 1880s, these two companies expanded into the area of building houses on the town lots they were subdividing and selling. The reason for the move into construction was primarily to attract buyers for the lots. Potential purchasers were more willing to buy residential land if some houses were already built than if the salesman was huckstering an unbroken piece of sod.[7]

6. The ease with which tradesmen could become building contractors is outlined in Michael J. Doucet and John C. Weaver, "Material Culture and the North American House: The Era of the Common Man, 1870–1920."

7. The two companies in question were the A. J. King Realty Company, founded

These two companies and the few others like them across the country were the exception rather than the rule in the late nineteenth century. Most urban houses went up along the lines of the patterns found in three formerly suburban portions of Boston during the last third of the nineteenth century. Small subdividers sold individual lots to small builders, who in turn rented or sold their completed houses and flats to occupants or investors. Even companies like the two in Kansas City did little more than survey the legal boundaries of lots and build some houses to attract buyers. The days of the planned residential community were still to come in the 1880s in all but a handful of instances.

Historians have paid little attention to these processes of land subdivision and housing construction in North American cities. While the records are generally available to encourage research into housing history, "the study of housing in both its physical and human contexts has been largely ignored by historians." Some studies have recently been completed on aspects of housing and land-development history, but the interpretive works are based almost entirely on the same inadequate body of primary research.[8]

A significant body of literature exists concerning "land jobbing" in rural areas in the nineteenth and early twentieth centuries, but speculative urban land-development ventures have gone largely unnoticed. One historian noted in 1982, "At the root of all urban growth is the land development process—the conversion of rural or vacant land to some sort of urban use. This process is, as yet, poorly understood for most nineteenth-century North American cities."[9]

Shortly after 1900 a young man undertook a subdivision and

---

in 1880, and the Fletcher Cowherd Company, founded in 1883. "King Developments"; "Kansas City Realtors Build 2000 Homes."

8. The quotation is from Jules Tygiel, "Housing in Late Nineteenth-Century American Cities." See, for example, David P. Handlin, *The American Home: Architecture and Society, 1815–1915;* Gwendolyn Wright, *Moralism and the Model Home: Domestic Architecture and Cultural Conflict in Chicago: 1873–1913;* Wright, *Building the Dream: A Social History of Housing in America;* Doucet and Weaver, "Material Culture"; Robert Fishman, *Bourgeois Utopias: The Rise and Fall of Suburbia;* Marc A. Weiss, *The Rise of the Community Builders: The American Real Estate Industry and Urban Land Planning.*

9. Doucet, "Urban Land Development in Nineteenth-Century North America"; Fishman, *Bourgeois Utopias,* 77–91.

building enterprise in the Kansas City area not much different from the examples already given. Jesse Clyde Nichols (known as "J. C." from his earliest days in the real estate business) began building speculation houses on strategic vacant lots in a small subdivision in Kansas City, Kansas, in 1903. Nichols had grown up in the small northeast Kansas community of Olathe. He graduated Phi Beta Kappa from the University of Kansas in 1902 and added a second B.A. degree from Harvard University in 1903, just before he began his subdivision work.

Two years later, at age twenty-five, he moved his main operations to a ten-acre subdivision a few blocks south of the city limits of Kansas City, Missouri. The young builder became a subdivider-builder. In 1908 he and some financial backers gained control of approximately one thousand acres of potential residential building sites, which Nichols called "The Country Club District" because the land surrounded the grounds of the Kansas City Country Club. Nichols and his planners improved and planned the residential setting according to the latest concepts in landscape design. By 1915 he had developed an overall plan for the set of subdivisions, which were laid out, beautified, and protected by a legal means from "harmful" uses. He had built a significant number of houses both for speculation and by contract with the landowners who had bought from his company. Beginning in 1914 Nichols expanded the plan to include associations of owners who were obligated by contract to protect the subdivisions. By 1920, the development included two shopping centers for the convenience of the residents and the profit of the J. C. Nichols Company. In 1922 he announced what has come to be considered his masterpiece, the Country Club Plaza, the first regional shopping center designed primarily to attract an automobile clientele. Nichols continued development work on a restricted basis during the 1930s and supported his company's move into middle-income housing after the close of World War II. He died in 1950 of lung cancer. (A more detailed listing of his land-development activities is given in the Chronology.)

The Kansas City developer did not initiate the first planned residential community in the United States. That achievement occurred at least as early as the 1850s, when Llewellyn Park, New Jersey, was planned. Obviously, Nichols was not the first real estate subdivider

This photograph of Nichols, taken about 1940, shows him preparing to enter the front doors of his company's offices on Ward Parkway facing Brush Creek in the Country Club Plaza. The ironwork on the doors shows a typical upper-income home in the Country Club District on one side and the facade of the building he is shown entering on the other. The symbolism is obviously intended to emphasize the major economic activities of the Nichols Company: residential land development, homebuilding, and shopping center construction and management. The front of the headquarters of the J. C. Nichols Company looks essentially the same in 1990. KC106, N2.

to build houses for sale on his lots, even in Kansas City. He was not even the first developer to have legal protection (called "deed restrictions") drawn up or to have homeowners' associations or shopping centers. Nichols was, however, one of the very first United States land developers to do all of these things on one site using large-scale operations to achieve economies of scale. Nichols and his company integrated the two types of development—land and construction—into a unified form. Even when others built houses on his lots, he sought to incorporate their activities into his overall plan through the self-perpetuating building restrictions and home-owners' associations. The company introduced shopping centers to serve residents, to increase community cohesion, and to provide the company with revenues from residents long after the original houses and lots had been sold. Moreover, his development pattern continued into the 1980s under the leadership of his older son.[10]

The Kansas City developer-builder has been cited as a key figure by historians of urban expansion, suburban growth, and housing development. Urban historian Sam Bass Warner, Jr., has indicated that Nichols's subdivisions comprised "the nation's only continuously planned residential developments." He called it, among other things, "a city planning triumph." One of the classic summaries of United States urban history, *A History of Urban America,* used the Nichols Company as a prime example of a suburban development company in the 1920s. A suburban historian has labeled Nichols "qualitatively, the most successful American developer." One architectural historian pointed out that the Nichols development "won international renown because of its extensive and effective controls." Marc Weiss credits Nichols's 1916 speech to the national conventions of both the National Association of Real Estate Boards (NAREB) and the National Conference on City Planning (NCCP) with "defining an agenda for public action" in the realm of city planning and zoning regulation as well as within the real estate profession itself.[11]

Nichols has not been without his critics. Warner tempered his enthusiasm for Nichols's work because of the restrictive nature of residential development in the Country Club District. In the same sentence in which he pronounced Nichols's work "a city planning triumph," Warner insisted that Nichols created "a social disaster" for Kansas City. Warner maintained that the "disaster" was inevitable because Nichols practiced class and race separation. Inherent in this argument is the implication that deed restrictions and racial segregation practices in housing originated with Nichols. It will be

10. Deed restrictions go far back in land history. See Chapter 5 for a thorough explanation of the background for these legal devices.

11. Warner, *The Urban Wilderness,* captions following 222; Charles N. Glaab and A. Theodore Brown, *A History of Urban America,* 276–78; Jackson, *Crabgrass Frontier,* 177; Wright, *Building the Dream,* 202. Regarding George Kessler, see William Wilson, *The City Beautiful Movement in Kansas City.* Weiss, *Rise of the Community Builders,* 64.

shown that in this instance Nichols simply followed existing practice. Both the praise of Nichols's planning and the condemnation of
his results merit further investigation.[12]

Other urban historians have stated that the key to Nichols's success lay in his exercise of extensive control over all aspects of development on or near his land. They have also pointed out that the
Nichols neighborhoods were marked by a sense of community spirit
fostered by special events such as lawn and flower contests and
unequaled recreational opportunities. Wright echoed the theme of
control when she discussed the developer's role in the creation of
restrictive covenants and mandatory homeowner's associations,
which were charged with enforcement of the covenants. Kenneth
Jackson praised Nichols's residential planning efforts and admired
the fact that the Country Club District was "*the* place to live in
Kansas City" in 1930. He also cited the importance of Nichols's
development of "the first of the modern variety" of shopping centers with the announcement of the Country Club Plaza in 1922. In
short, this array of historians have indicated the important aspects of
Nichols's work that merit further study. None of these authors
attempted to portray Nichols in any great detail; indeed, some of the
less important details that were included proved to be inaccurate.
These writers did indicate, though, that Nichols was an important
figure whose residential planning and commercial innovations
deserved greater treatment.[13]

This present analysis is a case study of what has been referred to as
the "city-building process." It is important to understand how one
section of a city's residential area may affect the development of
another section. It is also essential to delve into the elements that
make up one of the older planned residential communities in the
United States. If such suburban communities are truly marked by
what has been called "natural beauty and gracious civility, the col-

12. Warner, *The Urban Wilderness,* caption for figure 109, following p. 222.
13. Glaab and Brown, *A History of Urban America,* 266–67; Wright, *Building the Dream,* 202; Jackson, *Crabgrass Frontier,* 177–78, 258–59. As an example of incorrect minor details, both Wright and Jackson indicate that Nichols started accumulat-
ing land in 1907 and began housing construction in 1922. They apparently base
this observation on a similar statement made by Martin Mayer in *The Builders: Houses, People, Neighborhoods, Governments, Money,* 58.

lective idealization of individuality within the context of their social conformity," their origins must be studied in more detail and interpreted more fully than has previously been done.[14]

Nichols carefully observed one aspect of early twentieth-century urban life that was just then accelerating in Kansas City. Houses in residential neighborhoods that had previously housed upper-income families were being sold and converted to rooming houses or split up into several apartments. Sometimes the owners were able to recoup enough from the sale or rental income to compensate for the inconvenience of moving, but in most cases, the decline in use also meant a loss of economic value as well. Sections of Chapter 2 explore this situation more thoroughly, but it is little wonder that Nichols began to emphasize "planning for permanence" in his early Missouri developments. He never altered the emphasis throughout his lifetime.

Along with the study of the Country Club District as an early example of a planned residential community that was intended to retain its value, it is necessary to examine Jesse Clyde Nichols as an individual developer. Nichols was not so much an innovator in many areas as he was a synthesizer of other people's ideas. His values are a product of his era. The fact that many of those values were expressed through legal requirements and institutions he created made them more visible and susceptible to later criticism. Nichols was a keen observer of the urban pattern. He knew how to put his subdivisions in the path of growth among the people he most wanted to attract to his communities—the wealthy and upper-middle-class residents of Kansas City, Missouri.

The Country Club District is still *the* place to live in Kansas City, Missouri, just as the Country Club Plaza is still *the* place to shop in 1989. That much has not changed in almost sixty years. The questions of how this part of town came to have that status, of how it retained its position, and of how the District has affected Kansas City and the nation provide the framework for this study.

---

14. Lubove, "The Urbanization Process"; Stern, *Pride of Place,* 158.

1

PROTOTYPES

The processes of subdividing urban land and building houses were usually two separate business activities in the nineteenth century. This differentiation was mainly the result of the types of work done and the businesses most closely related to these functions. In addition, the fact that land could be readily financed with a small amount down while houses usually required a 50 percent down payment made the two commodities sell much differently.

Land subdividing was—and is—basically taking an acreage and having the land surveyed to be broken up into lots of sufficiently small size to be salable for building uses. Given the fairly uniform manner of land subdivision into ranges and sections set out in the Northwest Ordinance of 1787, it is a bit surprising to find that urban land subdivision has as much diversity as it does. Town building-site lots were as small as fourteen feet by forty-one feet or as large as a full acre. These lots were sold by the "front foot" in the nineteenth and early twentieth centuries, meaning that the price was so much per foot of frontage facing the street or road. Lot depths were not considered, except indirectly, in the price. This led to instances of lots too shallow for any practical use. Gradually the "square foot" method of sale, which placed a price on the entire area of the lot rather than on simply the amount of frontage, came into use.[1]

The land subdivider oversaw the process of breaking larger pieces of land into smaller ones and was also primarily responsible for marketing the land. These responsibilities led him rather naturally into the real estate business if he was not already part of it. Residential housing construction, on the other hand, was a natural outgrowth of the building professions. Often, a carpenter would gain sufficient capital and experience to put together a crew to build one or more houses a year. Large, organized building companies were infrequent; only since World War II have major companies building

1. Doucet, "Urban Land Development," 310–11.

hundreds and even thousands of housing units per year been very important. One student of housing theory suggests that another reason for this "Balkanization" in the housing industry was in the financing terms available to housing purchasers prior to the inception of the FHA and the widespread availability of the amortized long-term mortgage. Both were products of the New Deal. The less favorable terms available prior to FHA loans usually involved a maximum of 50 percent of the purchase price in a first mortgage with a five-year term, a second mortgage, often with the same five-year term, of 30 to 40 percent, and a down payment of 10 to 20 percent.[2]

The result of this often massive activity by so many unrelated individuals was that housing and residential neighborhoods usually were built up without much concern for what was going on in the next block or even the next lot. Chaos was brought about by countless private decisions made with little concern for the common good of the future, or even the current, residents. Nevertheless, a few isolated planned residential communities were actually being developed in the nineteenth century. By examining some of these exceptions, the role of J. C. Nichols as a transitional figure emerges more clearly.[3]

Some nineteenth-century examples demonstrated that real estate companies could offer something more of a finished housing product. The key to these instances lay in the rate of growth of the particular city. Where cities were growing rapidly, there seemed to be more demand for house-and-lot combinations on paved streets. This type of development occurred in San Francisco, Philadelphia, and Chicago, among other cities. In San Francisco, a group called the Real Estate Associates bought land and built houses in outlying districts of the growing city in the 1870s and 1880s. Some of the surviving "San Francisco Style" homes of that era, complete with gingerbread and cupolas, are examples of this early type of subdividing and homebuilding combination work. These disjointed areas of

2. Ibid., 327–31; Eichler, *The Merchant Builders*, xvi–xvii.

3. This theme of uncoordinated private decisions with a profound effect on the resulting housing and communities is best stated by Warner in *Streetcar Suburbs*.

substantial construction in that city are hardly examples of coordinated building and planning, however.[4]

In Chicago, the massive growth of the metropolis spawned several subdivisions and building contractors, some of whom developed rather large organizations for the times. Samuel E. Gross was the most famous of the Chicago builders. It has been estimated that he laid out more than forty thousand city lots in sixteen towns and one hundred fifty subdivisions in and around Chicago between 1880 and 1892. In addition, his people built and sold over seven thousand houses ranging in price from under eight hundred dollars to more than four thousand dollars. In many instances he installed water, gas, and sewer lines and controlled building designs and construction quality guidelines. Gross's most interested supporter pointed out, however, that his influence was limited to certain areas of Chicago. Most other parts of town were put up by subdividers and builders who did not work together or coordinate improvements beyond what was mandated by city law, which was almost nil. This was the pattern in most developing residential sections around the country throughout the last third of the nineteenth century.[5]

In Philadelphia the pattern was somewhat different. Wealthy residents laid out their small, exclusive planned community on the outskirts of the city along the main line of the Pennsylvania Railroad. Chestnut Hill, on the northern edge of the city, followed a similar pattern. Most of the housing in the city itself was built by men who put up a block of row houses at a time and sold them to workingmen and clerks. The degree to which planned communities were developed and flourished was minimal. Chestnut Hill, while no more planned than other sections, nevertheless had certain features that commended it to upper-income families. The provision of amenities such as the Wissahickon Inn, the Philadelphia Cricket Club, and the adjacent St. Martin-in-the-Fields Episcopal Church created sufficient levels of prestige and protection of values to ensure Chestnut Hill's survival as a picturesque enclave into the latter third of the twentieth century. However, the preeminence of

4. Tygiel, "Housing," 85.
5. Mayer and Wade, *Chicago*, 155, 174, 262, 267; Holt and Pacyga, *Chicago*, 121–23; Wright, *Moralism*, 40–45; Wright, *Building the Dream*, 99–100.

Chestnut Hill owes more to the tenacity of its residents than to the farsightedness of its developer.[6]

Several reasons account for the disjointed nature of urban residential development in post–Civil War America. One was most assuredly the reason cited by Sam Bass Warner: private interests pursued their own private plans. Any attempt at rationalizations by government or even trade associations would have been considered meddlesome interference. Another reason was the disinterest of American and foreign capital in investing in long-term projects with a great deal of initial cost. Until the entry of the United States into World War I, it was a debtor nation with more foreign investment coming in than U.S. investment going out. There simply was not enough money, foreign or domestic, to invest in large-scale development projects that offered only possible, rather than definite, financial returns in the future. Coincidentally, most of the planned communities developed in the nineteenth century turned out to be bad investments for the initial stockholders.[7]

A third reason for the paucity of fully developed residential neighborhoods lay in the lack of trained personnel to perform the necessary planning. Real estate entrepreneurs had almost no experience in this area; building tradesmen and small contractors who put up most of the houses had even less. The profession of city planning did not exist, while the role of the landscape architect, which became crucial in this type of development, was just evolving through the work of Frederick Law Olmsted and a few others.

Finally, there was the question of what the consumers wanted. For coordinated housing, land, and development work to be successful, it was necessary to sell some of the developed commodity. There is little evidence that in the nineteenth century most housing consumers thought very much about the value of the surrounding neighborhood. The wealthy certainly clustered near each other and coerced the municipal authorities to provide them with needed services and amenities. Most of these affluent urban dwellers, even

6. Tygiel, "Housing," 85. The observations about the degree to which Chestnut Hill has retained its charm and attractiveness are based on personal observations by the author, July 4, 1988.

7. Warner, *Streetcar Suburbs*, 153–68; see also Warner's *The Private City*.

in the rapidly growing cities of the day, did not expect the shape of the cities to change as rapidly as they did. Only near the end of the century did even the wealthy, who could certainly choose where and how they wanted to be housed, begin to realize that some planning and protection might be in order. That is just the point in time when planned residential communities began to be seen as possibly useful and profitable endeavors.

"Under all is the land." This slogan of the National Board of Realtors speaks to the primacy of land development over all other forms of urban expansion. Land is the essence of urban space. Subdivision of the land by specialists into useful parcels is a uniquely urban endeavor that has been overlooked, for the most part. Because so much of our thinking and legal framework comes from English experience, the land development practices of the British Isles are important for comparative purposes.[8]

The basic right of the individual to use real estate without restraint is based on British common law. Throughout most of England and her dominions this has been tempered by the concept of feudal obligations in which landowners have absolute sway in theory, but under which they had to accommodate the needs of their dependents, which meant all living on their land. In Kent County, England, however, a different sort of landholding held sway. Individuals did not receive land with the expectation of offering service, military or otherwise, in return. However, the Kentish men held their land by absolute title with no accompanying power or obligation over the people on or nearby their land. They were not kings of their domains, controlling the lives of others but also having to respond to their needs. They were, instead, clear title owners who could do to or with the land as they pleased. Only court injunctions *might* interfere with these rights. This sort of landholding practice became dominant in the English colonies in North America rather than the feudal style of landholding with reciprocal obligations.[9]

During the nineteenth century, England experienced tremen-

---

8. Warner gives a brief but useful summary of some of those interconnections in *The Urban Wilderness*, 15–17.

9. Ibid., 16.

dous population growth in and around its urban areas, particularly London. One suburb, Camberwell, grew phenomenally in the last half of that century. In that instance a relatively small number of persons or institutions held the land. They almost never sold parcels to individuals for building or other purposes. Ground rents were the rule, with improvements (including all houses or other structures) retained in the title to the land. Landlords granted leases of up to ninety-nine years to builders who would put up houses to receive the income over the life of the lease. The way in which land was used for housing was determined by the lessee unless the owner, or lessor, restricted the use of the land through covenants attached to the lease. In practice, the use of covenants ranged from no use at all to prescriptions for the placement of houses and for the materials to be used in construction.[10]

Probably the closest analogy to the London suburb of Camberwell in a United States setting is late nineteenth-century Boston and its closest suburbs. There the situation appears superficially very similar in that the homebuilders served as the determining agents of the physical shape of the city. The role of landowner and/or subdivider was almost entirely absent. The lack of attention given to the land subdivision process had the effect of focusing subsequent studies on the housebuilding aspect of urban development. The problem with this approach is that builders in Boston bought lots already subdivided by previous owners. They started building with lots, blocks, streets, and alleys already in place. The Boston builders thus determined the type and quality of housing stock, but they were not the designers of the city, whereas in the London suburb the lessee-builders were more the subdividers of Camberwell than the landowners or their agents.

In Boston and all other American cities, the builder could theoretically buy enough raw land to subdivide it and then build on it. As has been documented, however, most houses were constructed by small builders who did not have the resources to buy parcels of land large enough to subdivide. Thus, in North America, normally the owner of the acreage either subdivided his land himself or hired a

10. For Dyos's comments on landholding in *Victorian Suburb*, see particularly 39–42.

subdivider who specialized in this endeavor. The landowner might, and often did, sell to the subdivider, who proceeded to carve out streets, building lots, and other physical features on which the builders could construct their dwellings. This pattern is important because it produced a specialized form of real estate business in the United States that was little known in England—land subdivision. Because of the speculative aspects of this type of business, this development has been a mixed blessing for North American residential life.[11]

Some investigation into the origins of this specialization is essential to a study of J. C. Nichols and his work. The city-building process of laying out cities was normally gradual. In times of expansion, land subdivision "boomed," with hundreds of thousands of lots being carved out of the ranges and sections of former cropland. When the booms "busted," as they always did, several years might pass before enough of the excess subdivided land was utilized to stimulate further subdivision activity.

In the last third of the nineteenth century, the land development process was most commonly carried out by at least three different entities, including the subdivider. This real estate specialist took raw land in acre form and subdivided it into lots, streets, alleys, and the like. This was done by having a surveyor draw up a plat (essentially, a technical map showing relationships) of the land. The owner filed the plat with the county or city clerk; it was subsequently approved, amended, or disapproved in session by the city or county representative body. The governmental body based its approval on the recommendation of its civil engineer. In practice, the engineers and governing assemblies turned down very few plats.[12]

Until the 1880s real estate agents marketed almost all the subdivided land. These individuals and firms completed all kinds of real estate transactions, from commercial land sales to the resale of houses and lots. The sale of vacant, subdivided land was normally a

11. The best recent discussion of this process in historical perspective is Doucet, "Urban Land Development," 327–31. Tygiel, "Housing," 85–87.
12. Doucet, "Urban Land Development," 327. The role of the engineer is apparent in plat maps on file at the Jackson County Courthouse, Kansas City, Missouri.

sideline that became profitable only at certain times, such as during booms. Most often throughout the nineteenth century, a third entity, the builder-contractors, did whatever improvement to the land was deemed necessary to sell it to the consumer. Yet the builders' low capitalization allowed them just enough funding to build houses. They simply could not afford to pay for water lines, sewers, or street and sidewalk pavement, let alone such niceties as landscaping or playground construction. The common practice was for little property development to be done until the residents could band together to lobby the city or county legislature to fund in whole or in part such improvements as street pavement, sidewalks, sewers, and even water connections. Most often, the municipal officials simply agreed to be responsible for the arrangement of financing and collection of funds to pay off the improvement debt.[13]

Because these improvements were deemed to benefit the local landowner most of all, the special tax theory of special benefit districts evolved. Under this system, landowners paid most of the cost of these improvements over a period of time through special taxes levied by the municipality. Such taxes added to the cost of the land after the purchase and thus became for many a hidden cost of urban landownership. The manner in which this took place was quite uneven in different urban areas.[14]

One of the reasons for the extreme specialization of function, then, was the limited capital held by any of the participants in the process. Subdividers did not have money to go into marketing. Real estate agents sold services, not goods, and were not capital intensive. The cities effectively loaned the money for improvements to new residents, who repaid the loans through the special assessment taxes. With the significant expansion of urban population and wealth in the 1880s, some instances of combining these functions occurred.

One other limitation had existed up to this time: land was held by title, and whoever possessed the title to land had tremendous advan-

13. Warner, *Streetcar Suburbs,* 137–39.
14. Ibid., 138–39, 156. See Roger Simon, "The Expansion of an Industrial City, Milwaukee, 1880–1910," 105–10, for similar conditions in Milwaukee.

tage in any court proceedings concerning ownership or rights of mortgage-holders in case of foreclosure. The result was that land-owners required large down payments, often up to 50 percent, before they would sell to someone else since selling always involved giving title. Armed with the large down payment, the landowner was more secure because the purchaser would be unlikely to stop paying for land in which he already had a substantial investment. If he did default, the landowner had enough money from the transaction to go to court to regain legal title. This pattern held whether the loan was from the original landowner or from a bank that held the mortgage. Effectively, this meant that only the more wealthy who could accumulate enough for the large down payments could expect to own land. The observation has been made that land-ownership in mid-nineteenth-century North American cities was limited to a relatively small portion of the population—barely more than one-tenth in Philadelphia in 1860, for example. One historian has stated that the rewards for landownership were so great compared to other forms of investment at the time that a relatively small group of speculators dominated the market purely for profit. Certainly there is logic behind this conclusion, but he did not inquire into the method of money lending for real estate, which was at least as important in holding down diversity in landownership as was the desire for personal gain.[15]

At least as early as 1886 in the Cincinnati area, a new form of conveyance of real property came into use. A young man named W. E. Harmon introduced the idea of writing a contract for deed that would give the purchaser a legal document providing him with some rights to the property even before the conveyance of the deed or title itself. That conveyance would occur at a time specified in the contract when enough money had been paid in to warrant the transfer. The result was that the seller still had the deed and could repossess easily if default occurred, while the buyer could purchase without having to provide such a large down payment. Harmon's terms for his initial subdivision were two dollars down and twenty-five cents per week toward the purchase price of twenty-five dollars per lot. This type of pricing meant the introduction of installment

15. Doucet, "Urban Land Development," 316–20.

sales to land purchases. While it is quite possible that it was done in a small way earlier, Harmon's version of the origin of the financing method has been accepted within the real estate profession.[16]

Harmon worked hard to popularize the method. His first subdivision was done in partnership with his brother under the company name of Harmon Brothers. It contained 303 lots, all of which sold within four days of the initial offering. Realizing they had a profitable method on their hands, the Harmons recruited their uncle, a man named Wood, as their nonactive partner in Wood, Harmon and Company. With some of their own money and more of their uncle's, the Harmons bought more suburban land near Cincinnati, cut it into streets and lots, bought an ad in the *Cincinnati Evening Post,* and waited for buyers.

The terms offered for this second tract were even more generous than the first. Lots ranged in price from ten dollars to fifty dollars each; down payments amounted to 1 percent of the purchase price with no carrying charges; and the seller paid the taxes until the lots were paid in full. This second subdivision sold out as rapidly as the first one had. By 1924 Harmon could claim that his firm had subdivided over two hundred such areas in twenty-six urban markets. Wood, Harmon and Company had become one of the early national land subdivision companies.[17]

Given the low down payment and easy weekly or monthly payment terms of this method, the appeal obviously was directed heavily toward the workingman. There were many more people in that income bracket than in the one that would be able to buy land through the more traditional deed-and-mortgage method, which required a 30 to 50 percent down payment. The problem was that few of the workingmen who bought land on such easy terms could then afford to build a house. The pennies-down, pennies-a-week subdivision sale was not the only land business conducted using the installment sale method. Roland Park, a planned subdivision near Baltimore, used a variation of the contract-for-deed for land sales to

16. 1924 *Proceedings,* 30–31; Stanley McMichael, *Real Estate Subdivision,* 12; Pearl Janet Davies, *Real Estate in American History,* 50.

17. McMichael, *Real Estate Subdivision,* 12; Clark Timmons, "Why the Subdivider?"; 1924 *Proceedings,* 30.

its middle- and upper-income buyers. The houses, if built by the company, were sold on a first and second mortgage basis. When Nichols offered his first house and lot for sale in Kansas City, Missouri, in April 1905, he proposed terms of fifty dollars down payment "and small monthly payments from a good, reliable party with a steady job." This was the first home offering in what has become one of the premier planned subdivisions of the United States. Significantly, it began with an easy payment plan.[18]

Subdividers, armed with the tool of contract-for-deed, used the advertising broadside approach to boost initial land sales. After a few months, or at most a year or two in one location, they would move on to a new location in another part of town or near another city. As often as not, their legacy was phantom subdivisions in which many people owned land, but on which few houses were built. No sewers, paved streets, or other improvements that would transform the vacant land into a neighborhood were completed. Thus, these boomer subdividers cut up every possible vacant piece of land to make a profit when the demand was great and investors were hungry for a quick turn. There were, as well, other subdividers who took smaller pieces of property and marketed them each year on a continuing basis. If the number of subdivisions platted per year is any measure, then the boomer was the most common prototype, even if he operated only at certain times and in particular cities experiencing boom conditions. The long-term, small-scale subdivider was important but distinctly in the minority in terms of the total number of subdivisions available.[19]

A third type of subdivision activity in the nineteenth century had even less impact in regard to the total number of lots subdivided. In its effect on twentieth-century subdivision practices, however, this third type of operation was the wave of the future and the forerunner of the type of subdivision activity that would be done by J. C. Nichols. This alternative method was the planned subdivision,

18. E. H. Bouton, "Development of Roland Park, Baltimore," 21–29; Reed, Nichols & Co. advertisement in the *Kansas City Star,* April 2, 1905.

19. Harmon, "The Proper Handling of Subdivisions"; Helen C. Monchow, *Seventy Years of Real Estate Subdividing,* 67; Weiss, *Rise of the Community Builders,* 107–15.

which employed a landscape architect at its inception and presented a finished product, in terms of land, to the consumer. Unlike the boomer subdivider who staked out his lots and streets to sell the lots without improvements, these subdivision planners spent time and money to lay out on paper and then on the ground a design for all improvements. In most instances part or all of the proposed improvements—from streets to curbs, gutters, streetlights, and even street railway lines—were completed before land was offered to the public.

Possibly the first example of a planned subdivision for residential use is Llewellyn Park near Orange and West Orange, New Jersey. In 1853 Llewellyn Haskell bought twenty-one and one-half acres of land on the side of the Orange Mountains. Other friends bought similar acreages adjacent to his. A total of 350 acres were finally put under a single set of restrictive covenants, which specified that each homesite must be a minimum of one acre in area. Somewhat unclear records indicate that a landscape gardener named Eugene A. Baumann was responsible for the initial informal design, which took advantage of the rough natural setting. Architect Andrew Jackson Davis has been credited with much of the post–Civil War landscaping as well as the design of several houses, including one of his own.[20]

Llewellyn Park was a forerunner in several ways: the use of a landscape architect or at least an architect for land layout; the provision of extensive restrictions on what could be built or done on the land; the creation of a homeowner's association; and the overall emphasis on the development of a sense of community spirit. The landscape planning took advantage of the rather rough natural surroundings, including a meandering ravine that became known as "The Ramble." Roadways went up the sides of this area of untouched underbrush and natural ground cover. The development lent an air of wilderness never since attempted or achieved in planned subdivisions. Early promotional brochures and newspaper advertisements referred to the Park as a site for "country homes for

20. Samuel Swift, "Llewellyn Park, West Orange, Essex Co., New Jersey: The First American Suburban Community"; Christopher Tunnard, *The City of Man*, 183–85; also see Stern, *Building the American Dream*, 132.

city people." All streets were private drives; as late as 1903, the residents had to maintain their roadways themselves while also paying taxes on the open areas to the West Orange authorities.[21]

The Panic of 1857 disrupted Llewellyn Haskell's direct involvement by leaving him largely impoverished. Others decided to fund the further landscape development of the Park for their own benefit as well as that of their neighbors. Possibly because of its small size or its aristocratic overtones or the Perfectionist religious beliefs of Haskell and other residents, Llewellyn Park serves mostly as a footnote in the history of planned residential subdivision development. While it was probably the first such subdivision, there is little indication that later nineteenth-century landscape planners or subdividers used its positive lessons.

On the other hand, Llewellyn Park has had indirect influence on major architects of the nineteenth century. Not only did A. J. Davis live and design homes there, but Charles McKim of McKim, Mead and White grew up in Llewellyn Park. His partner, Stanford White, designed the monument on which a bust of Haskell was placed in the Park a few years after the founder's death.[22]

Another possible reason for the obscurity of Llewellyn Park until after 1900 in the thinking of land development men might have been the problems that ensued for its residents over time. The money assessed from each landowner to pay for upkeep of the common areas quickly proved insufficient to cover the actual cost. Since the Park was private, no city or county funds could be used. Further, some of the restrictions were legally more rigid than the state of New Jersey allowed, and in 1903 some residents were withholding payment of the small assessments because of a pending lawsuit. Although the use of deed restrictions was not limited to planned subdivisions, they were another distinguishing characteristic of this type of development. The mere fact that the landowners wished to control some of the ways the land would be used after it was sold implies a degree of planning. Generally, the more detailed the deed restrictions, the more planning and land preparation were actually done by the subdivider. Another major problem was the lack of an

21. Stern, *Building the American Dream;* Tunnard, *City of Man,* 186.
22. Swift, "Llewellyn Park," 329; Tunnard, *City of Man,* 183-86.

adequate sewage system or the ability to fund any improvement. In 1886 only thirty-eight of the one hundred thirty plots had been sold. It was anything but a financial success.[23]

In the 1980s Llewellyn Park continues to serve an exclusive and elusive set of residents, including the surviving son of Thomas A. Edison. One cannot enter the Park just to walk through it and view the harmonious treatment of architecture and nature without obtaining written permission from the owners' association weeks in advance. A guard at the gate and high wire fences ensure that residents get the privacy they apparently so earnestly desire. The main potential invasion of that privacy is by way of the home of the most famous former resident, Thomas Edison. In 1954 the Edison heirs gave the house (named Glenmont) and grounds to the United States government. It has since been administered as a national historic site, along with Edison's laboratory some two blocks east on Main Street from the entrance to the Park. Visitors to the laboratory can obtain passes (free of charge) to visit Glenmont in groups of eight to ten per hour. This entails them driving their own vehicles through the lower portion of the Park along the Ramble until reaching the thirteen and one-half acres of the Edison estate. Thus, one must use a ruse to see even a portion of one of the earliest planned subdivisions in North America.[24]

Similar in many ways to Llewellyn Park but better known in its own time, Lake Forest, Illinois, had its origins after a landscape architect had surveyed the property and laid out the plat. Lake Forest was initially intended as a year-round community surrounding the small Presbyterian-affiliated Lake Forest College. The institutional trustees also envisioned it as a summer residence area for wealthy Chicagoans who might take an interest in the welfare of the college.

Lake Forest lots were sold as a means of raising money for the college. The trustees sold the subdivision by the acre rather than the front-foot method common in most nineteenth-century subdivi-

23. Swift, "Llewellyn Park," 329–30, 332–35. Sales figures in 1886 are from "Glenmont," a pamphlet issued by the National Park Service to visitors to this national historic site.

24. Observations on the current status of the park and the means of legal entry are based on the author's experience, July 3, 1988.

sions. This led to a much more exclusive character for this area. In this way, Lake Forest was similar to Llewellyn Park, even though the Illinois site had more unified planning from its inception.[25]

The trustees consulted with Frederick Law Olmsted in 1857 to determine a plan of development. Olmsted, just then appointed superintendent of the proposed Central Park in New York City, recommended that the trustees select Jed Hotchkiss from St. Louis. Hotchkiss confronted a rough sloping topography slanting off toward Lake Michigan. Like Baumann at Llewellyn Park, Hotchkiss chose to wind the roads along the ravines that fed toward lakeside.[26]

A later innovation at Lake Forest held great portent for later planned residential suburbs: the creation of a golf or country club. In the early 1890s several residents bought a neighbor's two-hundred-acre estate and turned it into the Onwentsia Club. Soon the club ground included a golf course, polo grounds, tennis courts, and croquet courts. Part of the acreage was left natural so that members could call out the club hounds for an afternoon of drag hunting when they so desired. Not content with the outdoor sports, the members built indoor bowling alleys and squash courts. Understandably, the Onwentsia Club became one of the premier country clubs in the United States.[27]

Lake Forest became first the summer home and then the year-round residence for members of the A. B. Dick, Armour, Farwell, and many other influential Chicago families who could afford to live some twenty-eight miles north of the city and still commute regularly. Its larger size and the high incomes of many of its residents made it better known in Chicago than Llewellyn Park was in New York. Neither were really examples for subdividers to follow, however, because of the limited market for these high-rent subdivisions in the last third of the nineteenth century. The closest parallel to Lake Forest among planned subdivisions was Pierre Lorillard's Tuxedo Park, begun in the Catskills above New York City in the 1880s. The Chicago suburb became a year-round residential area about the

25. "Lake Forest: The Beautiful Suburb of Chicago."

26. Stern, *The Anglo-American Suburb*, 23.

27. Ibid., 266–67; Peter J. Schmitt, *Back to Nature: The Arcadian Myth in Urban America*, 44.

time Tuxedo was being laid out. In this instance, at least, Chicago was not the "Second City" as far as exclusive planned subdivisions for wealthy city dwellers in search of play areas.[28]

Just after the Civil War, the Chicago area was the scene of another planned subdivision that ultimately resulted in one of the most publicized nineteenth-century subdivisions. The key to its popularity lay not in the real estate firm or subdivider but in the company's choice of a landscape architect. The suburb of Riverside, southwest of Chicago, was begun as a planned speculative subdivision in the late 1860s under the auspices of the Riverside Improvement Company. Emery E. Childs served as president of the company and as chief negotiator on its behalf with their architectural and engineering consultants—Olmsted, Vaux and Company of New York. Considered by his profession to be the father of landscape architecture, Olmsted has also been called by Lewis Mumford "the foremost exponent of ecological planning and regional design."[29]

Olmsted had only a small connection with Lake Forest. He knew of Llewellyn Park at the time Childs approached him to design Riverside. Olmsted, Vaux and Company had presented a proposal to the park commissioners of Newark, New Jersey, to construct a parkway connecting Llewellyn Park with Newark in 1868, the same year they made their proposal for Riverside. Indeed, a central aspect of the Riverside plan was the landscaping of a "Long Common" along the Des Plaines River, which meandered through the property. This feature closely resembled Llewellyn Park's Ramble, which wound up both sides of a ravine running through the center of the development. Another fact that has brought continuing attention to Riverside is that the Olmsted firm remained in business for over a century and kept its records. Thus, it is possible to document the origins of Riverside to an extent not possible in the earlier cases of Llewellyn Park and Lake Forest, where records have generally not survived in great quantity.[30]

28. Swift, "Community Life in Tuxedo"; Frank Kintrea, "Tuxedo Park."

29. Albert Fein, *Frederick Law Olmsted and the American Environmental Tradition*, backpiece.

30. Olmsted's knowledge of Llewellyn Park is documented in Fein, *Frederick Law Olmsted*, 32, 157.

Riverside enjoyed some early acceptance in the late 1860s. Olmsted's partner at that time, Calvert Vaux, indicated that by 1870 fifty houses were built or underway. He also pointed out that prices for the lots had risen from three hundred dollars each prior to the start of improvements to forty dollars per front foot, or four thousand dollars per lot on the one-hundred-foot frontages, by that time.[31]

Olmsted was a self-taught landscape architect; no formal training in the subject existed in the mid-nineteenth-century United States. Much of his experience prior to getting the job as superintendent of construction for Central Park in 1857 had been as a farmer on Staten Island. Olmsted used his writing skills in September 1868 to lay before the Riverside Improvement Company his firm's ideas for the development of Riverside as a suburban subdivision. Many of these ideas are important because of their later application by Nichols and other developers of planned subdivisions. A believer in the salubrity of suburban living from his days as a Staten Island farmer, Olmsted sounded a theme in 1868 that would be repeated by Harlan P. Douglass in his 1925 classic, *The Suburban Trend*. The suburbs were the hope of humanity as places to live in or around large cities. Olmsted told the real estate men that in suburbs "are to be found . . . the most attractive, the most refined and most soundly wholesome forms of domestic life, and the best application of the arts of civilization to which mankind has yet attained." Thus, suburbs were improvements on town life, and it was clear to him "that no great town can long exist without great suburbs." Chicago needed Riverside as much as Riverside needed Chicago.[32]

The report called for a boulevard to connect Riverside with Chicago by the most direct diagonal route, curvilinear streets to break the flatness of the overall site, the planting of additional trees in occasional locations (and definitely not in rows), restrictions with the deeds that specified thirty-foot setbacks from the streets and owner maintenance of trees, and the provision of an open park area

31. Hubbard, "Riverside, Illinois"; Fishman, *Bourgeois Utopias*, 121–24; Jackson, *Crabgrass Frontier*, 61–67.
32. For a listing of Olmsted's works, see Fein, *Frederick Law Olmsted*, 166–70. The Olmsted quotations are from Hubbard, "Riverside, Illinois," 258, 262.

of some size. Houses were required to cost a minimum of three thousand dollars to construct and had to be placed on lots at least one hundred by two hundred feet in area, and front-yard fences were prohibited. The connecting boulevard never materialized. However, the curved streets and tree-lined drives, the common setbacks, and the Long Common all continue to exist in the 1980s as testimony to much of Olmsted's foresight. It is interesting to note that Olmsted limited the suggested deed restriction in his proposal. Specifically, he stated that the control of house design was beyond the purview of the subdivider. Olmsted's firm, under the leadership of his stepson and son, reversed this stance and required the review of plans for other planned subdivisions. Although it would appear that Riverside was a success, it did not become so until late in Olmsted's active life. The Panic of 1873 ruined some of the backers. A hotel built for a summer resort in the early 1870s was converted to an apartment house in 1879 to boost revenues. Not until the return of better financial times in 1885 did Riverside begin to attract much building interest. Olmsted's basic plan survived all of this, however; and the suburb retained a residential appeal that never existed in most southwest Chicago suburbs.[33]

While Llewellyn Park and Lake Forest have enjoyed degrees of success as resorts for the well-to-do, Riverside slowly assumed the character of a neighborhood of upper-middle-class homes in the 1880s and 1890s. The planned subdivision that has had the most impact on the industry as a whole, however, started as Roland Park, a small suburb of Baltimore, Maryland, on the eve of the economic distress of the 1890s. Ironically, given the Kansas City focus of this study, the roots of Roland Park go back to the Kansas City land boom of 1886–1887. During that wild, expansive period, the mania for a quick turn of profit was as seductive to newspaper people as to anyone else. These hustler-promoters who helped to fuel the boom in Kansas City also had nationwide connections that would prove important after the Kansas City boom had died.

33. See Harlan P. Douglass, *The Suburban Trend*, 304–27. Thomas Bender, *Toward an Urban Vision: Ideas and Institutions in Nineteenth-Century America*, 181–84; Stern, *Pride of Place*, 135; Mayer and Wade, *Chicago*, 183–86. The 1980s observation is based on a December 1984 visit to Riverside by the author.

In the 1880s Kansas City had three major newspapers: the *Journal*
and the *Times* were morning papers, while the *Star* was an evening
sheet and the latecomer of the group. The *Journal* was edited by
long-time resident and Kansas City promoter Robert Van Horn,
who had been involved in railroad promotion and speculation in the
1860s and 1870s, but he did not encourage real estate as an investment for himself or for others. The *Star*'s publisher, William Rockhill Nelson, owned significant property on the south side of Kansas
City and lobbied the city for improvements leading to it. This land
became the Rockhill District just after the turn of the century and
had an important impact on J. C. Nichols's developments.[34]

In relation to Roland Park, however, the *Times* was the important
paper. Its publisher was a nonpracticing physician named Morrison
Mumford. In 1886 the editor was Charles Grasty, who became a key
figure in the Kansas City–Roland Park connection. Publisher Mumford had long been a land speculator, and during the 1880s he made
some money at it. He not only allowed his employees to do the
same; he encouraged it. Grasty became involved with the land and
building speculations financed by the Jarvis and Conklin Trust
Company, which was primarily a conduit for English industrial
money to be invested for profit in growing American cities like
Kansas City. Another young man who worked with Jarvis and Conklin, Edward H. Bouton, helped superintend the building of houses
on some of the lots in new subdivisions between downtown and
Nelson's southside properties. Grasty invested his money and
arranged for others to do the same.[35]

The land boom in Kansas City sputtered in 1888 and died the
next year. The English money people represented by Jarvis and
Conklin wanted to invest in a more active area. In 1890 Grasty
moved from Kansas City to Baltimore to become editor of the
Baltimore Evening News. He became acquainted with William H.
Edmunds, president of a trade newspaper, the *Manufacturers'*

34. Brown, *Frontier Community*, 90–93; Glaab, *Kansas City and the Railroads: Community Policy in the Growth of a Regional Metropolis*, 194–211; Reddig, *Tom's Town: Kansas City and the Pendergast Legend*, 44–45.
35. *Kansas City*, 108, 110. See Roland Park Papers, particularly letters from J. T. Harwood to Bouton, May 3, May 29, and July 17, 1891.

Record, in Baltimore. Edmunds wanted to develop one hundred acres that he owned about five miles north of downtown Baltimore. It was bordered by a railroad and a little lane leading up to Lake Roland further north.[36]

Grasty thought he knew just the people to accomplish this task. He contacted Bouton, Jarvis, and Conklin in the spring of 1891. They journeyed east and met Albert Fryer of the Lands Trust Company in London at the site north of Baltimore. They reached an agreement whereby Jarvis and Conklin would buy for the English syndicate the one hundred acres, plus an additional three hundred eighty-six acres for residential building purposes. Actually the agents for the British interests owned only 55 per cent of the initial stock. Richard Capron, from whom they had purchased a large part of the land, owned the other 44 percent, with one share each held by Grasty, Bouton, and three minor landholders in the area. Jarvis and Conklin formed the Roland Park Company on July 30, 1891. The new company issued ten thousand shares at one hundred dollars, par value, for an initial paper capitalization of one million dollars. The basis for this stock was the land purchased by Jarvis and Conklin, the land owned by Capron, and $59,300 in cash subscribed by the shareholders. Though the company often advertised that it was capitalized at one million dollars, the basis for this was shares issued in return for title to artificially inflated land values.[37]

Thus the beginning of Roland Park as a planned residential subdivision was little more than another real estate speculation. Bouton had moved to Baltimore to run the company partly because he had to escape his creditors in Kansas City. Jarvis and Conklin were in financial trouble at the time, although it did not catch up with them until 1894, when the firm went into receivership. The Englishmen who wanted to make money in America stayed with Roland Park until 1903, when they sold their stock to Bouton and a local Baltimore syndicate he had organized. The company received approx-

36. The Edmunds-Grasty-Bouton connection is from the *Kansas City Star,* December 11, 1911; and from *Roland Park: A Reminiscence,* Roland Park Papers, n.p. See also a copy of the original company charter dated July 30, 1891, Roland Park Papers.

37. "Purchase by Edward H. Bouton of the Stock of the Roland Park Company Owned by the Lands Trust Company," July 1, 1903, n.p., Roland Park Papers.

imately four hundred thousand dollars for their controlling stock. This was considered half the par value of the stock held by the English syndicate, but it probably represented some profit to them in that their initial investment was in land bought by the acre twelve years prior. The operating company had achieved profitability by the late 1890s.[38]

Speculation in land subdivision can yield both positive and negative results in residential developments. That Roland Park proved to be a positive, influential development can be determined by examining its planning and design as well as its long-term impact on the suburban development of the United States. Once Jarvis and Conklin closed the deal for the land with the help of Grasty, they appointed Bouton as general manager and assigned a young landscape architect named George Kessler to lay out the first section. They were, in 1891, also developing residential sections in a suburb of Cleveland named Euclid Heights and near Ogden, Utah. Kessler was hired to do initial landscape designing for all of these, and the English money was involved in each venture. Unfortunately, records are lacking about the relative success of the other ventures.

Kessler had studied in Germany and had done some work on the Central Park project under Olmsted. He had come to Kansas City during the land boom of the 1880s. There he helped design a small park around which Jarvis and Conklin financed the construction of upper-middle-income homes. He also worked for the Kansas City, Ft. Scott & Memphis Railroad (later the Frisco), which was then headquartered in Kansas City. By 1892, Kessler was the consulting landscape architect for the development of a park and boulevard project for Kansas City. He did not continue his involvement in the Roland Park planning.[39]

Kessler's plan for the first plat of Roland Park was not the constantly curving street layout that Olmsted had created for Riverside. Where Olmsted had only the winding river to consider besides the flat landscape, Kessler confronted an existing roadway and a heavily

38. Fishman, *Bourgeois Utopias,* 125.

39. Kessler's involvement with other projects for Jarvis and Conklin is indicated in his correspondence with Bouton. See letters from Kessler to Bouton, May 17, 1891, and August 20, 22, and 24, 1892, Roland Park Papers.

wooded and deeply cut site. The financial backers also wanted smaller lots of more regular shape than the one-hundred-foot curving frontages Olmsted created at Riverside. The first Roland Park lots generally were fifty-foot frontages with depths of approximately one hundred fifty feet. Some streets curved in relation to the established route of Roland Avenue, but more corners were squared off for even lot size than were rounded or that formed a triangle.

When Bouton wanted to open a new part of the acreage for development in 1898, he went to the Olmsted firm for his landscape design. Since Frederick, Sr., had retired, the founder's son, Frederick, Jr., and his stepson, John Charles, were in charge. Their first effort resulted in a second platted area of Roland Park. Kessler's plat had been of a flatter, upland area; the Olmsteds dealt with a rougher valley and called for a distinctly more curvilinear street layout with larger, more irregular lots. Either through the Olmsteds' influence or Bouton's own altered thinking, Roland Park took on a more informal planned appearance.[40]

Roland Park, though the product of speculation, was much more carefully prepared for sale than almost any of its competing subdivisions across the country. The land was assembled and the company officially in place by July 1891. The first public offering of lots appeared almost one full year later, on June 15, 1892. Bouton estimated in 1903 that the land syndicate had spent more than $115,000 in the first twelve months putting in streets, sidewalks, gutters, and storm drains. He attempted to save all existing trees, even routing sidewalks around them at times, as well as planting new ones where necessary to improve homesites. The Roland Park Company also thought it necessary to build houses on some of the lots in order to give a more completed impression of the development to potential purchasers. Bouton built a home for himself in 1892; Grasty, who had become editor of the *Baltimore News* in 1892, built a home for his family the following year. A brother of Edmunds who was among the original backers also built a home. The first sale of a house and lot to a noninvestor occurred in 1893.[41]

40. The two plats are shown in Weldon Fawcett, "Roland Park, Baltimore County, Maryland: A Representative American Suburb," 180.
41. Ibid., 183–84. Also see "From the District's Archives."

Good transportation was one of the essential elements of such a suburban subdivision. From the beginning, Roland Park residents could catch a train on the Maryland and Pennsylvania Line, which formed the eastern border for the first platted section. But the Maryland and Pennsylvania was not primarily a commuters' railroad and did not serve to heighten interest in the subdivision. Overland transportation by carriage was even more precarious because of poor connecting roads during the 1890s; rains could quickly mire a buggy. By early 1893 the Lake Roland Elevated Electric Railroad was carrying cars back and forth to city center in thirty minutes. According to Sam Bass Warner, this was about the maximum travel time that nineteenth-century people would endure regularly.[42]

A lack of shops nearby was an early drawback. Before Bouton and his local group assumed the ownership in 1903, the company had built a business block with grocery, drug store, and post office, all located in one connected set of buildings designed to blend in with the surrounding houses. This block, land for which had been reserved in all the plats and restrictions, was set back from the street to enhance this initial impression. Outside this area, the company prohibited by deed restriction the building or occupying of any store, saloon, or business property of any nature. The Roland Park Company was not the first to use deed restrictions as a means of establishing and maintaining the appearance and character of their subdivision, but it carried the legal method far toward its final formulation as established by J. C. Nichols in Kansas City.[43]

In addition to the ban on business establishments, the restrictions that were applied to the initial sale of lots set out the *minimum* cost for houses, which varied from two thousand dollars to five thousand dollars in pre-1900 values, required setbacks of thirty to forty feet, and prohibited the raising of hogs and the construction of privies or vaults or "other nuisances noxious or dangerous to health." These restrictions were to run with the land

42. Fawcett, "Roland Park," 180; "From the District's Archives," 4. Warner's estimates on travel time are interpreted from *Streetcar Suburbs,* 21–29.

43. The presence of the shopping block in 1903 is supported in Fawcett, "Roland Park," 190. The restrictions on business usage are best described in a *Baltimore American* article on May 16, 1912, 12.

in the deeds in perpetuity for the first lots only. Bouton later revised the length of the restrictions to limit them for twenty-five years, and later still he revised them to allow for the landowners to renew them for all the lots in the plat by majority vote.[44]

With the opening of the second section, and on the advice of the Olmsteds, Bouton instituted a requirement that all building plans had to be approved by the company. This was part of the sales contract rather than the deed restrictions in Roland Park. Bouton maintained that this was both "one of the most troublesome and from my standpoint the most necessary of all restrictions we have." The goal was not so much to dictate housing styles as to gain architectural consistency. To Bouton this control was most needed by the development company to insure continued high property values for themselves and their other buyers.[45]

Charges for the maintenance of roads and common grounds were part of the restrictions in Plat 1 from 1891 onward. This included the cost of lighting the streets, since that was done by a subsidiary of the company rather than by the city until the area was annexed into Baltimore in 1912. The company later included the cost of garbage, ash, and rubbish collection as part of the charges. These charges were not to exceed twenty-five cents for front foot per year, or twelve-and-a-half dollars per fifty-foot lot per year. The agreement stipulated that the funds were not for improvements but for maintenance of existing conditions only.

As the development progressed, lot shapes became more irregular. After the turn of the century, the square-foot method of assessment replaced the front-foot method, assessing the cost over the whole lot, regardless of frontage. By 1923 Bouton established a set amount for each lot owner to pay annually according to the amount of impact he thought the lot had on the overall development. This charge was established before the sale and attached to the deed through a restrictive clause. Under this method, no two landowners would necessarily have the same charges.[46]

44. "From the District's Archives" includes information from a June 18, 1893, advertisement that lays out all the restrictions cited here except the time limit. Bouton, "Development of Roland Park," 26–29.
    45. Bouton, "Development of Roland Park," 24–25.
    46. Fawcett, "Roland Park," 195; Bouton, "Development of Roland Park," 25–26.

As early as 1897, Bouton organized what he called the Roland Park Civic League to control and direct the receipts and disbursements of these maintenance charges. This worked well for some years, but in 1907 the Civic League objected to an increase in the company-provided water rates. This led in 1909 to the creation of the Roland Park Roads and Maintenance Corporation. Both residents and company officials served on this corporation's board of directors, which removed some of the pressure from the parent company. Even more relief was provided when the city annexed Roland Park and environs some three years later.[47]

The details of the development of Roland Park are significant to the background of the Nichols developments for several reasons. First, the initial landscape design in both areas was either done by George Kessler, in the case of Bouton, or apparently influenced by Kessler, in the case of Nichols. It will be shown in Chapter 4 that Nichols began to work with Kessler as early as 1909 in the Sunset Hill subdivision of the Country Club District. Secondly, the relatively complete nature of subdivision improvements provided by Bouton at Roland Park demonstrated to Nichols what a more fully developed planned residential community could be after twenty years of work. While the younger Kansas City developer did many things differently from Bouton after their first contact in 1912, Nichols sent his men to Roland Park on several occasions and corresponded frequently with Bouton until the latter's death in 1940.

A third result of these men's association was the expansion of horizons that each brought to the relationship. Bouton had been involved in the development of his own area and in that of Forest Hills Gardens in Queens, New York, by 1912. He was not an overly outgoing man, however, and seems to have been reluctant to push forcefully in public gatherings for the gospel of planned residential development. Nichols, on the other hand, was really just beginning his work in 1912 and had no real experience outside his own subdivisions. He did, however, have a good deal of willingness to share what he believed with the real estate profession. In later years he

47. See "Deed and Agreement between the Roland Park Company and the Roland Park Roads and Maintenance Corporation," dated July 26, 1909, Roland Park Papers.

arranged for Bouton to make presentations to realtors' conventions, and Nichols constantly referred to Roland Park as a major inspiration for his own efforts. Thus Bouton exposed Nichols to new ideas and different settings, while Nichols returned the favor by publicizing Bouton's work in ways that the rather shy little man from Baltimore would never have done on his own. They never engaged in any business ventures together, but there seems to have been a rich collaboration between these dissimilar men who enjoyed the same vocation—exclusive land development and homebuilding.

None of these nineteenth-century planned subdivisions should be considered as the norm for such work during that period. Most subdivisions were comparatively unplanned beyond the preparation of a plat map, with improvements usually being limited to marking lots and streets. Roland Park went as far in the other direction as any nineteenth-century suburb could go. Its ability to survive as a development company was unique when compared to the other commercial ventures mentioned as planned subdivisions in this brief survey.

Planned residential communities were an almost foreign idea to Kansas City in 1905. The subdivision history of the city was not at all remarkable when compared with the other growing metropolises of the day. In order to understand Nichols in his environment thoroughly, it is necessary to examine the land development history of Kansas City, Missouri, in some detail.

2

THE CITY OF KANSAS

When readers of the *Kansas City Times* opened their newspapers Thanksgiving morning, 1984, they discovered an entire section of the issue devoted to an analysis of the current importance and historical background of the J. C. Nichols Company. The piece was of interest on that particular day partly because the centerpiece of the Nichols Company's empire, the Country Club Plaza, would that night be the focus of the city's most important rite of Christmas—the turning on of thousands of colored lights outlining the buildings of the shopping center. The special section of the paper on the Nichols Company was primarily concerned with the degree of control this privately held company had exercised in the 1980s on land use and commercial properties in Kansas City and the immediately adjacent counties.[1]

The justification given for the investigative report was that the Nichols Company controlled land and institutions that had come to be thought of as "owned" by the public in Kansas City. The Country Club Plaza, where the lighting ceremony was imminent, had become a second downtown for the metropolitan area. Indeed, its shops encompass more square feet of retail space than the original downtown retail section. Further, unlike the first downtown area, which had become almost exclusively a "daytime only" environment for office workers and convention participants, "the Plaza," as Kansas Citians prefer to call it, offers extensive shopping, restaurants, entertainment, and office space that are open well into most evenings. The Plaza has even become something of a convention center, with two Nichols-owned hotels and several other hotels around its periphery. While Kansas Citians tend to identify the Nichols Company primarily with the Plaza, the shopping center is only the tip of an iceberg-shaped wedge of urban development stretching eight miles to the southwest across the Kansas state line.

1. Paul Wenske, "Fulfilling a Vision: The J. C. Nichols Company; A Family's Vision Helps Shape a City."

Christmas lights on the Country Club Plaza, about 1935. This trademark of the Nichols Company, which has become the central feature attracting holiday shoppers to the Kansas City area, began with just a few strings of electric lights in 1929. By the mid-1930s, it was already a tradition. In the foreground is an example of one of Nichols's "decorative filling stations," located approximately in the spot occupied by Swanson's in 1990. The larger building with the tower is the Plaza Theatre, Kansas City's first showplace theater to be constructed outside the downtown area, completed in 1929. KC54n55.

The company has not developed all the land inside that wedge, but its practices and communities have greatly influenced even the development done by others.

When Jesse Clyde Nichols opened his first small development in 1905, there were a few scattered farmers' settlements inside the southwest wedge south of Brush Creek. The only real attraction was the Kansas City Country Club, which occupied the site of present-day Loose Park. Nichols knew an attraction when he saw one; he made the most of proximity to one of the area's most exclusive clubs by naming his developments "the Country Club District" in 1908. Twenty-five-year-old Nichols recognized between 1905 and 1908 that the residential patterns of the wealthy were changing. As was occurring in many other American cities, the old elite neighborhoods adjacent to the original downtown center were deteriorating rapidly. Many of these privileged people, who could choose where they wanted to live, had already demonstrated their willingness to move straight south from their former neighborhoods. Nichols used the magnet of the Country Club, along with carefully planned land development, to lure them on across Brush Creek, then a sluggish little trickle meandering from Kansas across the southern limits of the city toward the Blue River valley to the east. Between 1905 and the growing impact of the Great Depression in 1930, Nichols and his company transformed a ten-acre tract of residential lots into homes, parks, new country clubs, and shopping centers for more than twenty-five thousand of the more prosperous citizens of the Kansas City metropolitan area. By the time of his death in 1950, the number of residents was approaching fifty thousand.

It is important to note that Nichols's home developments and shopping areas held their appeal from the earliest years well into the 1980s. While previous neighborhoods such as Quality Hill, just west of the downtown section, and Hyde Park, between downtown and Nichols's Country Club Plaza, lost their attraction and value in the first and fourth decades of this century respectively, Nichols's subdivisions retained their appeal throughout the century. Even the rapid changes of the 1950s and 1960s did not significantly affect appearances and values in these sections. J. C. Nichols not only advertised that he had "planned for permanence"; the goal was achieved.

In order to understand how this portion of the city-building process in Kansas City came about, it is important to visualize the demographic patterns prior to and following Nichols's activities. The developer alleged later in his career that his plans had changed the direction of residential growth in the metropolis. To assess this claim, it will be necessary to reconstruct the growth patterns between 1900 and 1905. A differentiation must be made between general demographic growth and specific movements of the more wealthy segment of the population.

Every city has its own development pattern. This is not to say that cities determine their own destinies; rather, various human and

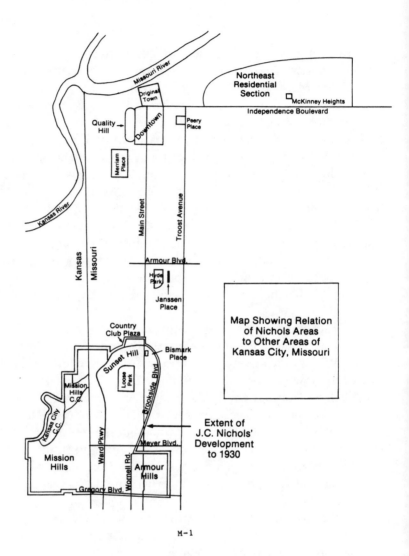

M-1

geographic realities join to influence the direction and quality of physical growth in urban areas. In North American cities, nearly all of which have been created within the last two hundred years, these patterns are comparatively easy to discern with the proper analytical tools. Some of the more useful tools for studying land development patterns are the books of plat maps of subdivisions and additions to the city. Municipalities have required that land be surveyed and pictorially represented in the divided form of streets and building lots before any land can be sold in parcels of an acre or more. Thus, sets of plat maps give the area and sequence of land development and indicate which individuals were involved in the initial plans for selling the land for urban use. Plat maps are readily available in the clerk's office of any American county or township.

Many American cities, including Kansas City, commissioned surveyors or civil engineering firms to draw up books of plat maps illustrating the improvements on the land as well as the prospective land subdivisions. Insurance companies often used these plat books for the purpose of rating different sections of the city for insurance purposes. Thus, the books showed the placement of commercial buildings, houses, outbuildings, and other significant structures, along with streets, water mains, and sewer lines. In the case of Kansas City these plat books were usually updated after major subdivision and/or building activity had boomed. The books show the degree of construction on the subdivisions at different times, in addition to the land surveys themselves.[2]

Subdividers and developers have long used the plat maps of preceding subdivisions to help them determine what areas are still available for development and who owns the land in question. Land lists, which keep track of the sales of particular parcels of land, aid in this search. These lists are also available in county clerks' offices. Developers planning to put up a building or starting a major remodeling job were required to take out a building permit stating what was to be built, the approximate cost, and the name of the contractor. These records are available from the local city or county clerk's office. An examination of either or both of these sources provides a good overview of the progress of building. As an aid in understanding the degree of Nichols's originality and influence in his type of subdivision work, these and other sources can reveal the growth patterns of Kansas City, Missouri, prior to J. C. Nichols's first land sales in 1905.

Kansas City's reason for existence was its location at the convergence of two rivers, the Missouri and the Kansas. The Missouri

2. The Kansas City Plat Books, 1886, 1891, 1903, and 1925. Sanborn's Insurance Map Books serve much the same purpose at other intervals. All are available in the Missouri Valley Room of the Kansas City Public Library.

River, the larger of the two, originates in Montana and flows through the Dakotas to form the boundary between Nebraska and Iowa and between Kansas and Missouri. Then it meets the other river—the Kansas. At the junction of the two rivers, the Missouri, which has tended to the southeast for hundreds of miles, bends directly east to cut across the midsection of the state of Missouri. Just above St. Louis it joins the Mississippi to roll toward the Gulf of Mexico.

Back at the juncture of the Kansas and the Missouri, a French trading village grew up on the Missouri side during the 1820s and 1830s. In 1836 a small group of investors bought some land from the widow of one of the French traders. They organized the Kansas Town Company and called their city-to-be "Kansas" because it lay at the mouth of that river. The confusion that would come because the larger Kansas City was in Missouri did not occur until much later. Everything west of the little town of Kansas was Indian Territory until 1854, when Kansas Territory was organized and opened to white settlement. Because Kansas City abuts the state of Kansas to the west, the city's development was always restricted on that side. With the Missouri River forming a major obstacle to northerly development, Kansas City necessarily had to grow east and south.

In 1853, by act of the Missouri legislature, the town became "The City of Kansas." The official designation as "Kansas City" did not come until the 1880s. The name was appropriate because the City of Kansas has always depended for its livelihood on the development of the tributary area of the river for which it is named. The fact that the state of Kansas became a major wheat-growing and cattle-raising state did much to determine the industrial and commercial development of the City of Kansas, Missouri.

The best estimate of Kansas City's population at the opening of Kansas Territory in 1854 was just under 450 persons. Six years later, on the eve of the Civil War, the official census tallied 4,418. The tenfold increase in population was largely a result of increased trade with the Kansas Territory to the west. The Kansas settlements south of the Kansas River had direct overland routes into Kansas City, Missouri.[3]

3. W. H. Miller, *The History of Kansas City*, 50, 74.

At the start of this period of rapid growth, the physical limits of Kansas City were legally confined to an area of approximately 440 acres hugging a rock landing at the edge of the Missouri River just below the mouth of the Kansas. Even within the six-year spurt of population growth from 1854 to 1860, the city grew officially to more than seven times its original area. A total of forty-two subdivisions and resurveys were filed with the county authorities during this period. This was Kansas City's first economic take-off period, and it was punctuated by a land boom.[4]

One of the earliest subdividers, Kersey Coates, platted several subdivisions during this eventful time. The three most important ones with regard to later Kansas City residential patterns were Coates' Addition (platted June 2, 1857), Peery Place (platted July 15, 1857), and Lucas Place (platted March 2, 1860). Coates had come to the City of Kansas to promote Free State interests supporting the immigration of antislavery advocates to the newly opened Kansas Territory just west of the little community. He had bought land in the City of Kansas for his financial backers in Pennsylvania. When they wanted to sell the land because of threatened disruptions in Kansas Territory and in the City of Kansas itself, Coates mortgaged his belongings and bought their interest.[5]

Coates' Addition and Lucas Place became very important addresses west of the small downtown section for upper-income Kansas City residents during the 1860s and 1870s. There was little in the physical design of the subdivisions that determined this status. The lots were fifty feet by one hundred twenty-five feet and were laid out in rectangular fashion. Coates did attach a building restriction to his deeds requiring the construction of brick buildings. This single restriction effectively screened out the construction of working-class homes, rooming houses, and cheap storefronts, which were almost always frame structures for reasons of economy.[6]

4. Ibid., 71.
5. Ibid.; Brown, *Frontier Community*, 107–9.
6. In 1889 brick residences in Kansas City, Missouri, cost an average of just under six thousand dollars to build, according to building permits. On the same basis, frame residences cost an average of just under twelve hundred dollars to build. Except where a contract-for-deed (essentially an installment sale) was possible, even the average frame house would have been far beyond the means of a

Kersey Coates laid out his Peery Place subdivision twelve blocks east of Coates' Addition (and eight blocks east of the newly developing downtown section) with a different idea in mind. He placed no brick-construction requirements on this property. After the Civil War, Coates began selling these lots in blocks of two and three to builders and speculators. He donated land to the black Baptist church and to the newly formed school board for a site for the new Lincoln School for black children. Coates appears to have been acting on his abolitionist principles in donating land to black institutions and in being willing to sell land, either directly or indirectly through builders, to blacks at all, for these were not common practices in the 1860s. Coates did not create a legally segregated subdivision, but it became, by 1868, the second-largest concentration of black families in the city.[7]

Coates' Addition and Lucas Place became known informally as "Quality Hill" in the 1880s. Wealthy newcomers, particularly those born and raised north of the Mason-Dixon line, bought lots from Coates and had tall, narrow brick residences constructed along Penn and Jefferson streets just west of the downtown area. In the 1980s this section of Kansas City has been the focus of much redevelopment activity, including some restoration and much new construction of housing and community facilities. The new residents are typically young professionals who aspire to some of the wealth and prestige held by the original residents of Coates's Quality Hill.

In Peery Place a curious pattern developed. Despite the presence of black churches and the school, there was a constant pressure for property occupied by blacks. Many wealthy whites who had either lived in Kansas City since the 1840s or who had moved there from Missouri and other former slave states had settled on land in Thomas A. Smart's subdivision and McGee & Holmes' Addition, located just west of Peery Place. The wealthy whites built substantial homes on the high ground along Cherry and Locust streets between Ninth and Fourteenth streets. As the white sections grew, Peery Place land

---

worker making less than six hundred dollars per year.

7. Grantor lists for Jackson County, 1865–1870. Black residence locations are from Kansas City *Directory and Reference Book for 1867–68.*

values rose, which forced rents higher than blacks could pay. The white landlords of black rental housing sold to other whites who wanted to build their own houses. This was the first instance in Kansas City history of what has come to be called "invasion and succession," in which one ethnic group moves into another's neighborhood and takes it over. In the 1950s and 1960s whites applied the term to blacks who moved into formerly white neighborhoods, but in the 1870s it was the whites who moved into formerly black neighborhoods.

This "invasion" meant that blacks had to retreat to areas east of Troost Avenue by the 1880s. There, south of Twelfth and centered along Vine Street, the black community found itself in a ghetto that remained intact until the 1950s. In 1913 white social workers referred to the black community south of Twelfth Street and Vine as "The Bowery" to signify it as the part of Kansas City most in need of rejuvenation. The seeds of Kansas City's division into class and racial neighborhoods thus originated in the land boom before the onset of the Civil War. The full development of these patterns, though, came after the disruption of the war years was over and a new land boom was underway.[8]

If the opening of new trade territory caused dramatic growth in Kansas City in the 1850s, railroad speculation and construction did even more for the small city after the Civil War. Literally dozens of railroad schemes were hatched in and around Kansas City during the period from 1854 through the 1880s. When overall economic conditions allowed optimism, there was always a railroad promoter ready to take investors' money.

Speculation about possible rail connections had partially fueled the 1850s land boom, but the City of Kansas had no completed rail service to the east until after the Civil War. Almost as soon as hostilities ceased between North and South, the pressure for railroad development began anew. A most important connection with the Burlington system, providing a direct connection with Chicago, resulted when Congress approved funding for a railroad bridge to

---

8. Maps illustrating subdivision locations are available in the *Atlas of Jackson County, Missouri*, n.p. The social workers' designation of "The Bowery" is in *Social Prospectus of Kansas City, Missouri*, 9–11.

span the Missouri River at Kansas City in 1867. The bridge was completed and service began during July 1869.

The construction crews, the increased trade, and the sheer anticipation of greater things to come started a new boom. Population increased sharply every year after the war until the Panic and Depression of 1873. From the 4,418 inhabitants of 1860, the city declined during the war to about 3,500 at its close. The next federal census in 1870 revealed that Kansas City had outgrown its rival cities with an official count of 32,286. Directory estimates of population in 1873 listed 40,740 inhabitants.[9]

In the land subdivision business, those were heady times indeed. Forty-two new subdivisions and resurveys were filed between the close of the war and the opening of the Hannibal Railroad Bridge for the Burlington route in 1869. (See Table 2-1.) Much of the activity took place in the largely industrial area of the West Bottoms at the mouth of the Kansas River, where rail depots, grain elevators, and packing plants vied for locations. The Kansas City Stockyards, founded by an eastern syndicate in 1871, took up even more West Bottoms space. Workers understandably wanted to live close to their workplace.[10]

The residential subdivisions created during this boom were more numerous than the industrial sites, but they were no more innovative in their layout. Almost all the subdivided land, whether intended for industrial, commercial, or residential use, was surveyed into rectangular blocks of similarly rectangular lots. Whether the land was flat or hilly, the rectilinear grid system of city planning reigned supreme. The main reason for this uniformity was the conviction among subdividers and investors alike that land use would change over time. They believed that in a rapidly growing city, a fine residence district of one period would eventually become a retailing or even an industrial site. In Kansas City this had been the case with the original townsite. By the 1870s the small houses that had clus-

9. Miller, *History of Kansas City,* 129, 144. Brown in *Frontier City* suggests a more likely figure of 20,000 to 25,000 in 1870.
10. Miller, *History of Kansas City,* 123–24; Glaab, *Kansas City and the Railroads,* 168–69; Sherry Schirmer and Richard McKinzie, *At the River's Bend: An Illustrated History of Kansas City, Independence and Jackson County,* 43–45.

TABLE 2-1

PLATS OF ADDITIONS TO KANSAS CITY, MISSOURI, 1865–1905

YEAR	NO. OF PLATS FILED
1865–1869	42
1870–1872	28
1873	4
1874–1877	6
SECOND ONE-HALF OF 1882	18
1883	40
1884	38
1885	93
1886	150
1887	282
1888	68
1889	44
1890	20
1891	13
1892	8
1893	6
1894	5
1895	7
1896	12
1897	17
1898	16
1899	17
1900	26
1901	34
1902	33
1903	34
1904	52
1905	76

Sources: Miller, 129, 143–144, 163. Jackson County Plat Books B-2, B-3, B-4, B-5, B-6, B-7, B-8, B-9, B-10, B-11, B-12.

tered about the levee and market square had given way to ware-houses, railroad shops, and trading emporiums. This expectation of changing use caused landowners to shape their lots as regularly as possible so that they could take advantage of any future rises in land values for commercial or industrial use. This anticipation of change in land use was summarized for real estate owners and agents in the idea of "highest and best use," an economic term that can be trans-lated as "the use that will bring the highest ground rent or sales value." The idea had been mentioned as early as 1903.[11]

The expectation of changing use led to the predominance of twenty-five-foot frontage lots in the 1870s and 1880s because that was a useful size for later storefronts. Such narrow lots could be combined for residence use or larger shop or warehouse space. A by-product was that cheaper rental housing was placed on twenty-five-foot lots, which resulted in crowding even though Kansas City was predominantly a single-family-home city in the nineteenth century.[12]

The 1865–1872 Kansas City land boom was choked off by the onset of depression accompanying the national Panic of 1873. The demand for new land flattened out. Twenty-eight new subdivisions had been platted from 1870 through 1872, but only four were platted in 1873. Six more small subdivision plats were filed during the next three years. The second Kansas City land boom had clearly bottomed out.[13]

One result of each nineteenth-century land boom in Kansas City was the annexation of newly subdivided land into the city. In 1873 the city council petitioned the state government for annexation of a comparatively small but important area south from Twentieth Street to Twenty-third and east from Troost and Lydia to Woodland. This move brought the Exposition Grounds and surrounding environs under city control.[14]

11. Henry V. Hubbard, "The Influence of Topography on the Layout of Land Subdivisions"; Richard M. Hurd, *Principles of City Land Values*, 87–88.

12. Jackson County Plat Book B–2. On the single-family-dwelling predominance in Kansas City (and other cities), see Tygiel, "Housing."

13. Miller, *History of Kansas City*, 143, 163.

14. A. Theodore Brown and Lyle Dorsett, *K.C.: A History of Kansas City, Missouri*, 247.

Just as railroads were the primary stimulus to city growth in the 1860s, meat packing became locally important in the 1870s when the firm of Plankington and Armour located its first branch outside Chicago in Kansas City. Throughout the decade the grain trade continued to improve as Kansas farmers began to adapt to climatic conditions by planting hard red winter wheat. The stockyards and grain elevators in Kansas City expanded to meet the greater demand. Population increased significantly during the 1870s, although not as spectacularly as in the previous half-decade. From the inflated census count of 32,286 or the more realistic estimate of 25,000 in 1870, census takers counted an increase to 55,813 in 1880. The bulk of the increase probably came between 1876 and 1880 as economic fortunes began to rise locally and nationally.[15]

The first newcomers in the 1870s found space in existing subdivisions. There was probably not enough money in circulation until late in the decade to stimulate much land speculation in excess of immediate demand. Only three new subdivisions were platted in 1878, but the number quadrupled to thirteen in 1879 and doubled again to twenty-seven in 1880. Land was beginning to be seen as a favorable investment again.

Intracity transportation had some effect on residential development decisions prior to the 1880s. Kansas City had mule-drawn cars after 1869 between downtown and Westport. During the 1870s mule lines to the northeast sector of the city were added. The result of these lines in residential patterns was a lengthening of the Quality Hill sections to the south and an expansion of the Independence Avenue high-value residence section to the east, areas where the transportation services were best. A string of houses also extended south along either side of Grand Avenue almost to OK Creek (now approximately Twenty-third Street). This built-up area was stimulated by the Kansas City-to-Westport line.[16]

Technological innovation was a major factor in the expansion of

15. Ibid., 201.
16. Ibid., 188, 202; Karl Peterson, Jr., "Color and Romance in History of Cable Cars," ; "History, Early (1876)," in Clippings File, Missouri Valley Room, Kansas City Public Library; George Ehrlich, *Kansas City, Missouri: An Architectural History, 1826-1976*, 34-42. Ruger's "Bird's-Eye View of Kansas City," c. 1878, is reprinted in Brown and Dorsett, *K. C.,* frontispiece.

the 1880s. The application of steam power to transportation helped power the first cable street railway in San Francisco in 1880, and by 1882 steam generators were used to power central stations for electrical output. Kansas City began to feel the effects of this innovation in 1882 when a central power station for illuminating electric arc street lights went into service. This was not the first such substation in the country, but the innovation was introduced in Kansas City the same year it appeared in other cities. Also in that year the city council granted the first franchise for a cable car line to the Kansas City Cable Railway Company. Construction was begun in 1883, and service on what became known as "the Ninth Street Line" commenced on June 15, 1885.[17]

Kansas City authorities granted franchises to several other cable traction companies during the 1880s. These firms built lines primarily south through Quality Hill and Merriam Place to Westport and directly east along Independence Boulevard and parallel streets to the south. One company built a spur south on Troost Avenue to serve the eastern edge of a growing affluent neighborhood near Hyde Park. The result of all these competing cable lines, built between 1885 and 1889, was a cross-hatching of the city along the lines dictated by topography. From Independence Avenue on the north to Eighteenth on the south, lines radiated from Main to Elmwood and Cleveland streets, where the land fell away into the Blue Valley, with resulting rapidly declining property values. Going to the south, lines traversed the OK Creek Valley (later the rail route serving the now-closed Union Station across from the Crown Center development) at five- to ten-block intervals to the highlands rising from Twenty-third to their summit at Springfield Avenue (later Thirty-first Street).[18]

One other type of traction service existed in the 1880s. Steam-powered "dummy lines" traversed the outlying territory from Kansas City in three directions by 1890. These smaller-scale steam rail-

17. Helen C. Monchow, "Finding a Base-Year for the Study of Urban Problems"; "Rich Chapter of the City's History in Evolution of the Street Car," *Kansas City Times*, June 8, 1937, page D.

18. Henry Van Brunt, "Early Farm at Linwood and Troost is Now 'Crossroads of Nation,'" *Kansas City Star*, November 2, 1947, real estate section; Peterson, "Color and Romance."

roads were called dummy lines because their engines were hidden behind the familiar siding of a horse car in order to prevent frightening real horses that passed the line on its intracity routes. One of these dummy lines ran south from Westport across Brush Creek to a little community near present-day Eighty-seventh and Brooklyn named Dodson. After crossing Brush Creek it followed a brook that meandered through a wide arc to Sixty-third Street. When J. C. Nichols bought his first piece of Missouri land in 1905, it lay within two blocks of the Dodson dummy line.[19]

The best level of streetcar service ran east and west. The greatest degree of land speculation took place between the northern bluffs running east from downtown and extending from Front Street (or First Street) to Eighteenth Street on the south. Cable lines, real and projected, stimulated interest in these sections. The highlands between OK Creek (about Twenty-third Street) and the Brush Creek Valley (just south of present Forty-seventh) formed the secondary area of land speculation; fewer cable lines were projected into its broader expanse. Development, as well as speculation, was noticeably slower in these sections. Since the southern highlands were not as rapidly developed, and because the northern elite families from Quality Hill and Merriam Place wished to maintain continuity with their youngsters setting up households, these people were more often attracted to the many available sites further south than east. They could better afford the horse and buggy necessary to convey them to downtown offices since mule-car and cable service was minimal to their sections.

An early leader in this movement to the far south, Charles F. Morse, was the financial representative of the Bostonian Adams family interests, which owned the Kansas City Stockyards and other properties. He had lived on Quality Hill since the early 1870s. In 1887 he moved his family to a large home he had built at Thirty-sixth and Warwick. This site was just over the crest of the highlands, where it would catch the summer breezes and be somewhat protected from harsh winter winds. It lay about eight blocks east and

---

19. Calvin Manon, "Street Cars Have a Long and Varied History in Kansas City," *Kansas City Times*, June 18, 1957, 28; "Nehemiah Holmes: Father of K. C. Street Car System," *Kansas City Journal*, April 16, 1922.

some twenty-six blocks south of his old homesite on Penn Street on Quality Hill. Morse built his mansion in the eastern part of a subdivision called Hyde Park, which had initially been laid out in 1886 by two mortgage bankers named Mastin and their real estate agent, Frank Baird. The Mastins had inherited part of the land through their wives, both of whom were daughters of Westport pioneers. Hyde Park was really part of Westport geographically, but the filed plat called it an addition to Kansas City. Strictly speaking, it was outside the city limits of both municipalities at the time.[20]

The development side of the Hyde Park subdivision, and the Kenwood subdivision directly east of it between Thirty-sixth and Thirty-ninth from Oak to Holmes, is the story of a conscious effort to expand the residential preferences of wealthy Kansas Citians. Morse was himself quite comfortable in his new surroundings in the 1880s, as were the Mastins, who built homes along Main Street two blocks west of Morse. They worked with two young Kansans who had moved to Kansas City in 1880 to enter the land-mortgage business, Samuel Jarvis and C. C. Conklin. These two mortgage bankers also built homes in Hyde Park in the late 1880s, directly across the street from each other. All these families built quite large homes and encouraged friends and associates to do the same.[21]

The two subdivisions were separated between Thirty-sixth and Thirty-ninth streets by a deepening ravine running south toward the latter. In other parts of Kansas City this type of area, even near a wealthy enclave such as Quality Hill, often developed into a neighborhood of shacks and squatter huts because the broken ground was considered unsuitable for large homes.[22]

20. From residential location studies done by Richard P. Coleman for his forthcoming study of the changes in upper-class Kansas City life from 1885 to the 1970s. Henry Van Brunt, "Elegance of Old Quality Hill Lives in Shadows of Progress," *Kansas City Star,* March 15, 1953, 4E, 9E.

21. On Jarvis, see his biographical sketch in Theodore B. Case, *The History of Kansas City,* and Albert H. Hindman, "Old Mansions on Warwick Boulevard Recall Era of Spacious Hospitality," *Kansas City Times,* December 31, 1951. On Morse, see E. R. Schauffler, "This Was Quality Hill in the Dollar Gold Piece Days," *Kansas City Star,* February 7, 1943, C1.

22. Clifford Naysmith, "Quality Hill: The History of a Neighborhood," Mis-

Jarvis and Conklin hired young George Kessler to landscape the ravine into a pleasure park for nearby residents. He laid out walks, croquet grounds, and scenes of natural beauty. Later residents became so obsessed with privacy that they put up an iron fence with locked gates, to which only subscribing residents could obtain keys. The initial goal of a scenic park to attract future land and home buyers became a monument to the exclusiveness of the neighborhood, much like Louisburg Square in Boston and Llewellyn Park yet today.[23]

In addition to building their own homes in the area and financing the improvement of potentially damaging surroundings into an attractive, if exclusive, park, Jarvis and Conklin embarked on a speculative homebuilding campaign to attract even more buyers to the area. They hired Edward H. Bouton to superintend the construction of at least four houses in the Kenwood subdivision in 1888 and 1889. One of these was purchased by a business associate, Henry M. Beardsley (who later became mayor of Kansas City), but the remainder were purely speculative. When these houses were going up in Kenwood in 1888–1889, the boom had passed, and houses and lots were becoming harder to sell in Kansas City. Jarvis and Conklin then began to look for other investment opportunities, including the one in Baltimore that evolved into Roland Park.[24]

The land boom of the 1880s can be examined to a limited extent with the beginnings of the Hyde Park exclusive residential section in a more slowly growing part of the city, but the dynamics of the boom are better illustrated in the northeast sections of the city, which fluctuated most rapidly in value. Simple numbers give some indication of the interest in land investments and sales during this period. Expensive residential property in the northeast section was platted and sold during the land and building boom of the 1880s. One example is an eight-block subdivision offered in 1886 that was located directly east of the site later chosen by lumber magnate R. A.

souri Valley Room Series, no. 1, Kansas City Public Library, 1962, 24.

23. Ann White, "Old Hyde Park Was a Child's Wonderland," *Kansas City Star,* August 15, 1957.

24. Kansas City Chapter, AIA, *Kansas City,* 108, 110.

Long for his huge mansion on the bluffs overlooking the East Bottoms. Named McKinney Heights after the most recent landowner, the small subdivision became part of one of the more exclusive residential areas of Kansas City.

Advertised attractions were elaborate for such property. The agent had all tree trunks up to the height of the fences painted white like the fences themselves, "making you imagine you were in a fairy land." The view from the adjacent bluffs was one of the more spectacular in the area. No malaria was expected, thanks to a grove of catalpa trees, which was thought to be "an antidote to the missimatic poison." Deed restrictions were quite extensive. Cesspools were banned. Business establishments were excluded. The central street of the subdivision had a thirty-foot setback requirement, and the secondary streets had twenty-foot setbacks. Two of the streets had minimum house price requirements of $5,000. Side streets carried $3,500 restrictions. One advertisement explained that these restrictions were necessary because "it is desired to make this beautiful suburb the home of the CULTURED, REFINED, and ARISTOCRATIC." Prices were not quoted in the newspapers for land in McKinney Heights, as befitted an exclusive subdivision. The agent did suggest that because of new railroad development in the East Bottoms below the subdivision, he foresaw land values doubling in one year.[25]

Such inducements and restrictions, while not common across Kansas City, appeared in some instances (even during boom times like the 1880s) to ensure a certain level of property values for the near future. However, no one during this era put together enough property with similar requirements to have the overall impact that J. C. Nichols would have some twenty-five years later.

Residential real estate could be offered in a variety of ways. In the spring of 1885 lots in Henwood's Addition on Eighteenth Street received the following advertising support:

$950.00 [or] $350.00 and $75.00 every 3 months will buy a 40 ft. lot on E. 18th St., on the high ground near Chestnut Ave. Has a fine view

25. Both quotes are from a classified display advertisement in the *Kansas City Journal*, June 6, 1886.

of the city. The six adjoining lots have been sold in the last 5 days, and 6 2-story frames will be built at once. Street cars, sidewalks, perfect title, full abstract, health, happiness, and a great bargain with each and all of these lots. See and be satisfied. George Law, sole agent of Henwood's Addition. Sheidley Bldg. 9th and Main Streets.[26]

This revealing advertisement illustrates the type of offerings made in residential real estate during the boom. The cost per front foot of land was $25. The streetcars mentioned in the advertisement were planned, but not yet in service; the line along Eighteenth Street did not open until 1887. The sidewalks were usually made of boards. The $350 down payment and the $75 every three months made the purchase of such land impossible for working-class people, who might make only a little more than that in a year. The cost of building, when added to this land cost, meant that only speculators could invest in such property. The statement that six lots had been sold and that six new frame houses would be going up shortly on adjacent lots clearly indicates that speculators had bought the other land. During the boom, this type of activity often resulted in the quick construction of cheap frame dwellings from which the speculator might derive rental income. Construction for owner occupancy would have been financially difficult.[27]

Ultimately, the boom was self-liquidating. Land values were boosted so artificially high that no one would buy. Real estate sales dropped, and land subdivision lost favor with investors. Boomers moved on to other cities like Los Angeles or Chicago or Baltimore. The resulting depressed real estate values lasted until 1900, according to one observer.[28]

Just as the glow faded and the economy slipped toward depression, a fifteen-year-old movement for parks gained more strength. People had argued for and against park space for Kansas City since

26. *Kansas City Evening Star,* April 15, 1885, classified section.
27. Kersey Coates's son-in-law, Homer Reed, wrote a revealing commentary on boom-era speculation in *The Science of Real-Estate and Mortgage Investment,* 46–53.
28. Ibid., 80.

the close of the second boom in 1872. William Rockhill Nelson had used his *Kansas City Star* to widen support for the effort. Through a series of legal twists, a permanent planning and administrative body was established in 1891. This group named George Kessler to be its paid secretary and unpaid engineer–landscape architect. By 1893 Kessler had surveyed the city, laid out a plan of parks connected by broad boulevards, and submitted a written report.[29]

The report has been heavily studied by critics of the so-called "city beautiful movement." It has usually been evaluated for what it was not intended to be—an urban renewal document sixty years ahead of its time. It was, in fact, a call for public funds to bolster private real estate values. Kessler was aware that some less desirable residential sections would be demolished to make room for the boulevard system, but he was more concerned at the time with shoring up values or creating potential home sites for middle- and upper-income Kansas Citians.[30]

Kessler deplored the deterioration of residential neighborhoods through invasion by shops or other business uses. He planned for his boulevard system to accomplish the goal of "fixing and classification of residence sections." He argued that "such a system, if carefully planned, if it give due weight to existing conditions and adapt itself to the topography, avoiding as much as possible forced routes and forced construction, will give a permanent residence character to certain sections of the city and will determine and fix for a long time to come, if not permanently, the best and most valuable residence property."[31]

As a result of this commercial emphasis, the parks were primarily intended to be playgrounds and "breathing spaces" for the poor and working classes, while the boulevards were supposed to ensure high residential property values for middle- and upper-income residents. The reason for this two-fold argument is not difficult to guess: the plan required public approval. Tax money was required to finance the proposed projects, and these taxes had to come from special benefit districts, assessed according to property value. The public

29. Wilson, *City Beautiful Movement,* 45.
30. Ibid., 49.
31. *Report of the Board of Commissioners of Parks and Boulevards,* 14.

and the decisionmaking bodies needed reassurance that it was going to be worth the cost.

In the northeast section of the city, the boulevards were largely placed along what were already high-value residential streets such as Independence Avenue. There the attraction was the protection of existing value. In the southern part of the city (and, in fact, beyond the southern city limits), South Boulevard was projected to run along Thirty-fifth street from Lydia west to a continuation of Broadway on the west side. In this section the boulevard plan actually helped create value, as intended. After South Boulevard was officially included in the plan, several members of the Armour meat-packing family built homes along its tree-lined right-of-way. South Boulevard was renamed Armour Boulevard in 1899 after the death of original park board member S. B. Armour, who happened not to be one of the Armours living on the boulevard.

Construction began on the park and boulevard system in 1895 and continued into the 1920s. As one historian has pointed out, the system was essentially an effort at zoning at least ten years prior to the enactment of zoning laws in Los Angeles. Its effect on the residential patterns of Kansas City lasted until the close of World War II. Ultimately, however, the park and boulevard system could not prevent the decline of property values. Only one census tract (the one surrounding Janssen Place, a private boulevard) along the original boulevard system still ranked high in property values in 1980. J. C. Nichols's restrictions have proven much more effective long-term protectors of property values.[32]

One offshoot of the parks and boulevards movement was a private attempt at residential boulevard development. The plan called for a private-street type of exclusive subdivision, which had thrived in St. Louis. In 1896 Arthur Stilwell was in the midst of building what would become the Kansas City Southern Railway. He had built a large home in Kenwood Addition facing south on Thirty-sixth Street between Holmes and Locust streets in 1892. The section of Kenwood subdivision to the south of his home had not been built upon as late as 1896. He determined to fill that space with a "pri-

32. Wilson, *City Beautiful Movement,* 49.

vate place" like the private streets he had seen and admired in St. Louis.

Announced in a front-page news story of the *Star*, Stilwell's Janssen Place was avowedly patterned after Vandeventer Place in St. Louis. He had a massive limestone gate erected at the single entrance off Thirty-sixth Street. Lots were subdivided into seventy-five-foot frontages with two-hundred-fifty-foot depths. The street was laid out for two blocks and was divided in the center by a curbed boulevard strip. Stilwell planned for the planting of trees and the placement of fountains and statuary in the boulevard strip. Houses had to cost a minimum of ten thousand dollars. Land costs to buyers were projected at thirty-five to forty dollars per front foot.[33]

Stilwell had intended to build a mansion for himself on Janssen Place, but by 1899 his railroad fortunes had changed. Both his own home plans and the further development of Janssen Place were put aside. Lots gradually sold over the years. Large homes were built on most of the lots by the 1920s; by then, however, the private street had become more of a dividing line between the homes of the elite of Hyde Park and Kenwood to the west and the merely wealthy or upper-middle-income residences to the east toward Troost. Residents of Janssen Place fell into the merely wealthy category and were not accepted into the inner circles of Kansas City's elite.

The information concerning residential locations of "Capital S" society and "lower-upper-class" Kansas Citians is derived from the unpublished research of Richard P. Coleman on the changes and continuities in that city's upper class from the 1880s through 1975. The determination as to who fits in which categories was painstakingly arrived at through research concerning membership lists and directories of boards of businesses, financial institutions, and charitable organizations, and through interviews with long-time residents. In 1915, the breakpoint of Janssen Place is most clear. Of the

33. "Homes Around a Park," *Kansas City Star*, January 10, 1897, 1; "The Entrance to Janssen Place," *Kansas City Star*, January 30, 1897, 8; Henry Van Brunt, "City Developed 'Courts' and 'Places' in the 1880s," *Kansas City Star*, April 4, 1955.

members of Capital S society living in Hyde Park–Kenwood at the time, 83 percent lived west of Janssen Place, while only 17 percent lived east of it. None lived on the private street itself. For the "lower-uppers," the situation reverses. Only 35 percent living in Hyde Park–Kenwood in 1915 resided west of Janssen Place, while 60 percent lived to the east of it and 5 percent actually lived on the private street itself.[34]

The most important nineteenth-century Kansas City subdivision as it relates to the story of J. C. Nichols had its origins in the era of the booming 1880s, but the sections that laid the groundwork for the young Kansan were not begun until just after the turn of the century. The Rockhill District, overlooking the north bank of meandering Brush Creek, was the brainchild of the publisher of the *Kansas City Star*, William Rockhill Nelson.

The magnet for the Rockhill District was Nelson's massive native stone home, Oak Hall. Begun in 1887, the structure was enlarged several times. The grounds, covering more than six blocks between Forty-fourth and Forty-seventh streets, Oak to Cherry, allowed such additions without losing their sweeping grace because of their huge size. With his home complete, for the time being, by 1890, Nelson began to sell land around his estate that he had acquired during and after the boom of the 1880s. Land acquisition was a slow, steady process for Nelson, but by 1905 he had acquired 275 acres on both sides of Brush Creek in the immediate vicinity of Oak Hall.[35]

The Southmoreland section of the Rockhill District was intended as a site for impressively large homes. Nelson laid it out so that Warwick Boulevard, an extension of Grand Avenue, ended in Southmoreland, winding around the several large estates he planned to sell. Warwick was intended to be a southerly extension of the boulevard system's South (later Armour) Boulevard, but the park board did not accept the proposal. Nelson proceeded to petition the town of Westport to develop the street, while he himself contrib-

34. Coleman, unpublished research summaries in possession of the author.
35. "Rockhill District in Kansas City."

uted by planting trees so that it would serve as a fitting entry into his major area of development.[36]

His friend and ally in the effort to build parks and boulevards about Kansas City was August Meyer. The two worked out a large plot for Meyer across Oak Street from Nelson's own land. The estate Meyer built in 1896 was sufficiently large that it was later converted to an entire campus for the Kansas City Art Institute. Other Southmoreland landowners by 1904 included two members of the Armour meat-packing families, one Cudahay, a nephew of John Deere, several influential lawyers, and some grain merchants. Almost all had moved from Quality Hill or Merriam Place to Southmoreland.[37]

Many of the houses Nelson had built in his Rockhill District in 1904–1905 were small frame and stone houses. He planned to provide his employees at the *Star* with relatively inexpensive housing in a good neighborhood. In order to give these small company houses more room, he built them on only one side of the street in several areas, giving each house more of a view than would have otherwise been possible. Most of these small homes were retained by Nelson as rentals. Other lots in this new section were for sale. The stated goal of the owner was "to immutably establish it as a residence district of high class." This was possible because of the "high class" neighbors to the west and the protection of Gillham Road in the boulevard system on the east side of the property.[38]

Nelson constructed Rockhill Road as a privately developed boulevard just after the turn of the century. He extended the winding roadway from Oak Street at a point one block north of his residence, to the southeast, gradually up a hillside, and then down into the Brush Creek valley. At the creek he constructed a stone bridge as an indictment against what he called "tin bridges." South of Brush

36. Wilson, *City Beautiful Movement*, 18–19.

37. Display advertisement for "The Rockhill Neighborhood." Previous residential locations are from unpublished research by Richard P. Coleman in the possession of the author.

38. Landmarks Commission of Kansas City, "Nomination Form for the National Register of Historic Places," in "Rockhill" vertical file, Missouri Valley Room, Kansas City Public Library, n.p.

Creek the roadway curved irregularly back to Oak at Fiftieth Street.
Nelson planted trees all along Rockhill Road, extending the plantings south on Oak to Fifty-first and then west some ten blocks to
Wornall Road. This tree-lined route brought his homeowners and
renters to the gates of the Kansas City Country Club. His advertising exploited this proximity.[39]

Nelson attempted to deal creatively with the question of how to
treat the unsightly roadbeds of the much-needed trolley car lines.
He placed them on one side of the street rather than down the
middle, and further separated them from road traffic by using sidewalks and plantings. By 1904 Nelson had deeded enough right-of-
way to the Metropolitan Street Railway System to allow them to
build a modern trolley from Westport all the way through the Rockhill District to connect with a line to Swope Park coming down
Troost. The route came as close to Brush Creek as Forty-eighth and
Rockhill.

The Rockhill District became known for its low native stone walls
with overgrown flowering vines and bushy shrubs. Trees were
planted where needed, and roadways were curved to ease the grade
or to conform to the landscape contour. Nelson supervised the
construction of most of the houses that went up in the Rockhill
District; his trademark was the pioneering use of native stone as a
building material. When the William Rockhill Nelson Gallery of Art
opened on the site of Nelson's former manorial home in the 1930s,
the design for the sculpture garden on the grounds of the gallery was
altered to include the little stone walls that Nelson had so meticu-
lously maintained decades earlier.[40]

When J. C. Nichols bought his ten-acre plot just north of tree-
lined Fifty-first Street leading from Rockhill to the country club, he
consciously set out to mimic much of the work done by William
Rockhill Nelson. He was aware of the beginnings of the southerly
migration from Quality Hill and the examples of exclusive development set down by the Hyde Park and Janssen Place subdivisions. If

39. Ibid. See also classified advertisements in *Kansas City Star*, February 7 and
March 6, 1904.
40. Wilson, *City Beautiful Movement*, 18–19.

any single developer is responsible for the majority of upper-class Kansas City moving directly south after the turn of the twentieth century, it was Nelson. In 1905 Nichols began to deal with the problem of how best to capitalize on the lessons of these earlier developments, particularly the Rockhill District.

3

THE COUNTRY CLUB DISTRICT

Jesse Clyde Nichols started building houses in Kansas City, Kansas, in 1903 with a small subdivision created by an earlier subdivider. It lay just north of Quindaro Boulevard, one of the major roadways in the northern part of town. The Kansas River had flooded that summer, causing many working men and their families to lose homes in the river bottoms; Quindaro, though, was high and dry. Small homes were built there on thirty-foot-wide lots. The lot-and-house package was priced to sell for less than one thousand dollars on easy terms.

Nichols had raised the money for this venture by borrowing from farmers around his hometown of Olathe, Kansas. His father had been active in the local grange. Nichols had bought meat and produce from some of these farmers during his summers off from high school and college, then offering the goods at wholesale in the Kansas City, Missouri, marketplace. Using other people's money, the young man returned them a fair profit on their investment and reinvested much of his own earnings in his projects.[1]

Indeed, one of the hallmarks of J. C. Nichols's experience prior to launching into the land development and homebuilding business was his fervent effort to improve his economic situation through sales activities. As he remembered these experiences in later years, he sold everything from overripe bananas to United States maps. Though his parents were apparently willing to help pay for his education at the University of Kansas, Nichols appears to have insisted on paying his costs himself. He joined a prestigious fraternity (Beta Theta Pi) but chose to serve as chapter steward because that meant free room and board in return for managing the fraternity's finances.[2]

Upon graduation as a member of Phi Beta Kappa and valedic-

1. J. C. Nichols Company Scrapbook (hereafter cited as Scrapbook, followed by volume and page numbers) 1:19.

2. Ethel Treshadding, "Genealogy of Jesse Clyde Nichols," 11. This typescript was probably prepared in 1950 after Nichols's death.

torian of his class at Kansas, Nichols accepted the university scholarship for a year of study at Harvard with the intention of reading law. "Until I was at Harvard I had expected to be a lawyer; everything had been done with that end in view. I would have been in Harvard law school if my health had permitted," he recalled to a reporter in 1929. He had apparently been such an active student at Kansas that he had brought on a physical collapse of some sort.[3]

While at Harvard, he took a course in industrial history taught by Professor O. M. Sprague. As Nichols remembered the thrust of the professor's arguments in 1929, the central concept was that industry had historically moved south and mostly west from the northeast as it migrated toward more available natural resources. This was interpreted by the professor as a natural economic law—that industry would always relocate closer to raw material sources. Nichols indicated to an interviewer in 1929 that this was the idea that moved him toward land development.[4]

Nichols did not move directly into the urban land subdivision business, however. He spent a few months in the summer of 1903 traveling through the remaining territories of Oklahoma, New Mexico, and Arizona, looking for land he might be able to buy and develop into a land colonization scheme to attract some of the thousands of potential homesteaders who were then flocking to those areas. Somewhere during this trip, he later remembered, he decided that the best place to develop land for sale might be much closer to his home base. This decision in 1903 brought him into partnership with two former Beta Theta Pi fraternity brothers, W. T. and Frank Reed, in land development and house building in Kansas City, Kansas.[5]

Significantly, Nichols seems to have transformed his ideas about growth in land values from an industrial history course into a practical experiment in urban land development. Nichols would continue to be a student of land-use patterns throughout his life. He bought up or gained sale control of land much in advance of its

3. Richard B. Fowler, "How J. C. Nichols Reached His Turning Point," *Kansas City Star*, December 8, 1929, 6C.

4. Ibid.

5. Ibid.

being offered on the market. This pattern continued after his death and into the 1980s, when the J. C. Nichols Company was credited with being the largest private landowner in Johnson County, Kansas, and a major landowner in developing residential suburbs to the east of Kansas City, Missouri.[6]

At the same time Nichols began to put his land-value ideas to work with the Reeds, the land subdivision and home construction business began to revive across the river in Kansas City, Missouri. Table 3-1 illustrates the turnover and fluidity in the construction and real estate businesses from 1887 through 1905. The term *architect* should not be construed to apply only to trained, artistic designers of buildings, for in this earlier era of elastic titles many homebuilders described themselves as architects in order to distinguish themselves from their less accomplished fellow tradesmen.[7]

The increasing number of people in the real estate business, particularly after 1903, indicates that there was a growing interest in the exchange of land and buildings after the mid-1890s. This developed into a small boom by 1905, when, for two years running, at least one hundred additional people entered some aspect of the real estate trade each year. The situation was ripe for a young man like Nichols to move into a position of prominence in a short time if he handled himself well.

Nichols and the Reeds bought land for residential sites on the far south side of Kansas City, Missouri. The young realtor convinced his farmer-backers from Olathe to go along with him as well. The plot he purchased with this financial backing lay south of Brush Creek across from the splendor of Southmoreland and the growing Rockhill District of William Rockhill Nelson. It had been subdivided in 1887 during the great land boom of the 1880s. Few lots sold at that time, and Nichols was able in 1905 to put together two city blocks of Bismark Place as the first site for his Missouri operations. In this early venture, Nichols aligned himself with people he knew and whom he hoped knew the real estate business. The Reeds

6. Wenske, "Fulfilling a Vision," *Kansas City Star,* June 4, 1950, C-1.

7. Gwendolyn Wright, in *Moralism and the Model Home,* 46–55, writes of the scorn professionally trained Chicago architects had for these builders, who adopted their title with no justifiable right as far as the trained architects were concerned.

TABLE 3-1

FLUCTUATION IN NUMBERS OF THOSE INVOLVED
IN THE HOME BUILDING AND REAL ESTATE BUSINESSES
IN KANSAS CITY, MO., 1887–1905

YEAR	# "ARCHITECTS"	# REAL ESTATE MEN
1887	47	689
1889	65	447
1890	59	336
1892	32	268
1893	32	249
1895	36	259
1896	33	275
1897	31	311
1898	40	339
1899	43	372
1900	46	388
1903	58	485
1904	60	568
1905	61	653

Source: *Hoye's Kansas City Directory* for the years indicated.

proved to be mostly silent partners and were only mildly supportive of the younger man's increasing interest in residential land development. From 1903 to 1908 they operated their business under the name of Reed, Nichols and Company.[8]

Bismark Place was located between Walnut and Main streets, Forty-ninth to Fifty-first streets. Brush Creek, which had to be crossed on Nelson's stone bridges to get to the Country Club, isolated Bismark Place from the real estate activity Nelson was devel-

8. Scrapbook 1:19.

oping above its north banks. The creek was marshy and tended to flood, and no successful residential development had been achieved as far south and west as this little ten-acre plot. What Nichols did have in his favor was the trend of well-to-do Kansas Citians to move as straight south or as straight east from downtown as possible. The southerly trend had been helped by Nelson's Warwick Boulevard, Southmoreland, and Rockhill District attractions. Nichols's small new subdivision was one block west of what would have been an extension of Warwick had it gone south of the creek. If Nichols had gone east along Independence Avenue for his new development, the land would have been costly, and not nearly as much would have been available.[9]

This phenomenon of the wealthy moving in a more-or-less straight line from their original neighborhoods near the center of the city toward its outskirts was observed by land development analyst Homer Hoyt. His "sector theory," based primarily on observations in the Washington, D.C., and Chicago areas, holds that the wealthy, who have the greatest ability to choose their residential locations, will decide to live within one or more wedge-shaped sectors of the metropolitan area. According to Hoyt's theory, they simply move outward within a rather narrow corridor. Hoyt used statistics gathered by FHA in the mid-1930s concerning the location of residents by level of rent paid. (Later in this chapter, a correlation will be drawn between levels of rent paid and values placed on housing by owner-occupants. An analysis will then be done of the changes in location of high-value housing from 1940 to 1980.) This concept had been stated in rough form as early as 1903.[10]

The much-advertised route to the Kansas City Country Club ran from downtown through Nelson's Rockhill area across Brush Creek. Participants in the golf games and polo matches at the club

9. Land values along Independence Avenue at the turn of the century are shown in Hurd, *Principles of City Land Values,* 153. Land was retailing at $150 per front foot on Independence Avenue at the time, while the most valuable land on Warwick Boulevard was $50 per foot, with prices declining further south from the Hyde Park section, where the highest values were located.

10. Hoyt, *The Structure and Growth of Residential Neighborhoods in American Cities,* 112–22; Hurd, *Principles of City Land Values,* 56–74, 149–59.

had to pass Nichols's subdivision in order to play their favorite sports, so members of the exclusive organization had to notice Bismark Place. The bridges over Brush Creek at both Oak and Rockhill Road provided access. Nichols was not bashful about pointing out the geographic proximity of his subdivision to those areas already accepted as potential homesites for the well-to-do; his first advertisement for the land, which appeared in 1905, stated that it was in the Rockhill District. Nelson seems to have taken offense at the incorrect statement about what was in the publisher's development, for he called the young realtor into his office to explain the boundaries. Later that year, Nichols was pointing out to potential customers that his subdivision overlooked Rockhill "Boulevard" to the east and the Country Club to the west. Another advertisement indicated that the land adjoined that of Nelson and two other prominent Kansas Citians. He was claiming value by association—a technique to which he returned on many occasions. It must be noted that another student of Nichols relates this story of Nichols's confrontation with Nelson somewhat differently. Gary O. A. Molyneaux states that Nelson was not aware of Nichols's development until 1909. This assertion is difficult to accept in that Nichols had advertised heavily in the *Star* since 1905 and Nelson's paper had done a major article on the announcement in April 1908 that Nichols and his backers had gained control of over 1,000 acres in the area. Based on circumstantial evidence, it appears that Nichols and Nelson must have made contact at least as early as 1905.[11]

"Buy low and sell high": Nichols followed that motto as closely as possible for the early land purchases. The price for the original acreage in Bismark Place was $800 per acre. Many of these lots sold for $6 per front foot, or $300 total cost for a 50-foot lot. Much of the rest of the early Country Club District was bought for approximately $1,000 per acre. He could get at least 7 building lots of 50-by-125 feet out of an acre, which meant there would be 350 front feet to sell per acre. The price per front foot on this newer ground ranged from $8 to $15. At $8 per front foot, a gross selling

11. Reed, Nichols & Co. advertisement, *Kansas City Star,* April 2, 1905, 18, 2d section. Also see advertisements, *Kansas City Star,* April 9 and May 28, 1905.

price of $2,800 per acre would be realized. At $15 per foot, the gross price jumped to $5,250 per acre.[12]

As he began to sell land and houses on the Missouri side successfully, Nichols sought out and was sought out by more wealthy and influential men who would back him. W. R. Nelson was the first of these backers, although he never put any money in Nichols's enterprises. The publisher-builder's main contribution was the favorable publicity he afforded Nichols's developments in the *Kansas City Star* and *Times*. Grain broker Frank G. Crowell became involved very early. When Nichols was a student at Kansas University, the young developer had met Crowell, who was a member of the Board of Regents and a partner in the grain commission firm of Hall, Baker and Company. Through Crowell, Nichols also met Crowell's grain partner, Herbert F. Hall, and their relationship proved most profitable for both Hall and Nichols. At one point in the mid-1920s, the J. C. Nichols Company declared a $950,000 dividend, which the three divided among themselves. Crowell and Hall had each invested $50,000 in this company in 1908. Nichols invested no money; he worked out his share through the sales that generated these dividends. The three had become involved in their first land deal together in late 1905.[13]

Hugh Ward, a neighboring landowner near Nichols's early developments, was another fortunate contact for Nichols. Ward, a young lawyer, inherited several hundred acres of land above Brush Creek and southwest of Nelson's Rockhill District from his pioneering father, Seth Ward. When the Kansas City Country Club determined to relocate from the confining area of Hyde Park just before the turn of the century, Ward had donated the use of a large pasture on his land southwest of Fifty-first and Broadway (now Wornall Road in this part of Kansas City). By 1906 Nichols was working with Ward in the development of the remainder of the lawyer's estate into Sunset Hill, ultimately Nichols's most exclusive Missouri-side de-

12. Treshadding, "Genealogy," 24; "Representative Real Estate Sales," *Kansas City Star,* July 16, 1905; also, advertisement, *Kansas City Star,* August 20, 1905. The prices listed were asking prices. Actual selling prices were probably less.

13. W. G. Clugston, "Kansas City: Gateway to What?" 275; Scrapbook 2:8; "More KATY Deeds Filed," *Kansas City Star,* December 10, 1905.

velopment. George Kessler was engaged to lay out the property for residential use. At least two years of intensive land preparation went into Sunset Hill, for it was not formally announced to the public until 1908.[14]

As Nichols filed new plats for land acquired during 1906 and 1907, the influence of a landscape planner became apparent. Particularly, the Rockhill Place plat, filed November 23, 1907, contains both winding streets rather than all-right-angle corners and blocks that are longer east to west than north to south. The standard block layout in Kansas City was the latter. This new arrangement, which was widely used in Sunset Hill, allowed houses to have more rooms with southern exposure and arranged the solid parts of the blocks so that they would break the prevailing northerly winter winds.[15]

Having a landscape architect prepare a plat was definitely more costly. In the years before collaboration with Kessler, Nichols and other subdividers were required only to have the land surveyed and mapped by a civil engineer. Anything done beyond that to improve the land for resale was purely voluntary. For most subdividers, including Nichols at the very start, the cost of a plat was merely for the survey and map preparation. When a landscape architect became involved, not only were his fees higher than those charged by a civil engineer, but the professional landscape man also always included plans for improving the property that were expensive to implement. The value to the developer depended upon the degree of acceptance of the landscape architect's ideas by potential land purchasers. After 1907, Nichols determined that this extra cost was worthwhile in the added salability it brought to his lots.

The plats also contained another important feature: restrictions on how the land could be used, what type of buildings could be constructed on it, and to whom it could be sold. These "deed restrictions" (sometimes called "restrictive covenants") were not uncommon in Kansas City, but prior to Nichols they were seldom filed with the plat, which was a map. Beginning with his plat map of Rockhill Park, Nichols always filed the restrictions with the plat.

14. The first advertisement for Sunset Hill was in a Sunday display ad by the Nichols Company, *Kansas City Star*, July 19, 1908, 13C.
    15. Rockhill Place plat, Plat Book B–14, 80.

Later, as the restrictions became more detailed, he filed and printed them separately and gave the copies to prospective and actual purchasers alike. In this way the statement of restrictions actually became a sales tool just as the plat map had been previously.[16]

The restrictions were initially considered to be a selling advantage because they would insure the stability of investment for land purchasers. Nichols soon discovered, however, that restrictions had to be rigorously enforced if they were to remain assets. This enforcement gradually became a dual responsibility of his real estate company and the homeowners' associations that he organized. The forerunner of the many associations that continue into the 1980s was the Country Club District Improvement Association, which had its organizational meeting on December 5, 1909.[17]

In addition to assuming a small role in enforcing restrictions, the association collected money from landowners, based on the amount of street frontage they owned, to maintain and beautify the Country Club District. The Nichols Company paid the same amount per front foot for land it still owned as did the private landowners. By October 1910, the association was arranging for local police patrols and for regular garbage collection. The Country Club District Improvement Association is covered in more detail in Chapter 8, which deals with the development and importance of the Nichols homeowners' associations.[18]

During the 1920s, J. C. Nichols spent a great deal of time and money to establish a sense of community spirit among his homeowners. Although Nichols's early years were centered on simply making the sale, by 1910 his advertising had already begun to emphasize the type of family community he idealized during the 1920s. Phrases like "Select Your Lot and Build in Southside Center of Ideal Home Life!" conjured up an image of a community where all homeowners were people "whom you would enjoy having as neighbors." In another instance he inquired through an advertisement, "Wouldn't You and Yours Enjoy and Take Pride in a Home

16. For examples, see plats in Plat Books B–14, 93, for Country Side; B–15, 33, for Country Side Extension; and B–15, 47, for Sunset Hill.

17. Scrapbook 2:193.

18. Ibid., 158.

Built in The Country Club District?" The section was then described as an area "where your children will get the benefit of an exclusive environment and the most desirable associations." The move toward organizing community activities where such associations could better take place was a natural one as the subdivisions grew. [19]

Because the district was twenty-five minutes from downtown by streetcar, Nichols concluded that some local shopping facilities were necessary. In 1907 the company put up a small building to house a "high class grocery and attractive pharmacy" at the temporary end of the extended streetcar line coming from Westport. From this humble beginning came the innovations in shopping centers that have come to symbolize the J. C. Nichols Company in the 1980s. These factors—landscape design innovations, more extensive and better-written deed restrictions, homeowners' associations, the development of a sense of community identity, and the strategic placement of profitable shopping centers—are the major aspects of J. C. Nichols's subdivision developments that distinguish them in many ways from others in Kansas City and link them to others scattered about the United States. [20]

In the real estate and land subdivision business, people sometimes worked for years to bring about an acquisition or expansion that might have seemed to others to come together all at once. For J. C. Nichols, such an acquisition came to fruition in the last week of April 1908. The confluence of events began on Monday, April 20, when Nichols tied up the loose ends on a deal with the last remaining Missouri-side major landholder in the area he wished to develop. E. S. Yeomans and his wife, Kate, owned an old farm that was surrounded by land Nichols and his backers had pieced together in the previous three years. Mrs. Yeomans had inherited it from her father and had resisted any kind of deal until 1908 unless she were given some cash up front. Nichols had no more cash to offer, for he had exhausted his last reserves of supportive capital closing

19. J. C. Nichols Co. advertisements, *Kansas City Star,* March 6, 1910, 4A; and April 17, 1910, 4A.

20. Reed, Nichols & Co. advertisement, *Kansas City Star,* July 14, 1907.

The first Nichols "shopping center" appears to have been opened in 1907. The Country Club trolley line was being electrified in that year. It ran approximately 250 yards to the right of the buildings in the foreground. As always, Nichols leased the space to retailers rather than running the stores himself. What appears to be the first house Nichols occupied (and either the first or second house he and John Taylor built) is visible behind the last column on the left side of the buildings. The Colonial shops, as this little center came to be called, still exists at 51st and Brookside, as does the house at the top of the hill. Because of the limited restrictions placed on this Bismark Place property, Nichols lost effective control of the later development of the area where the house is located. The neighborhood has changed substantially, with nonconforming apartment houses dominating the rest of the block on which the house is located. Probably for this reason, the company has not publicized the continued existence of its "first house." KC54n26.

two other deals that would come to fruition during this same week.[21]

What finally made the deal work was a buyer for a portion of the Yeomans' acreage. St. Theresa's Academy, an expensive Catholic girls' school that was one of the oldest schools in Kansas City, wanted to relocate from their campus on Thirty-ninth Street in Westport. Wealthy Protestants as well as Catholics sent their daughters to the school for tutelage by the Sisters of St. Joseph. Its

21. Ibid.

trustees offered to pay forty thousand dollars for twenty acres from Fifty-fifth to Fifty-seventh between Wyandotte and Main streets. With that money in hand, the Yeomans were amenable to a sales agency contract with Nichols.[22]

The next deal was a small but important one. Four acres at the southeast corner of Fifty-first and Main had also eluded Nichols's gathering up of loose parcels. Armed with the Yeomans' commitment, the developer worked out an expensive purchase funded by two of his main backers. E. W. Shields was a grain commission man who like Herbert F. Hall—the other participant in this deal—had been involved in Nichols's earlier land acquisitions. The two men were the buyers of record of these four acres at the price of $3,125 per acre. A news story on the sale noted that this completed ". . . an area of six hundred acres between Fifty-first and Fifty-fifth streets and Holmes street and the State line, which is to be made a high class residence neighborhood." The 600 acres did not include the 120 acres held by the Kansas City Country Club on long-term lease from Hugh Ward.[23]

The developer and his backers crossed the state line between Missouri and Kansas to buy land during this eventful week as well. Nichols completed a transaction on Thursday, April 23, to acquire 229 acres from Charles W. Armour. The land lay directly west of Hugh Ward's holdings on the east from the point where Brush Creek entered Missouri near Fifty-second Street south in a widening triangle to Sixty-third. The Nichols syndicate, made up of Nichols, Hall, Crowell, and Simonds, paid $75,000, or slightly over $300 per acre, for what would four years later be christened Mission Hills. This land, together with almost 800 acres on the Missouri side, had been assembled by Kirk Armour in the late nineteenth century for a registered Hereford farm. About 200 acres on the Missouri side had been sold previously. The front-page story indicated that the Armour family was going to hold the approximately 600 remaining acres "for high class residence development." Nich-

22. "Important Realty Sales of the Week," *Kansas City Star,* April 26, 1908. Also see Scrapbook 1:138. Nichols controlled more than half of his initial one thousand acres in 1908 through sales agency contracts.
23. "South Side Acres Sold," *Kansas City Star,* April 21, 1908, 1.

ols was credited with closing the deal and described as having "extensive holdings in this neighborhood which he is developing as a high class residence district."[24]

Over the next fifteen years Nichols and his backers did acquire the remainder of the Armour holdings. Whether the price was set at this early stage is unknown, but it seems unlikely. What is known is that during this immensely busy week, Nichols not only bought the land for his most exclusive development, for a quite favorable price, but also received at least a verbal agreement from the Armours to hold the rest of their land for his type of development.

These large land acquisitions were completed in a somewhat questionable manner, which came to light during the Great Depression of the 1930s. All of the purchases were for a specified down payment with regular payments to follow. All contracts for land purchases were signed by Isla Derr, an employee, but not an officer, of the J. C. Nichols Company. No company official signed the purchase contracts. It was as though Miss Derr were the actual purchaser. During the Depression the company was unable to keep up payments on most of these contracts, but the former landholders who held the contracts could not foreclose on anyone but Miss Derr. The company was thus insulated from suit. As a result, these landholders negotiated new payment terms with the company that gave payment and interest concessions to the company. The practice was common (and legal) in real estate development at the time, although it seems morally questionable from a later vantage point.[25]

That same day, April 23, the architectural firm of Wilder and Wight announced the completion of a seven-room home as part of a group to be built on a five-acre tract they had acquired from Nichols. The asking price for this particular house was $5,900. The purpose of the offering and the comparatively low price was "to advertise this district." Model homes would become a regular selling feature during the 1920s.[26]

24. "For South Side Acres: $75,000," *Kansas City Star*, April 23, 1908, 1.

25. Taken from comments by Frank Grant, company treasurer, reproduced in Scrapbook 10:291–92.

26. "Rockhill Park Home," advertisement, *Kansas City Star*, April 23, 1908, 13.

One other series of events crowded into the week. For five years Nichols had been in partnership with his fraternity brothers, the Reeds. By this time Nichols had worked out his own backing with men like Crowell, Hall, Ward, Simonds, and Shields. He had previously entered a separate land-holding partnership with Shields and Hall called the Brush Creek Park Land Company, for which Nichols served as secretary. The Reeds were lawyers who had continued to dabble in mail-order real estate on their own account. Nichols now believed he had found his niche in the area of local residential land development. The three agreed to a friendly parting of the ways. Nichols set up his own firm in a new location, and the Reeds continued in the old offices and along their old lines. Additionally, the Reeds retained title to some of the Bismark Place lots, which they could and did sell in their own name.[27]

To accomplish this change, Nichols formed an alliance with William T. Kemper of the recently reorganized Commerce Trust Company for financial backing and office space. In return, Nichols, only twenty-eight, was made the youngest director in the history of the bank. This arrangement was to prove profitable for both parties, and Commerce Trust remained the primary financial source for the J. C. Nichols Company into the 1980s. Nichols was assisted in creating this important financial connection by Hall and Ward, who were already directors of the bank, along with Kemper.[28]

The financial alliance with Kemper was only part of the relationship between these two men. They were both members of the Democratic party and supportive of the Pendergast faction when it served their interests. The leadership of that group within the Jackson County, Missouri, Democratic coalition passed from Jim Pendergast to his younger brother, Tom, in 1910. Until the Pendergast goals permanently diverged from those of Nichols during the 1937 period of labor unrest, Nichols worked with the faction to make sure that civic progress was favorable to their interests. Kemper

27. See plat for Rockhill Annex, Plat Book B–14, 22, for evidence of the company and its officers. "Real Estate Transfers," *Kansas City Star,* August 9, 1908, 12A.

28. Scrapbook 5:256. For listing of directorships, see Commerce Trust advertisement, *Kansas City Star,* July 17, 1908, 14.

sided with Nichols in most instances until the banker's death in 1938.

Thomas Hart Benton painted a visual interpretation of the alliance as part of his historical mural in the Missouri State House in Jefferson City. Boss Tom Pendergast is portrayed seated next to a local orator, and facing him from behind a table are the clearly recognizable faces of William T. Kemper and J. C. Nichols. The mural caused a political uproar when it was unveiled in 1938, but wisely neither Nichols nor his former banker objected openly.[29]

Two corporate entities were formed to carry on Nichols's plans. The first was the aforementioned J. C. Nichols Realty Company. Frank Crowell and H. F. Hall each purchased a quarter interest in the company. Nichols, his family, and working associates held the other half interest. Nichols controlled that half and effectively controlled the company. The second was the J. C. Nichols Land Company, in which Simonds and Shields were also involved, but over which Nichols had the managing interest, as in the other company.[30]

At the end of this eventful final week in April 1908, Nichols controlled over 1,000 acres (including the Armour purchase for Mission Hills and the Country Club grounds). He placed significant deed restrictions on these new acquisitions concerning the required minimum cost of construction, set-backs, landscape features, and the like. The slogan he began to use in advertising talked of the "1,000 acres restricted."[31]

Quick, inexpensive public transportation proved essential for any successful early twentieth-century subdivision, and Nichols's projects were no exceptions. At the very start, he advertised that prospective customers had to walk from the terminus of the Rockhill streetcar line at Forty-eighth and Rockhill Road. This "solution" entailed a five-minute jaunt from the car stop, across one of Nelson's stone bridges over Brush Creek, and up a hill to Bismark Place. It

29. Reddig, *Tom's Town*, 327, chronicles the downfall of T. J. Pendergast. Clugston, "Kansas City," 275–76, provides a muckraker's view of the alliance among Kemper, Nichols, and Pendergast. See also Reddig, *Tom's Town*, 354–56.

30. Scrapbook 2:7.

31. J. C. Nichols Co. advertisement, *Kansas City Star*, April 30, 1908.

Early in his development experience, Nichols erected large signs to advertise his property to passers-by on Brookside Boulevard, a street the Nichols Company originally constructed and then donated to the boulevard system, and on the Country Club trolley line. Later, the company would tone down the size and amount of wording on such advertising. In the background is a native stone-veneer house that Nichols often pictured in his early advertising. It still stands, facing Brookside Boulevard at 53rd Street. KC54n14.

was not an auspicious entrance for the people Nichols wanted to attract. A second mode of transportation existed near Bismark Place. Since the 1880s a steam dummy line had traversed the miles between Westport and Dodson, located near Eighty-fifth and Brooklyn Avenue. To use this line, passengers from downtown had to transfer at Broadway and Westport Road to this noisy and smoky little train consisting of one disguised steam engine and several open cars.[32]

As Nichols got underway, the public perception of the Dodson dummy line was that it constituted more of a nuisance than a transportation solution. Its only real assets were the tracks and right-of-way. The young subdivider-developer organized with Shields, Hall, Crowell, and others to form the Westport and South Side Improvement Association. Using the neighborhood improvement association technique that had worked well during the park and boulevard campaign of the 1890s, these investors raised $15,000 to buy out

32. Reed, Nichols & Co. advertisement, *Kansas City Star,* April 2, 1905, 18, 2d section.

the Dodson line interests. The association then turned the trackage and right-of-way over to the Metropolitan Street Railway Company for the traction firm to convert the line to electric service. This seeming act of generosity was motivated by the realization that the new subdivision had to have streetcar connections. The $15,000 premium was a small price to pay for the access and publicity the converted electric streetcar line brought to Nichols's subdivisions.[33]

Nichols began advertising the coming electrification and improved transportation service with the start of his 1906 spring advertising campaign. He also raised his asking prices from eight dollars per front foot to ten dollars per front foot. The rails were laid by July 1906. In October, he confidently forecast that service would begin before the first of December. All estimates of completion proved optimistic; service did not begin until the following March. The advertising impact was increased substantially when Nichols was able to get the Metropolitan Street Railway Company to name the cars that ultimately went south to his land "Country Club Cars." This meant that residents and potential land buyers could board trolley cars in the downtown area that were marked as going to the Country Club District.[34]

During 1908 and 1909, the company was busy preparing the Ward property for sale. The section that lay north and west of the Kansas City Country Club grounds was the first to be improved for sale. George Kessler planned the layout and landscaping. The Wards provided more than $100,000 dollars in 1908 to prepare the land for residential sites. The family paid an additional $60,000 to the Metropolitan Street Railway Company as a premium for a streetcar line to ascend into Sunset Hill on the west side of Nichols's development of Hugh Ward's land. The streetcar company repaid part of its obligation to the land donors by naming the new carline the "Sunset Hill line" when it commenced service in 1910. Nichols's agreement with Ward provided that the landowner was to pay for these im-

33. "A Brush Creek Parkway," *Kansas City Star,* January 14, 1906, 1; *Proceedings of the First Annual Conference of Developers of High Class Residential Property* (hereafter cited as 1917 *Proceedings*).

34. Reed, Nichols & Co. advertisements, *Kansas City Star,* March 18, 1906; May 18, 1906; July 22, 1906; October 21, 1906; and April 1, 1907.

Nichols and his backers subsidized both trolley and boulevard construction to attract buyers to the company's developments. The Sunset Hill line ran from Westport along Brush Creek and up the hill on Ward Parkway to give access to Nichols's most exclusive Missouri development, the Sunset Hill for which the carline was named. This photograph clearly demonstrates that early in his work, trolley access was more important than finished roadways. KC54n22.

provements. Nichols supervised the work in return for a 15 percent commission on future sales.

While he still considered the need for streetcar connections, Nichols was interested in the potential impact of the automobile on his subdivision work from 1908 forward. He foresaw the important role the boulevard system designed by Kessler in the nineteenth century would have for auto traffic in the twentieth century. His Westport and Southside Improvement Association lobbied hard for a boulevard connection either from the north or east. By 1910 he had succeeded in getting the park board to approve the extension of a boulevard south from Westport down the Mill Creek Valley to Brush Creek. Initially christened Mill Creek Parkway, it is now known as J. C. Nichols Parkway. The boulevard route provided wide lanes for traffic from downtown through Penn Valley Park and Westport right to the edge of the Country Club District.[35]

35. *The Wildwood Magazine*, Scrapbook 2:198; Scrapbook 3. See also Treshad-

At the same time that he and his backers were successfully getting the Mill Creek Parkway route approved, Nichols proposed that a wide boulevard that was to wind through the northern and western areas of Ward's land also be included in the boulevard system. Like Nelson's ideas for Warwick Boulevard, Nichols was initially unsuccessful because the proposed route lay outside the city limits. Nichols and his backers donated the land to the city for these two boulevards along with that for Brookside Boulevard, but before action could be taken, a court suspended a 1909 annexation of Nichols's developments into the corporate limits of Kansas City until hearings could be held. A Missouri Court of Appeals decision finally ruled the election valid in 1911. This allowed for final annexation and acceptance of a gift of the rights-of-way into the boulevard system during that same year.[36]

The boulevard route Nichols proposed was actually donated by Hugh Ward's heirs. The youthful lawyer died at the age of forty-five in 1909. As a tribute to him, the park board approved using his name on the portion of the boulevard system that passed through his family's land, and Ward Parkway quickly became the most prestigious street in Kansas City. The gentle grades cut for it to climb the bluffs above Brush Creek also served as the route for the Sunset Hill streetcar line.[37]

Just to the west of the Sunset Hill section and across the imaginary line between Kansas and Missouri (which became State Line Road), Mission Hills began to take form. In 1909 Nichols sold a lot to A. C. Jobes, a vice-president of the First National Bank of Kansas City. Jobes was also a director of the Atchison, Topeka and Santa Fe Railway and of Southwestern Bell Telephone Company. Both directorships hinged on his being a Kansas resident. Jobes wanted a prestigious home location in Kansas, and the lot was located at Fifty-ninth at State Line Road. Between Jobes's lot and the proposed Ward Parkway the land was totally undeveloped. As an inducement to Jobes, Nichols signed a contract to build a road connecting the

ding, "Genealogy," 37–38.

36. "Park Plans for South Side," *Kansas City Star,* January 16, 1910, 2A.

37. Scrapbook 5:213. See also 1910 map of the park and boulevard system in Ehrlich, *Kansas City, Missouri: An Architectural History,* 30.

Jobes home with "some rock road in Jackson County, Missouri; said connection not to be south of Fifty-ninth Street." Nichols put down a $2,000 guarantee that the road would be built. The road was necessary because Jobes was one of the first south Kansas Citians on either side of the line to commute to work by automobile.[38]

When Nichols opened Mission Hills to full-scale development in 1913–1914, his advertising emphasized this aspect of living in Kansas and working in Missouri. The advertising stated, "Mission Hills offers the first opportunity ever given to persons who may wish to reside in a restricted residence section in Kansas, yet share in the conveniences and social environment of Kansas City proper." There was restricted property in Kansas City, Kansas, near where Nichols had started in 1903, but that would not have been considered to be near "Kansas City proper." No self-respecting Missourian wanted to live on the Kansas side at that time.[39]

The advertising for Mission Hills, as well as that for most of the rest of Nichols's Missouri-side developments, was based on the creation of a desire to live in the best neighborhoods. From the beginning this approach is evident in the company's advertising. Bismark Place was referred to as "Kansas City's choicest neighborhood" in April 1905. References to living among the wealthy and influential showed up in May 1905 advertisements. By June of that year Nichols claimed that such lots would "soon equal Armour Boulevard," then among the most prestigious new addresses in the city. Other company advertisements during March 1906 proclaimed Bismark Place and the surrounding land that Nichols had assembled with his backers "the immutably established highest class residence district." This terminology was a copy of the description that had been used by Nelson for his Rockhill District in 1904. By the following year, advertisements proclaimed these subdivisions to be the "most protected and highest class region in or near Kansas City."[40]

The effect of the advertising and the cumulative decisions of many

38. Scrapbook 3:71–74.
39. Scrapbook 2:214.
40. Reed, Nichols & Co. advertisements, *Kansas City Star*, April 30, 1905; May 28, 1905; June 5, 1905; March 4, 1906; and July 14, 1907.

Nichols often spoke to groups about his ideas on residential development. Some of these were in Kansas City, but most were given at real estate conventions and city planning conferences. On many occasions he illustrated his talks with a lantern slide machine, forerunner of modern slide projectors. This picture is one that he regularly used to demonstrate how homes in older, exclusive Kansas City neighborhoods could be blighted by a lack of deed restrictions that would have prevented the construction of billboards such as these. KC54n16.

upper-income Kansas Citians to move from their homes on Quality Hill, in Merriam Place, near Independence Boulevard, along Troost Avenue, or in Hyde Park was becoming clear by 1915. Using designations and techniques developed by the preeminent analyst of Kansas City's upper class, it can be determined that the hypothetical "social center" of the center had moved far south by that year from its origin thirty years earlier. The social center in 1885 had been the south side of Quality Hill at Twelfth and Washington streets, just west of the downtown business center. The movement was slight between that year and 1900, when it was at Fifteenth and Walnut. No one lived at that address at the turn of the century, but the intersection formed the center of the distribution of wealthy residents.[41]

41. Richard Coleman, "The Kansas City Elite, 1914–1915," 5. Coleman has written (with Bernice L. Neugarten) the findings of a study of Kansas City class structure in *Social Status in the City.* Coleman and Dr. Lee Rainwater coauthored a

By 1915 this hypothetical center had moved to Thirty-seventh and Warwick. In that year more than 16 percent of the identifiable 495 upper-class families lived in Rockhill, and almost 10 percent lived in Nichols's Country Club District. This is a remarkable "pull" factor for a residential section only ten years old at the time. Nichols stated that a major goal of his planned neighborhoods was the creation of stable sections of the city that would not decline in value over time as Quality Hill and other elite areas had done. Not only did he attract the wealthy quite early to his developments, but the Nichols properties also continued to anchor the residential patterns of the wealthy in Kansas City into the 1980s. By 1930 the social center had moved much further south and back a little to the west at Forty-ninth and Wyandotte. By this date, more than 55 percent of the identifiable 625 men and nearly 700 women who comprised upper-class society in that year lived on land subdivided by the J. C. Nichols Company.[42]

As late as 1975, when just over 2,000 were counted in Kansas City's upper-class circles, the social center of the city was located just west of Fifty-ninth Street Terrace at Ward Parkway. In forty-five years this mythical point had moved only ten blocks south and about six blocks west. Most importantly for this study, the social apex remained solidly in J. C. Nichols country. Specifically, in 1975, 83 percent of the people identified in this class by the Century of Leadership Project lived on lots subdivided by the Nichols Company. Three-fifths of the Nichols subdivision population studied lived in Nichols areas on the Missouri side, with the remaining two-fifths in Nichols's Kansas subdivisions. Almost 20 percent of this population was housed in the relatively small confines of Mission Hills.[43]

Another way of measuring the impact of the Nichols residential areas over time is to look at the relative property values inside and outside census tracts given over to Nichols's neighborhoods. The

comparative study of class viewpoints in Kansas City and Boston entitled *Social Standing in America: New Dimensions of Class*.

42. Coleman, "Kansas City Elite, 1914–1915," 5; J. C. Nichols, "When You Buy a Homesite, Make Sure It's a Good Investment"; Coleman, "The Kansas City Elite, 1929–1930."

43. Coleman, "The Kansas City Elite, 1974–1975," 9–10.

data available for this type of analysis is beyond the time frame of this study because the United States Bureau of the Census did not start taking such information consistently until 1940. It is useful to look at data, however, even though it is later than the main period of analysis, because it indicates the lasting impact of the work done by the Nichols Company. By 1930 a major portion of the social framework of the Kansas City metropolitan area was cemented into place.

Among the majority of well-to-do Kansas Citians, the trend in choosing new residential sections was either to the east or south. Nichols simply built on that base. After the northeast section of the city was completely built up by 1915, Nichols attracted the sons and daughters of those residents as well as those from Quality Hill, Merriam Place, and Hyde Park to the friendly confines of the Country Club District. In 1940, ten years after the Nichols Company began to cut back development because of the deepening Depression, the residential property values remained highest in the areas of the city Nichols had developed. This was the case in both the median value of owner-occupied dwellings and the median rent in tenant-occupied dwellings.[44]

The highest-value census tract in Kansas City, Missouri, in 1940 was Tract 84. All but a small section facing the west side of Ward Parkway between Fifty-ninth and Sixty-third streets was developed by the J. C. Nichols Company. There were 954 dwellings in the tract in 1940, with a median value of owner-occupied housing of $13,412. Next highest in value was Tract 85, an area developed entirely by the Nichols Company. It contained 881 dwellings in 1940, with a median value of $10,571 for the owner-occupied units. Then came Tract 86, a little over two-thirds of which was Nichols's area originally. This section had an owner-occupied median value of $7,116. In fact, out of the top ten tracts (of ninety-two in all), only three were entirely outside a Nichols development.[45]

The median value for all owner-occupied housing in the incorporated limits of Kansas City, Missouri, in 1940 was $3,085. Of the

44. Ernest Mannheim, *Kansas City and Its Neighborhoods: Facts and Figures*, 38, 41, 47, 50, 56, 62, 65, 70, 74, 77, 80.
45. Ibid., 47.

ninety-two tracts, only twenty-nine were above the city-wide median. All the tracts that included subdivisions developed by Nichols were in the highest eighteen tracts and well above the metropolitan median level. The lowest Nichols subdivision in terms of median value of owner-occupied housing was the Plaza-area tract, where only 9 percent of the housing units were owner-occupied. Most residents lived in apartments in that tract. It had the fifth highest median rent of any tract in the city.[46]

As with the measurements of the "social center" of the city, so it was with the more matter-of-fact measurements of property values for owner-occupied housing. Thirty-five years after the beginnings of Nichols's Country Club District in 1905, the wealthiest and most socially influential people tended to cluster in Nichols's neighborhoods. Sunset Hill had the highest value and was the most socially prestigious section. Possibly an even more significant test of the staying power of property values occurred during the period between 1940 and 1980, when the Johnson County, Kansas, suburbs boomed after the war. Meanwhile, the population of the incorporated city limits of Kansas City, Missouri, expanded from 399,178 in 1940 to 448,159 in 1980. The small increase was located entirely in areas not incorporated in 1940. Population fell absolutely within the limits of 1940 Kansas City.[47]

Within the incorporated limits of Kansas City in 1980, the same census tract had the highest median value of owner-occupied housing as it did in 1940. Census tract 84, a J. C. Nichols area, had a median value of $103,000. A second Nichols subdivision, Tract 85, was the fourth most valuable tract with a median of $88,600. The exact social center of the metropolitan area, noted above and on the accompanying map of census tracts, was located in this section in 1975. Social desirability and high property value generally coincide in 1980 as they did in 1940. Of the top ten tracts in median value in 1980, two were Nichols tracts of the pre-1940 era. A third tract, 101.05, was largely made up of a newer Nichols development, the

46. Ibid., 47, 38.
47. U.S. Bureau of the Census, *1980 Census of Population and Housing: Census Tracts: Kansas City, Mo.-Kans. SMSA*, P-3, P-4.

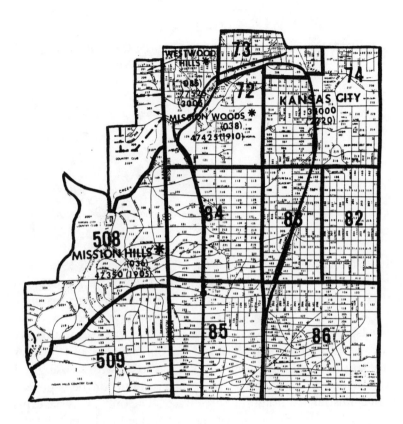

Map of Census Tracts

Red Bridge area. Tract 101.05 also is the second highest in value in the entire city in 1980, with a median of $91,900.[48]

The comparison of values in 1980 of similarly aged and styled housing shows dramatic differences between Nichols and non-Nichols neighborhoods. Table 3-2 demonstrates the similarities of three tracts in 1940 and the differences in 1980.

Tract 87 was not developed by Nichols and lies east of Troost. Its

48. Ibid., H–38–39.

TABLE 3-2

COMPARISON OF PROPERTY VALUES IN NICHOLS-BUILT
CENSUS TRACTS WITH THOSE IN NON-NICHOLS-BUILT
TRACTS, 1940 AND 1980

TRACT #	1940	1980
87	$4,201	$20,700
86	$7,116	$54,700
85	$10,571	$88,600

Source: 1980 Census. Mannheim, *Kansas City and Its Neighborhoods:
Facts and Figures*, 47.

values are below the median for the city of $30,700 in 1980. Tract
86 was developed by Nichols except for a seven-block area in the
southeast corner of the tract. It substantially increased its margin of
value over Tract 87 during the forty-year transition. Tract 85, on the
other hand, is entirely a Nichols area and was the second highest
value section in the city in 1940 and the fourth highest in 1980. Part
of the disparity among the three tracts has to do with housing style
and initial cost, but such factors do not account for the degrees of
change illustrated among the three tracts. The only plausible explanation is that the Nichols areas have continued to be perceived as
having higher value.

Nichols set out to create a residence section that would attract
and retain the more wealthy and influential residents of Kansas City
in his subdivisions. That he accomplished his goal is evident from
both the social-center analysis and the property-values study. Because Nichols accomplished his goal of social and property value
protection as well as he did, it will be important to understand in
the next chapter the methods he used.

4

THE PLANNING OF AN AMERICAN RESIDENTIAL COMMUNITY

————

Cities are the handiwork of the real estate man. Whether our cities are physically bad or physically good is our responsibility.

—J. C. Nichols[1]

It is the Realtor subdivider who is really planning our cities today, who is the actual city planner in practice.

—George B. Ford[2]

The similarity of these two statements is not a coincidence. Both speakers were interested in encouraging real estate brokers and agents to support the possibilities of what they understood as city planning at that time. Nichols was a realtor himself, calling upon his fellow realtors to take up the good fight to plan carefully and to protect effectively the growth of North American cities in a profitable manner. Ford was a planner who hoped to curry favor with a profession that had been less than totally enthusiastic about city planning in the nine years since Nichols had given his speech in 1916 to a national gathering of realtors in New Orleans. Nichols had then given essentially the same speech to a meeting of the National Conference on City Planning (NCCP).[3]

Despite the similarity of their initial remarks and overall goals, the

———

1. Nichols, "City Planning," 277. This was the text of a speech to a general session of the ninth annual convention of the National Association of Real Estate Exchanges, March 29, 1916.

2. George B. Ford, "City Planning and Unbuilt Outlying Areas," 247. This, too, was the text of a speech, given in this instance to a general session of the eighteenth annual convention of the National Association of Real Estate Boards (NAREB).

3. Weiss, *Rise of the Community Builders*, 64–68, recognizes this Nichols speech as one of national significance in the effort to combine the support of realtors/subdividers with that of planners for the implementation of zoning and regulatory legislation in the nation's cities.

two speakers diverged at particular points. Ford wanted city planning to be a factor in improving the lot of all city dwellers, whether they wanted that to happen to them or not. Nichols, on the other hand, was most concerned with the use of zoning and other city planning tools to safeguard his particular developments. Ford worked to achieve what would prove to be an impossible goal for planners—the control of the development of entire cities. Nichols, while not unconcerned with the city as a whole, was more involved with what he knew to be a fully realizable goal—the control of the development of his own subdivisions. Nichols was simply interested in getting the city to provide additional support by forcing his nearby competitors to play by the same rules he had outlined for himself.

During the 1910s, the real estate profession was hard at work to make itself just that—a profession, instead of a collection of people who floated in and out of the land and building business according to economic swings. Nichols's remarks to the realtors in 1916 were aimed to inspire them by emphasizing their work's importance. When the Kansas City developer delivered the same remarks to the planners' convention, he wished to convince them that the real estate profession was getting its house in order to support planning goals. Ford recognized that he, as a planner, could accomplish very little if realtors did not work with his growing profession.

Actually the two groups were initially antagonistic because the real estate men saw the planners' tool of zoning as a device limiting the real estate men's authority in their own sphere. J. C. Nichols was a central figure in encouraging real estate dealers to accept some limits in order to achieve a greater economic good in the long run. His 1916 speech was one step toward achieving such a goal. Real estate operatives slowly came to realize that by accepting zoning and getting themselves appointed to zoning boards and commissions, they could influence governmental and public decisions in their favor to an even greater degree than before.[4]

The issue of motivation is quite important in any study of plan-

4. Nichols, *Real Estate Subdivisions: The Best Manner of Handling Them*. Nichols was considered by some in Kansas City to have been the main person responsible for getting the city planning ordinance passed in 1921; see Scrapbook 5:256.

ning and planners. With Nichols, the relationship between planning and his subdivisions is quite clear from existing correspondence. When accepted planning objectives and methodology could be reconciled with his strong profit orientation, Nichols was more than willing to champion the need for increased city planning. When proposed planning objectives conflicted with or diverged from Nichols's clear conception of what was in his best interest, he normally supported the position that upheld his financial interest. This is not necessarily "bad" or "good," but is normal in our capitalistic economic life.

The best example of when stated public planning objectives differed from those of Nichols occurred in the 1930s when planning for additions to the storm sewer system touched on his areas. Using his influence on the Executive Committee of the Ten-Year Plan, Nichols appears to have squelched the original plan to pave Brush Creek as it passed through his properties and the Plaza. The Pendergast-aligned city manager, H. F. McElroy, justified this effort as a storm sewer improvement. Nichols often expressed verbally and in his subdivision design the wish to retain waterways in a rustic and picturesque condition. In spite of the recommendation of Nichols and of the Executive Committee, the concrete floor for Brush Creek in the Country Club District was approved at the final city council session on the subject. It should be noted that this was during the Pendergast era, when the machine controlled the council and the city manager position, and that the concrete used for the paving job came from Pendergast's own ready-mixed concrete company.[5]

Nichols had begun attending the NCCP in 1912. In 1913 he was named to the General Committee of the NCCP. In 1914, he was selected as a member of NAREB's City Planning Committee, along with E. H. Bouton of Roland Park; Paul Harsch of Toledo; Robert Jemison, Jr., of Birmingham, Alabama; Duncan McDuffie of Berkeley; King Thompson of Columbus, Ohio; and Lee J. Ninde of Indianapolis. This NAREB committee took the initiative to start discussions of the topic with planning advocates from NCCP. Five years later, Nichols and the other City Planning Committee mem-

5. See *Where These Rocky Bluffs Meet: Including the Story of the Kansas City Ten-Year Plan*, 153–60.

bers decided to meet annually to discuss mutual problems and share ideas in addition to the time they shared at the planning sessions. They called their organization the Annual Conference of the Developers of High-Class Residential Property. Since in 1917 Nichols served as chairman of the Committee on General Arrangements for the NCCP in Kansas City, the first High-Class Developers' conference took place in conjunction with the planners' sessions. This organization was a direct forerunner of the Home Builders' and Subdividers' Division of the NAREB, created in 1923. During the World War II period, both the Urban Land Institute and the National Association of Homebuilders were established to coordinate and promote activities by subdividers and housing construction companies. Nichols was involved in the formation of all of these organizations. No other subdivider in the United States became so involved so early in the effort to plan America's cities.[6]

Not all real estate people reacted favorably to Nichols's ideas and proposals. Some thought him to be an impractical dreamer, but he was really quite practical. He recognized that personal control of the development was essential. He also recognized that if the government, through its zoning power, could assist him in retaining that control, then it should be allowed to do so. Another tool that aided the developer in working toward controlling his development was the physical layout of the land. In 1929 a thoughtful student of real estate practice suggested that "the subdivider's control consists of his plan for the area and the restrictions which he places in the conveyances to insure the fulfillment of that plan. The plan is the initial step."[7]

The fact that Nichols had a plan at all set him apart from most of the subdividers and real estate men of his day. More importantly, his plan obviously accomplished its goal, since the Country Club District has retained its attraction for Kansas Citians into the 1980s. The plan had several facets, the most important of which was the physical layout of the subdivisions. It is necessary to examine the

6. Davies, *Real Estate*, 154–55; 1917 *Proceedings*, 9. The connections of Nichols with the NCCP's General Committee and the NAREB's City Planning Committee are also made in Weiss, *Rise of the Community Builders*, 56–57.

7. Monchow, *The Use of Deed Restrictions in Subdivision Development*, 9.

elements of that physical plan and the methods Nichols used to attain its goals in order to understand why he found additional protection devices to be so essential.

By 1908, Nichols had embarked on a mode of subdivision design that would distinguish his land developments from most others in Kansas City and across the country. Much later in life, he assigned his inspiration for using the topography as a guide for street layouts to a trip he made in 1901. He and a friend from Olathe traveled by cargo ship to Europe, where they bicycled through parts of England and the Continent. In 1937, he recalled, "My interest was aroused by the stability, beauty, charm and orderliness of the villages and cities as compared with our American communities."[8]

Recent historians of suburban development have construed this statement to mean that Nichols had visited the "garden city" constructions of England on his tour. That is impossible, for Nichols traveled in 1901, but Ebenezer Howard's brainchild, the first English garden city of Letchworth, was not begun until 1903. Nichols and his classmate probably visited villages that became models for the early English suburban developers cited by Robert Fishman in his recent study, but the articles written by Nichols give no indication that the boys visited the actual suburbs themselves. Moreover, Nichols did not use topographically oriented planning in his early work in Kansas City, Kansas, or in his earliest subdivisions on the Missouri side.[9]

While only a few planned subdivisions across the country predated Nichols's work, even in Kansas City W. R. Nelson had set the pattern for much of Nichols's later work, though by no means all of it. George Kessler, father of the Kansas City park and boulevard system, was a friend of Nelson and may very well have been con-

8. Nichols, "Realty as a Profession." The article quotes part of a Nichols speech to an eight-state real estate convention that he had chaired in St. Louis in his capacity as an officer of the NAREB.

9. Fishman, *Bourgeois Utopias*, 66–68, cites an early suburban designer's use of the " 'characteristic beauties' of the picturesque village" in designing the Park Village suburb of London's Regent Park. Both Boorstin, *The Americans: The Democratic Experience*, 272, and Jackson, *Crabgrass Frontier*, 177, carry the interpretation of English influence on Nichols. With regard to the beginning date of Letchworth, see Mel Scott, *American City Planning*, 89.

sulted on the planning for the latter's Rockhill District. Kessler was a key figure for Nichols in that he knew of Roland Park and had participated in its early planning. Nichols and Hugh Ward were using Kessler's consulting advice on the layout of Sunset Hill by 1907. Thus, Kessler's public and private planning activities provided the overall context and much of the connective tissue between Nichols's areas and the downtown section where most of Nichols's early residents worked.

That Nichols or the founders of Roland Park consulted with a landscape architect at all put them in a select group of developers across the country. As late as 1929 Helen Monchow observed that the hiring of a landscape architect to help lay out a subdivision made developers "above average in the business." Bouton at Roland Park had been doing this for almost forty years at the time, while Nichols had been working first with Kessler and then with Sid J. Hare as landscape consultants for over twenty years. Sid Hare did not have a large amount of formal landscape architecture training, but he sent his son, Herbert, to the Harvard School of Planning, the first such academic unit in the United States. Father and son formed a partnership in 1919 and were the landscape designers for all of Nichols's subdivisions from 1913 through the onset of the Great Depression.

Another factor that distinguished such developers from the average subdivider was whether they joined the national association for such work—the Home Builders' and Subdividers' Division of the NAREB. Nichols was the founding president of the forerunner of this organization as early as 1917. When the division was formed in 1923, he was unanimously selected for a three-year term on the board of directors. His selection to both offices indicates that Nichols and his ideas about land planning for residential purposes were nationally important in the formative years of that line of work.[10]

Across the United States at the turn of the century, the adherence to rectangular platting was almost universal. Such land designs have been in use since the ascendancy of Egypt and Assyria in the Middle East. The Romans used a gridiron as their plan for military camps, which often turned into cities, from England to Asia. In this coun-

10. Monchow, *Use of Deed Restrictions*, 27. See also 1923 *Proceedings*, 9.

try, dependency on the rectangular style was confirmed by the land ordinances of the Continental Congress passed in the 1780s.[11]

A few pioneering subdivisions had employed landscape architects in their planning and as a result had curvilinear streets that conformed to the topography. As late as 1900 these planned subdivisions had little effect on the overall planning of subdivisions, which, in turn, comprised the major portion of planning done in any American city. A survey of the residential sections in ten North American cities in 1903 revealed only one in which an appreciable portion of the residential area of the city had curvilinear streets in subdivisions. Seattle developers utilized the inland edges of Lake Union and the city shores along the extension of Puget Sound as sites for upper-income neighborhoods that featured such planning, but even in Seattle, only three fairly large subdivisions out of several hundred used the variation in land treatment.[12]

The use of longer blocks on an east-west pattern was somewhat more common in the ten cities studied, but the north-south pattern certainly predominated. Cities that were built up along a major stretch of riverfront, such as Richmond, Toledo, and New Orleans, generally had streets running either perpendicular to the riverfront or parallel to it, as did the original townsite of Kansas City itself. When the river curved as it went through the city, it resulted in such irregular patterns that the predominant orientation of blocks is difficult to determine in the downtown sections. The major exception to this entire pattern nationally was the Manhattan Island portion of New York City. All blocks there ran lengthwise between the Hudson and the East River in the great metropolis of 1903.[13]

Kansas City's basic plan involved the use of rectangular blocks of relatively short length. Kessler's park and boulevard system altered that rigidity to a degree with roadways that were laid out to conform

11. Hubbard, "The Influence of Topography on the Layout of Land Subdivisions," 188–90.

12. The cities included in the survey were Salt Lake City, Seattle, Richmond, Toledo, Kansas City (Missouri), Columbus, Atlanta, Minneapolis, New Orleans, and New York City. The survey is summarized in Hurd, *Principles of City Land Values,* 147–59.

13. Ibid., 147–59.

to the topographical features of the city. The city's boulevards affected the residential sections that fronted onto the rights-of-way, but these curvilinear streets had no effect beyond a block on either side of the boulevard. Land subdividers continued to lay out grid-iron-plan residential sections.

Nichols filed his first subdivision plat with streets laid out to conform to topographical features of the landscape in the spring of 1907. The subdivision, named Rockhill Park, was a small beginning toward the planned landscape he evolved over the years. Roughly equivalent to four normal Kansas City blocks, Rockhill Park had two features that suggested the need for different planning for it than had been given adjacent subdivided areas: a small stream ran through the property on its way to Brush Creek, and the right-of-way of the old Dodson dummy railroad line, then undergoing electrification on its northern section, ran on a slightly diagonal pattern parallel to the streambed.[14]

Nichols adjusted the roadway on the eastern side of the small subdivision so that a grassy strip remained between it and the track right-of-way for most of the distance. He also laid out a curved street to follow the streambed as it angled more sharply toward the west at the lower end of the area. Probably because the right-of-way and the streambed would have prevented the most economical platting of lots in the almost universal long north-south block method then used in Kansas City, Nichols made the blocks longer east and west. Later he justified his extensive use of such blocks by saying that they helped to break the prevailing winds.[15]

There is no direct evidence that anyone other than Nichols was involved in laying out Rockhill Park. It is known, though, that he was working at the time with George Kessler as a consultant for the Sunset Hill section owned by Hugh Ward, and it is certainly possible that Kessler reviewed the plat before it was filed. The final design of Sunset Hill includes both streets that conform to the rough topography in certain sections and blocks that are longer east and west than north and south. Regardless of the source, the result is the

14. The plat of Rockhill Park was filed by J. C. and Jessie (or Mrs. J. C.) Nichols on April 24, 1907. Plat Book B–14, 39.
15. Nichols, "Financial Effect of Good Planning in Land Subdivision," 98.

first instance of a pattern that would be heavily used by Nichols and a few other developers in Kansas City after this date.[16]

Prior to the platting of Rockhill Park by Nichols in 1907, the only extensive example of private platting of curvilinear streets to adapt to the topography was William Rockhill Nelson's Rockhill District, platted in 1905. Nichols has been described by one source as having "the good fortune of having 'Baron' Nelson take him under his wing when he [Nelson] retired from the real estate game." This "good fortune" is nowhere as apparent as in the ground plan developed by Nichols and his unspecified planner(s) in 1908.[17]

Within this curvilinear plan, there were still many largely rectangular lot arrangements because of the need to maximize salable land within the improved and beautified subdivision. Nichols confronted the question of having these mostly rectangular spaces conform to the other constant in Kansas City urban geography—blocks that were longer north and south than their east-west axis. He chose to reorient the elongation of rounded blocks along the east-west direction rather than the widely accepted north-south format.

There were some precedents in Kansas City for Nichols's commitment to the east-west arrangement. The downtown blocks were almost square from Sixth to Fifteenth streets. As the streets were extended eastward into residential neighborhoods along the gridiron pattern, the narrow north-south side of the downtown blocks became the short side of the longer residential blocks in the northeast section of the city. It must be noted that this was not so much the result of conscious planning as it was a simple extension of an existing pattern.[18]

One subdivision outside the northeast sector using this method

16. There are several plats for different sections of Sunset Hill. The earliest was filed on February 18, 1909, Plat Book B–15, 47. Other early Sunset Hill plats were filed on August 11, 1909, Plat Book B–15, 89; and on May 1, 1910, Plat Book B–16, 45.

17. An overview of platting patterns prior to 1910 can be seen in the map of the city reproduced in Ehrlich, *Kansas City,* 30. Plat Book B–13, 66–67. The quotation about the relationship between Nelson and Nichols is from Clugston, "Kansas City," 275.

18. The best representation of block patterns in Kansas City as Nichols was getting underway is Ehrlich, *Kansas City,* 30.

was being laid out and developed at the same time Nichols was beginning his work. Santa Fe Place was located between Twenty-seventh and Thirtieth streets on both sides of Benton Boulevard, a part of the park and boulevard system. Nannie J. Bell, widow of the cofounder of Long-Bell Lumber, had the land she had inherited from her father laid out in strict rectangular fashion. Benton Boulevard ran along a straight north-south ridge through the property, with the land sloping slightly to the east and west on either side. The unknown plat designer made the blocks run lengthwise along that east-west pattern. The lots were given greater depth than was usual for Kansas City, while some of the blocks ran to more than a thousand feet in length. Santa Fe Place was first platted in 1906.[19]

Shortly after Nichols platted Rockhill Park in 1906, a number of subdivisions were platted that adopted the curvilinear style of street development. The timing is so close to Nelson's Rockhill plat and Nichols's Rockhill Park that it is difficult to determine sources of influence. Quite possibly, Nelson's example was more influential simply because, as editor and publisher of the *Star*, his plans would have attracted more attention than those of the relatively unknown Nichols. Of the other subdivisions, only Marlborough was large enough to rival Nichols's development efforts. Located far southeast near Swope Park, Marlborough became the site of many large homes, but it was never accepted as a truly prestigious home location and did not fully build up until after World War II.[20]

The importance of the use of curvilinear streets in subdivision planning is best illustrated by the comments of Henry Wright, later the developer of the much-publicized Radburn subdivision in New Jersey in the later 1920s. In 1916 Wright suggested that the use of curving streets that followed the topography of the subdivision was possibly ". . . the chief device which differentiates the old and new school of design." Wright went on to justify the use of curving

19. Ibid. The filing of the plat for Santa Fe Place was done on the same day Nichols had filed his Rockhill Park plat, April 24, 1906. See Plat Book B–13, 86, for the design of Santa Fe Place.

20. The following subdivisions were platted between 1906 and 1908 with curvilinear features: Neosho, Hampden Parkway, Shyrock Heights, Marlborough, and Coleman Highlands. See Plat Books B–13, 93, 95; B–14, 26, 41, 64.

streets according to the lay of the land by pointing out that such street designs drew people into the interior of a property and tended to raise the value of interior lots to a point closer to what could be obtained for the corners. Sociologically, Wright believed that such curving streets helped to create a feeling "of community spirit" and to diminish the feeling of residents that they were "just around the corner" from everyone else in the subdivision. He believed that this would lead to better neighborhood interaction.[21]

The subject of streets was much broader than simply the question of their being straight or curving. Nichols knew that if he was to attract the type of customer that he desired and had to have, given the prices he paid for the land he was developing, he had to provide high-quality streets. In most Kansas City subdivisions of the time, subdividers marked out the streets and graded them. Gravel or crushed rock might be laid down in some of the higher-priced areas. In contrast, Nelson paved his streets in Rockhill. Nichols determined to do the same in his areas and even borrowed road-building equipment from Nelson during the earliest years. As early as 1908, he was putting in two-foot cement curbs and gutters along the edges of the macadamized streets. Four-foot-wide "granitoid" sidewalks were put on both sides of the streets. The term *granitoid* referred to an asphaltic type of sidewalk that could be laid more quickly and cheaply than concrete; the term was intended to imply permanence by its derivation from *granite,* but such sidewalks were, in fact, inferior and were usually replaced by the city at a later date. All of these improvements were put in to conform to city standards even before the subdivisions were taken into the city in 1911.[22]

During the first years of development, Nichols had specified that his roads should consist of an eight-inch base of crushed stone overlaid with two inches of macadam surface. By 1917, he had increased this to a twelve-inch base of crushed stone under the

21. Wright's comments were in response to a speech given by Nichols to city planners in 1916. See Nichols, "Financial Effect of Good Planning," 115–16.

22. "Rockhill District in Kansas City"; Reed, Nichols & Co. advertisement, *Kansas City Star,* April 26, 1908; Scrapbook 12:283; J. C. Nichols Co. advertisement, *Kansas City Star,* October 29, 1911, 7A.

During the World War I era, Nichols was developing areas toward the southern end of the original 1,000 acres acquired by 1908. The street construction pictured looking south on Belleview to the dead-end intersection with 60th and 61st streets illustrates aspects of Nichols's improvements to the site. Heavy curbs and sidewalks are featured, along with a divided roadway in the last block visible. A row of street trees was planted on either side of the sidewalk. The street base was large crushed stone, which would then be overlaid by smaller stone and, often, penetrated by oil. Note the three houses grouped at the end of the street. This kind of speculative construction of groups of housing was something of a trademark of the construction division during this period. KC54n23.

macadam because of the increased weight of vehicles using the streets. Both the Guilford section of Roland Park in Baltimore and St. Francis Woods in San Francisco were using a six-inch concrete base overlaid by asphalt. This quality of construction, which far exceeded municipal requirements in those cities, was considered to be a positive sales tool in the high-income subdivisions.[23]

The Nichols Company was always very proud of its street improvements. In 1912 an advertisement announced to Kansas City that the company had laid thirty-five miles "of heavy asphaltic macadam pavement," all of which was in good repair. At that time the rest of the city was getting piecemeal paving in residential sections— at best. Few streets were paved through entire blocks without some gaps or holes. While this was merely bothersome for old-fashioned

23. 1917 *Proceedings*, 22, 75.

The finished street in a World War I era Nichols neighborhood might be simply crushed stone. The transition from horse-and-buggy to automobile transportation is exemplified by the tell-tale reminder of horse traffic in the middle of the street alongside the parked auto. Electric streetlights were also a part of the Nichols landscaping plan. Where existing trees were available (which was not often, as witnessed by the illustration on the facing page), they were incorporated into the plan; note the curvature of Huntington Road to include the large tree at left center in the street tree design. The slightly upward diagonal white line beyond the large tree is the Country Club trolley. Part of a non-Nichols development, Morningside Heights, is pictured in the background center. This latter development was carried out by the Cowherd Realty Company to take advantage of the increased property values generated by proximity to a Nichols neighborhood. KC54n20.

steel-rimmed wagons, such gaps were disastrous for automobiles with fragile rubber tires. Good streets were essential to attracting motorized residents, and the Nichols Company strongly emphasized continuous, high-quality paving as a sales tool.[24]

The Nichols Company paid for these expensive street improvements with funds borrowed from Commerce Trust. The bank granted loans on the basis of Nichols's financial condition, the financial condition of his backers (Hall, Crowell, Simonds, and Shields), and the potential worth of the improved land. Nichols's close working relationship with William T. Kemper allowed the

24. J. C. Nichols Co. advertisement, *Kansas City Star,* October 20, 1912, 3A.

company to borrow this money on open notes without mortgages. This practice had a drawback for the banks: it put them in a less advantageous position to foreclose upon Nichols when he could not pay on notes during the Great Depression. The use of open notes is one reason why the Nichols Company was able to survive that calamity when it was so badly extended on land purchases for which it could not pay.[25]

The ability to obtain financing for Nichols's various projects was essential to his success. In his early developments, Nichols relied on his fraternity contacts and his father's friends from Olathe. By 1908, he had obtained the partnership agreements alluded to above with grain merchants Crowell, Hall, Simonds, and Shields. As was noted in Chapters 2 and 3, Nichols also entered into sales agency and land development agreements with Hugh Ward and the Yeomans family as a means of controlling the development of land that he could not buy through partnership or syndication. It has not been possible to obtain detailed records of Nichols's dealings with Kemper's Commerce Trust other than to document that he served on the Board of Directors from 1908 until his death. While it is no longer considered legal or ethical for banks to loan money to their directors, except in so-called "arms-length" transactions, in the first part of this century banks often had major borrowers act as directors.

As Nichols's operations grew in the 1920s, he appears to have also obtained financing from insurance companies and retirement fund investments such as the Teachers' Insurance and Annuity Association (TIAA). When he reorganized his companies in 1944 into the single entity of the J. C. Nichols Company, part of the motivation appears to have been to obtain refinancing that would remove some of these large corporate lenders, but the available evidence is sketchy on the motivations and the results.[26]

The importance of street improvements lay in the rapidly growing number of automobiles in Kansas City as Nichols was getting his housing developments underway. While there had been only 391

25. 1917 *Proceedings,* B49.
26. The best source on the early financial transactions and financing is in the Scrapbooks. Also see Nichols's correspondence with his son, Miller, available in the J. C. Nichols Collection, Western Historical Manuscripts Collection.

licensed vehicles in Kansas City when he gained control of "the thousand acres restricted" in 1908, by 1914 the number had soared to 9,774. That number, in turn, would nearly double to 18,900 in 1918. Nichols also knew that a quite high percentage of those 9,774 vehicles in 1914 were used on the streets and housed in the garages of his Country Club District. At the same time Kansas City was experiencing this increased number of autos, there was a corresponding explosion of automobile ownership nationally. In 1905, only 8,000 autos were registered in the entire United States. By 1915, the number had grown to 2,332,426. In the fifteen years between 1905 and 1920, the national ratio of autos to persons fell from 1,078 to 1 (1905) all the way down to 13 to 1 (1920).[27]

Occasionally, however, Nichols misjudged things, if only briefly. In 1909, he had gotten his financial backers to donate land and pay a subsidy to the Metropolitan Street Railway Company to extend a car line up the middle of what would become Ward Parkway, running through his top-of-the-line Missouri subdivision, Sunset Hill. With great advertising fanfare the company announced in 1910 that streetcars going south from Westport were traveling on the "Sunset Hill Line" and that cars would be so designated from downtown locations. Residents of Sunset Hill could board cars marked for their subdivision in the downtown area and arrive home without having to transfer once.[28]

During the following year the courts settled the annexation battle that would bring his development inside the legal limits of Kansas City, Missouri. The struggle to get his area included in the city's limits had begun with a successful vote by the citizens of incorporated Kansas City in 1909. The election had been contested, though, and Nichols was forced to wait until its resolution to get the city to expand its boulevard system into his property.[29]

Two years later, in 1913, the Parks and Boulevards Department completed a boulevard connection from downtown via Penn Valley Park and Broadway through Westport. It was named Mill Creek

27. *Kansas City Star*, May 14, 1919, 3A; Jackson, *Crabgrass Frontier*, 162–63.

28. J. C. Nichols Co. advertisements, *Kansas City Star*, November 11, 1909, and October 23, 1910, 16B.

29. Ibid., March 26, 1911, 8A.

Boulevard for the stream valley in which the roadway was built. Mill Creek Boulevard tied in with the beginnings of Brookside Boulevard, which Nichols had constructed on the east side of his property. A branch was constructed to intersect with the initial stages of Ward Parkway, which followed Brush Creek almost to the State Line and then climbed to run nearly straight south through Sunset Hill and (later) Romanelli Gardens.[30]

The first major advertising campaign for the Mission Hills section began in 1916. Using full-page spreads in the *Star*, the Nichols Company announced, among other things, that while a streetcar ride from the development to downtown at Twelfth Street and Grand Avenue took thirty minutes, the same distance could be covered by automobile in only eighteen minutes. Three weeks later a similar advertisement appeared for the unsold portions of Sunset Hill. This time streetcar connections to downtown were mentioned only in passing, but the fact that it took only fifteen minutes to travel from Sunset Hill to Twelfth Street and Grand Avenue by automobile was specifically asserted. This may not be the exact transition point between streetcar and automobile suburbs for Nichols and Kansas City, but it is very close to it.[31]

Less than three years later, the Metropolitan Street Railway announced that it was putting the Sunset Hill Line on what it called "stub service." This meant that transfers were required beyond Forty-eighth Street, where the Plaza shopping area is now located. Service would not be nearly so frequent as before. This rationale was given: "The scanty patronage alleged to prevail on the Sunset Hill end of the Westport Line is attributed to the general use of motor cars in that district." Significantly, Mission Hills, lying directly west of Sunset Hill, never had a streetcar line within its boundaries; it was an automobile suburb from the start.[32]

When the Parks and Boulevards Department constructed Ward Parkway along Brush Creek and south through lands Nichols controlled, he was compelled because of his previous policies to advertise that the company would pay for the roadway construction rather

30. Ibid., April 20, 1913, 3A.
31. Ibid., September 17, 1916; October 8, 1916.
32. *Kansas City Star*, July 27, 1919, 1A.

than the potential customers. New residents would pay their share of the boulevard cost indirectly through the higher cost of the land they purchased. That the company followed this policy is demonstrated by the fact that lots in Romanelli Gardens, located along Ward Parkway, were offered for fifteen dollars more per front foot in 1925 than were similar-sized lots in Armour Fields that same year. Land acquisition costs had been roughly equal for the two tracts, but more expensive street improvements in the Romanelli subdivision resulting from the Parkway were part of the cause for the higher price.[33]

An expensive irony of the practice of the company's payment for improvements came back to haunt Nichols in the 1930s when Ward Parkway was extended as a wide street beyond the limits of his developments. The owners of the more southerly tracts were not willing or able to pay for the land and the road construction themselves. Thus, the Parkway south of Gregory (Seventy-first) was paid for by special assessment taxes. Because the Nichols Company was an adjoining landowner, it was assessed for some of the construction costs beyond its boundaries even though it had paid the entire cost of the construction through its own lands when the Parkway was built. Nichols was understandably bitter about this experience, but his only suggestion for avoiding this problem in the future was to have written agreements with the Park and Boulevard Board to exempt the company from special taxation in years to come.[34]

Nichols was enough of a student of changing patterns to recognize by 1917 that increased reliance on the automobile had drawbacks as well as attractive features for a developer. He noted to a small group of subdividers of similar properties that he feared that heavy traffic on boulevards was beginning to make lots facing boulevards more difficult to sell. Previously, they had been the most popular type and the most expensive. This was a novel idea to Edward H. Bouton, who was also present at the meeting, but Elmer Rowell, a codeveloper of St. Francis Woods in San Francisco, had

33. J. C. Nichols Co. advertisements, *Kansas City Star,* July 16, 1916, 11A; and April 12, 1925, 2D.
34. J. C. Nichols, "Mistakes We Have Made in Community Development," 3.

The use of small triangular "parklets" became something of a trademark of the Nichols Company at intersections of curving streets. This 1914 scene is a reverse view, back to the west from Brookside, from that shown in the illustration on p. 101 above. Note the plantings in the parklet and the smaller size of the sign advertising the area. The house at the right of the photograph was built for H. F. McElroy, then a competing realtor and later Tom Pendergast's notorious "country bookkeeper" and city manager. The sleeping porch over the front porch was a later addition by McElroy. That it was allowed under the building restrictions demonstrates the flexibility that Nichols's restrictions generally provided within broad limits. KC54n15.

already noticed declining values along Portola Drive near his development.[35]

Once the automobile had become the chosen mode of transportation for Nichols's suburbanites, he and his landscape architects began to plan subdivisions with that fact in mind. Beginning in 1913, Nichols worked with local landscape architect Sid J. Hare, who had trained under George Kessler. Hampstead Gardens subdivision was Hare's first project in that year with Nichols. There the landscape consultant continued to use the long block running east and west, and he increased the usage of curving streets and small triangular parklets at intersections to direct traffic and beautify through landscaping. Hare was also involved in the planning of Mission Hills in 1913. Certain factors, such as the location and general shape of the Mission Hills Country Club golf course, were established at the outset. In Mission Hills he and Nichols created a

35. 1917 *Proceedings*, B106.

wonderland of irregularity revolving about one central straight avenue they dubbed "Colonial Court." Many of the blocks were quite
large, averaging ten acres each, with one block containing well over
thirty acres. These oversized blocks were bisected at intervals by
landscaped pedestrian walkways. Cul-de-sacs cut into four blocks,
providing access to the interior portions. No park space as such was
provided because of the proximity of the almost one hundred acres
of Mission Hills Country Club, to which most residents could
belong by reason of purchase.[36]
    It is useful to compare Mission Hills with the description of the
Radburn subdivision in New Jersey, which one urban historian has
called "the most highly praised suburban development of the decade [the 1920s]":

Radburn, advertised as "A Town for the Motor Age," had carefully
planned road systems for separating pedestrian and vehicular traffic.
The roadways formed "superblocks" of thirty to fifty acres. Within
each superblock, narrow cul-de-sac streets led to the houses, which
faced large interior parks, and an elaborate footpath system. Children
could walk almost anywhere without crossing traffic, and adults could
reach their automobiles quickly.[37]

There were, of course, differences. Radburn was subsidized by the
New York City Housing Corporation and was intended for middle-
income, white-collar workers. Mission Hills was always aimed at a
more affluent clientele, and Nichols intended to make a profit from
the sale of land. Mission Hills did not feature quite the degree of
planning for foot traffic that Radburn had, for it was planned as a
lower-density area. Otherwise, the design characteristics of the Kansas suburb developed by Sid Hare in constant collaboration with
Nichols appear very similar to Radburn. The biggest difference is
that Mission Hills was planned in 1913–1914, while Radburn was
developed in 1929 and after.

    36. Scrapbook 1:118; "Area 2," "Metropolitan Kansas City Living, Missouri
and Kansas," n.p.; Scrapbook 1:118; "Area 3," "Metropolitan Kansas City Living," n.p.
    37. Wright, *Building the Dream*, 205–7.

Other utilities were necessary besides good streets. By 1910 a significant number of land purchasers expected water, sewer, and either electricity or gas connections. In most subdivisions, however, purchasers had to fend for themselves until proximity, incorporation, or annexation brought them under the wing of municipal services. Often, the city was willing to extend services only when forced to do so because of expanded boundaries. This fact made high-cost developers who provided full utilities even more unusual.

Sewers were usually more difficult to obtain than water mains. The city assessed developers and/or homeowners for the cost of building sanitary sewers. The hygienic importance of adequate sewers was recognized, but the cost of pumping and treating sewage was so great that the city would not do it out of general funds or from anticipated revenues. The method of payment in Kansas City and in most other North American cities at the turn of the century was to collect this through special benefit taxes, just as with street and sidewalk construction. The unusual nature of high-amenity development began to change in the first third of the twentieth century as more suburbs resisted annexation into cities. Nichols's drive to be annexed was resisted by a few residents and real estate investors in the previously existing limits of Kansas City who did not want more territory included in the parks and boulevards plan. The opponents of annexation simply did not wish to pay higher general or special taxes. This situation reversed the sides drawn in most annexation battles around the country, for normally suburbanites resisted incorporation and city residents voted for the inclusion of surrounding territory.[38]

In general, high-cost developers across the country had to develop part or all of their own utility systems. Bouton at Roland Park had to develop an entire electrical, water, and sewer system with no municipal assistance. He believed in 1918 that this construction and maintenance of water facilities had cost his company much good will among residents who believed that their maintenance payments might be going to subsidize other services of the company. All bills for water, electricity, sewers, and general maintenance came from

38. Jackson, *Crabgrass Frontier,* 138–56.

the Roland Park Company until it spun off a homeowner-controlled maintenance organization in 1910.[39]

Generally, subdivisions developed inside or adjacent to the city limits of a metropolis were able to buy city water and sewage services and did not have to build their own. The further the development was from the central city, the more likely it was that the developers had to provide these essential services themselves until after World War II. Many of the high-cost developers, though, were building in areas isolated from the main city utility connections, as was true at Roland Park, at Highland Park near Dallas, and at an exclusive subdivision near Indianapolis called Brendonwood.

Nichols did not have sewer service provided to his subdivisions, except in exclusive Sunset Hill, until after the annexation battle was over in 1911. Instead, his first houses were equipped with septic tanks. These individual sewage treatment plants worked well enough, provided there was sufficient room for a large treatment field for the tank overflow to seep through. With houses built on fifty-foot frontage lots, as most of those built on Nichols's land were prior to 1911, the possibility for build-up and surface overflow was great. Septic tank overflow was a source of resident dissatisfaction that threatened the viability of the entire project if annexation and city sewers had not come when they did.[40]

In 1906 Nichols advertised the availability of city water to his subdivision even though the land still lay beyond the city's legal limits. Kansas City, Missouri, following a tradition set by many North American cities, offered water to developers without a great deal of up-front cost. The city anticipated growth as a result, with higher tax revenues generated by the new areas. Another argument used by developers in some areas was that provision of city water outside the city limits was necessary to preserve the good health of those who lived in the city as well as those outside it. The cost was borne by water bonds funded from existing sources of revenue and in anticipation of new revenues.[41]

39. 1917 *Proceedings*, 16–17, 265–68.
40. Scrapbook 1:148.
41. Reed, Nichols & Co. advertisement, *Kansas City Star*, March 4, 1906. For

Nichols avoided much of the cost of providing utilities because private utilities, such as gas and electricity, matched the Missouri city's water department policy. The Kansas City, Missouri, department sold water to the Nichols Company for Mission Hills, Kansas, beginning in 1913. The privately owned gas and electric utilities did the same thing in their areas, and even the sewage was piped back into Missouri through municipally owned lines. The only time that Nichols wavered in his devotion to providing all needed services in one packaged price was when the sewers became available. When the Missouri Court of Appeals issued its decision in March 1911, Nichols advertised that buyers could "profit by the immediate effect of city sewers on values in the Country Club District, 1000 Acres Restricted." His potential customers knew they were going to have to pay before they profited from any increased land values; thus, Nichols had to advertise in July that it would cost no more than $1.50 per front foot, or $75 per 50-foot frontage, to install the sewers. The city would allow this special tax to be paid over four years.[42]

It became apparent over that summer of annexation that Nichols had educated his buyers too well; they were accustomed to a fully improved lot with no assessments to pay besides their principal and interest payments. Nichols compromised in September (and compensated himself in the process) by raising prices to $2.50 per front foot, which was a dollar more than his advertised price just two months earlier. By following this policy, he got the sewers when he wanted them installed and took for his company the four-year payback initially offered to landowners. If it could sell the lots at the higher prices quickly enough, the Nichols Company would have the money for the sewers for some time before the final payments had to be made to the city. Everyone—the purchasers, the city, and Nichols—benefited, but Nichols benefited more.[43]

From this point forward, Nichols could truthfully advertise lots

comparison with other cities' water policies, see Jackson, *Crabgrass Frontier,* and Wright, *Building the Dream,* 106.

42. J. C. Nichols Co. advertisements, *Kansas City Star,* April 2, 1911, 5C; and July 24, 1911, 5A.

43. Ibid., September 24, 1911, 8A.

at a single price "with all improvements in." This meant that for a small down payment of 10 percent and a monthly payment of 1 percent per month plus interest calculated at 6 percent, a white-collar worker could buy a lot in the Country Club District, secure in the knowledge that his payments would not be increased by special benefit taxes in the future. It was an important selling point.

The coming of sewers was apparently the most important factor in stimulating home construction in areas under the control of the Nichols Company. In the month following the March 1911 approval of annexation, construction began on nearly fifty homes. The building spurt continued into the fall of 1911, so that by October nearly one hundred houses were underway, seven of which had been started during the last week of September.[44]

From this point until the entry of the United States into World War I, the Nichols Company sold lots with far greater frequency. Nichols had embarked on his subdivision activity at an auspicious moment in Kansas City real estate history. The excessive subdivision of the 1880s had dragged the market down through the recession of the 1890s. In 1900 there was only $10,966,600 in real estate transfers, less than one-eighth of the boom year of 1887. By 1905 this had improved to more than $30,000,000. The banking panic of 1907 held down the rise in that year and the next, but 1909 and 1910 were both years of over $50,000,000 in transfers throughout the city. The situation never boomed in 1880s style between those years and 1917, but a great deal of real estate changed ownership. Higher land values were common during the period.[45]

To a significant degree, Nichols used the country clubs and parkways as his parks. Relatively few specially designated park areas were laid out in Nichols neighborhoods. The Kansas City Country Club (KCCC) predated Nichols's Missouri-side subdivision work by some nine years; it had been started with a nine-hole golf course in Hyde Park in 1895. A fire consumed the club house the following year, and the members decided to move further south. One member, Hugh Ward, contributed land for lease to the club south of Brush Creek.

44. Ibid., April 23, 1911, 8A; and October 1, 1911, 16B.
45. Ibid., January 1, 1911, 11A.

The KCCC occupied the land now owned by the city as Loose Park until 1926, when it moved into Kansas to form the lower western boundary of Mission Hills. Its golf course adjoined that of the Mission Hills Club, which Nichols organized in 1913 to provide an alternative for his new residents who were not or could not become members of the older KCCC. Nichols also organized the Community Golf Club, which evolved into the Indian Hills Country Club, for the same purpose. The golf links of this club form the western boundary of the newer portions of Mission Hills south of Sixty-third Street. Thus, Nichols organized all the country clubs on his property with the exception of the already existing KCCC. They were not corporately owned clubs, however, for his control of membership policy and other matters was accomplished through board membership by either himself or his employees. The Nichols Company paid much of the organizational costs, but title to the lands and buildings remained with the membership through its board of directors.[46]

Nichols strongly believed in using the country club locations as open spaces and as protective barriers against possible undesirable uses of land adjacent to his developments. The KCCC site protected Sunset Hill and the Ward Parkway section from the less prestigious, non-Nichols subdivisions east of Oak and the streetcar line by Nichols's less affluent areas. First the Mission Hills Country Club and then the new KCCC sites protected Mission Hills residences on the north and west. The presence of Sunset Hill served to protect or increase values on the eastern flank of Mission Hills. By the late 1920s, the Indian Hills golf course and the new Community Golf Club course (located in what is now the Sagamore Hills subdivision below Sixty-seventh Street) formed an effective barrier against non-Nichols and lesser-value Nichols neighborhoods to the south. Everywhere possible, Nichols and his landscape architects planned for open spaces as protective screens.[47]

In addition to the use of golf courses, Nichols became very interested in creating artificial lakes as a means of beautifying Mission

46. Scrapbook 1:132A, 132B; Scrapbook 3:4.
47. "Area 3," "Metropolitan Kansas City Living," n.p.; J. C. Nichols Co. advertisement, *Kansas City Star,* September 17, 1916; Scrapbook 3:4–12.

Hills. Two were created: Lake Hiwassee at Sixty-third Street and Indian Lane, and nearby Willow Lake at Sixty-third and Ensley Lane. Lake Hiwassee was his showpiece in 1924, containing two islands with shelters built on them. The islands were connected to each other and to the surrounding land by rustic bridges, and the company placed picnic ovens to encourage informal family gatherings at the site. Unfortunately, in some cases picnickers chopped up the rustic bridges and surrounding fences for firewood.

Lake Hiwassee was formed at the junction of two branches of Brush Creek, which was ordinarily a lazy, picturesque stream. When it rained, however, Brush Creek carried ever-greater amounts of water and silt from its upper watershed as streets were laid out and homes were built there by the Nichols Company and other developers. By 1944 the vandalism and silting combined to make maintenance of Hiwassee as a lake too expensive to continue. The Nichols Company filled it in at its own expense and returned the site to being a junction of branches of the stream instead of an artificial water attraction.[48]

In the Crestwood and Wornall Manor subdivisions, the Nichols Company and Sid Hare planned interior parks in the middle of blocks that could only be reached from the backyards of the houses in the block, or the "garden side." These were intended to be recreational areas for the residents of those blocks only. These interior park areas were equipped with play equipment, sand boxes, and the like. By 1945, the company had found that continued maintenance of these interior parks was difficult because the homeowners' association could not cope with the vandalism and the concerns from residents about burglars lurking in the play spaces after dark. All but one interior park were resubdivided back into the surrounding lots. The sole surviving interior park in the 1980s was located in Crestwood.[49]

The concept of interior parks originated in the Guilford section of Edward Bouton's Roland Park area in Baltimore. The plans and

48. Scrapbook 7:178–79; Scrapbook 16:337.

49. Scrapbook 5:32–33. Nichols preferred to use the term *garden side* to refer to what others call *backyard*. Nichols, "Mistakes We Have Made in Community Development," 3.

restrictions for use and maintenance of the parks in Guilford were drawn up in 1908. They gave the owners of lots adjacent to the private parks the right to vote to remove the parks and take the property back into their own land after January 1, 1923. Many of them did so, just as the homeowners did in Crestwood and Wornall Manor. Thus the experience of private parks was quite similar in Baltimore and Kansas City, as problems with control and maintenance prompted their early demise in most instances.[50]

The largest public park in the Country Club District was not planned for that use at all. In 1926 the owners of the old KCCC site planned to turn that area into an expansion of Sunset Hill. Mrs. Hugh Ward had remarried in 1921, and her new husband, Dr. A. Ross Hill, a former president of the University of Missouri, was particularly interested in developing his new bride's property. They took back the Sunset Hill agency that had been first granted to Nichols by Hugh Ward in 1907, and they then gave notice to the Country Club that it would have to move when its lease ran out.[51]

By the time the Hills got possession of the land, the building boom of the middle 1920s was fading fast into the coming Depression, and there seemed to be little demand for the high-priced property they had to offer. Nichols went to the widow of the founder of Sunshine Biscuits, Mrs. Jacob Loose, and persuaded her to donate the funds to buy most of the old golf course site and then to give the property to the city for a park to be named in her husband's honor. Hence, what should have been Ward Park or even Hill Park came to be named Loose Park for its benefactor, who had never lived in the area. It is significant that Nichols was the one responsible for obtaining the funds to convert the country club site to park use. He had always planned for the KCCC to occupy that spot; had it gone for further development, even of the low-density variety the Hills planned, the loss of the open space would have

50. "Guilford Information for Buyers, Owners and Architects," 29, in the Roland Park Company Papers, 1921, Manuscript Collection, Olin Research Library, Cornell University.

51. Scrapbook 5:49–53.

drastically changed the appeal of the surrounding residential sites for many potential purchasers.[52]

One of the more successful dual-purpose recreational and scenic additions to the plat design was the inclusion of a lily pond in the wide middle planting area of Ward Parkway north of Meyer Circle. In the summer the pond was occasionally used as the site of model sailboat regattas that greatly impressed many young residents, including author Evan Connell as he grew up in the Country Club District. He included the regatta as an event in his second novel about life in the district, *Mr. Bridge*. (Connell's earlier and more widely known book, *Mrs. Bridge*, contains many other insightful anecdotes about the social customs of the Country Club District.) In the winter the company employees kept the pond flooded so that it would freeze to form a shallow ice-skating rink for the enjoyment of residents.[53]

One of the reasons Nichols devoted relatively little space for parks was the comparatively large size of the lots in his subdivisions. Other than a few forty-foot-wide lots in Bismark Place, Nichols had a minimum width of fifty feet for his lots. He preferred sixty-foot minimums and sold many one-hundred- and two-hundred-foot frontages in his more expensive subdivisions. This gave room for private beautification through lawns and flower gardens. With all this open, private space, Nichols's landscape designers and nurserymen did a great deal of planting of flowers, shrubs, and trees. In anticipation of his big opening sale in 1908, Nichols ordered the planting of five thousand flowering shrubs, ranging from crimson ramblers to honeysuckles, Virginia creepers, lilacs, and rosa rugosas. With the development of Sunset Hill in 1909–1911 under the direction of George Kessler, Nichols had his men take particular care to protect the natural trees they found and to plant new ones to enhance the variations in the rough topography that made (and make) Sunset Hill such a picturesque residential section. His advertising

52. Scrapbook 10:195.
53. Evan S. Connell, Jr., *Mr. Bridge*, 98–104; Scrapbook 7:164. During the fall of 1989, much of a film version titled *Mr. and Mrs. Bridge*, produced by and starring Paul Newman and Joanne Woodward, was filmed on location in the Country Club District.

used this plant-filled environment as a positive selling point: "Boys and girls reared in a place of flowers, lawns and shrubbery, of clean air and sunshine have an unquestioned advantage over the children from closely built houses, apartments and dusty traffic streets." On another occasion his advertisements waxed positively poetic: "The green of grass blades and leaves of shrub or tree, a background against which the bridal wreath in snowy banks is heaped; gay colored flowers, that splash along the walks and garden nooks; the song of birds, returned to their haven; open spaces, with views of distant hill or winding stream; it's springtime in the Country Club District."[54]

Normally, street trees were planted in double rows on each side of the street between the curb and the sidewalk in "the parking." Such plantings make clear the use of the term *parking* to describe the strip next to the street in American towns and cities: it was intended to be an area of parklike beautification, with trees and grass planted for visual effect. In certain boulevard situations, Nichols had his crews plant the trees in three rows per side even though the city-wide standard was two rows per side. During the 1920s the company planted trees in areas that had been purchased but were not yet slated for full development. Nurserymen arranged the trees in a random pattern to reproduce a forest effect in the sections where the land was relatively barren. This was especially necessary in the southern parts of the Missouri property because the previous owners, the Armour family, had used it as a grazing farm and therefore had cleared trees.[55]

Sidewalks proved to be a major expense for the company and a significant design question for the landscape architects. For Nichols, the lowly sidewalk was the symbol of all that he was fighting for in city planning. While landscape architects and other developers were divided on the question of appearance, he saw in the reduction of width and frequency of sidewalks the opportunity to reduce development costs and to increase the semirural appeal of his sub-

54. J. C. Nichols Co. advertisement, *Kansas City Star,* April 26, 1908; October 8, 1911, 11A; March 17, 1912, 5A; May 13, 1923, 4F.

55. Ibid., September 15, 1912, 6A; May 1, 1921, 4B; June 18, 1911; "The Nichols Organization and Its Activities."

divisions. The sidewalk was important to Nichols only partly because it provided a means of human communication; that was a
decreasing need with the advent of the motor car. He was more
convinced that sidewalks, if present at all, had to be cost effective.
Otherwise, the expense of the sidewalk added too much to the price
of the land. This cost consideration prompted Nichols to sacrifice
sociability for economy. He initially advertised a six-foot sidewalk,
but by 1917 he asserted that a three-and-a-half-foot sidewalk was
sufficient for two people to pass comfortably and thus adequate for
the needs of a suburban development.[56]

In Mission Hills and other low-density subdivisions, Nichols
advocated having a sidewalk on only one side of the block. He told
his buyers that the single walk gave the owners on the side without
the walk more privacy and more yard. Then, too, with only one
walk, fewer people would stop to pick the flowers from the landowner's lawn and garden on the opposite side of the street. The
proposed reduction in sidewalks combined with other factors—
including the disappearance of the front porch, Nichols's emphasis
on orienting houses toward "the garden side" or backyard, and the
increase in block size to discourage walking—to create a more private, insulated living environment in Mission Hills and other parts
of the Country Club District. The arguments were not entirely
convincing to his fellow realtors when he first proposed them.[57]

One of the more important aspects of landscape design and management for the purpose of selling land is keeping the vacant or
unimproved ground clean and clear of weeds or other foreign material. Nichols set up the deed restrictions so that the charges for
continued maintenance would be assessed on owners of vacant
ground, including his own company, just as they were on the owners
of improved property. The funds raised could be used to maintain
the appearance of vacant lots as well as for the other purposes for
which they were intended. Always looking for a less expensive way
to do these everyday things, Nichols for several years during the

56. Nichols, "City Planning and Real Estate Development"; 1917 *Proceedings*,
58–63.
57. 1917 *Proceedings*, 58–63.

1920s hired the sheep of a local farmer to graze down the grass and weeds on the unimproved sections of south Mission Hills.[58]

If unkempt vacant lots seemed at times to Nichols to be the bane of his existence, the possible presence of unwanted neighbors to his developments was even more upsetting. In one instance in the years just before World War I, Nichols and his financial backers bought back a piece of land they had previously sold to the Kansas City School Board. The board had decided to locate the proposed school elsewhere and to sell the land. A lumber yard was bidding for it, but Nichols was even then planning for the Country Club Plaza shopping center in the valley below the site, so he and his backers repurchased the land to keep the lumber yard from getting it.[59]

Even worse than a *potential* lumberyard, from Nichols's point of view, was an *existing* brickyard located on a hillside overlooking the future site of the Plaza. The Lyle Brick Company was a long-time Kansas City operation. The problem for Nichols was that brickmaking in those days included several processes, including the firing of the kilns, which necessitated the burning of coal. Often during the fall a northerly breeze caused black clouds of smoke to billow over the northern reaches of his subdivisions. Just as bad, during the summer the prevailing southerly breezes wafted coal smoke and soot over the valley where Nichols was planning to build his masterpiece, the Country Club Plaza. Nichols knew he had to remove the brickyard.[60]

The great legal difficulty of the situation was that the brick company had been there first. Nichols had to go to court and have his lawyers argue that the area had become a residential section and was no longer compatible with the land use practiced by the rock quarry and brick kilns. Finally, in 1920, two Missouri courts ordered the brickyard and rock-quarrying operation to cease and desist operations. The argument that won the case for Nichols was similar to

58. Scrapbook 7:71; J. C. Nichols Co. advertisement, *Kansas City Star*, October 3, 1909, 19C.

59. Scrapbook 2:201.

60. A photograph showing the effect of the Lyle Brick Company kiln on Brush Creek Valley is reproduced in the *J. C. Nichols Company, 75 Years: A Commemorative Publication*, n.p.

The original development of the Plaza site resulted in many lot sales, but few houses. The two pictured above were almost alone in Brush Creek valley. Note the apparently unused small storefront to the left of the center house. The dark cloud above the house is actually dust from the rock crusher at the Lyle Brickyard, which Nichols fought to have removed. Almost invisible beyond the trees to the extreme upper left is the outline of the E. C. White School (now the site of the Plaza Library), which orients this picture looking toward the southeast. The weeds in the foreground were really the dominant feature of Brush Creek valley before the Nichols Company built Chandler Floral and the riding academy on the site during the World War I era. KC54n21.

those used by residents who build homes near existing airports and then sue for implementation of noise abatement: the neighborhood had changed and no longer could permit unrestricted noxious activity by previous users. For two more years the two sides wrangled over price, and then in March 1922 Nichols was able to announce to his residents that his company had purchased the hated brick and rock lands. Later that same month the company announced plans for the Plaza area, including the construction of apartment buildings on the site of the former brickyard and rock quarry. Apparently, the seventeen-year struggle was the last roadblock before the company could proceed with its forward-looking business center plans.[61]

61. See Chapter 5 for a more detailed explanation of this idea of changed land use, which courts usually refer to as the "changed neighborhood" doctrine. Scrapbook 6:105–11.

Beginning in the 1920s, Nichols used imported statuary to accent the small parks and public spaces that were provided. This triangular park at Edgevale Road and Main Street illustrates "granitoid" sidewalks winding to the stone-walled statuary garden. To the right is one of the few examples of the provision of children's play equipment in a public park space by the company. A tennis court occupies the intermediate space between the statuary and the playground. Open spaces such as the area across the street from the park were common as development progressed at an uneven pace, but in the expansive early 1920s, when this photograph was taken, the vacant lots in view were occupied by completed housing only one year later. KC54n46.

A landscaping trademark of Nichols's developments was the placement of outdoor statuary and decorative objects at intersections. By varying the theme or historical period of the statuary, Nichols was able to give each neighborhood a distinctive flavor. His local competitors followed his lead by the 1920s. When he first began to place these pieces in the subdivisions, Nichols wrote in his company's newsletter to residents that his company was "confident that the residents of the district have such an appreciation of things beautiful that these ornaments will be as safe as they would be on a private lawn." In spite of this optimistic opening statement, vandalism did wreak havoc on some of the sculpture and ornamentation. In 1923, the company had placed a series of Chinese figures that formed a small musical band in whimsical style around a pond in one neighborhood on Mission Road. Just over a year later, vandals struck, stealing some of the figures and defacing others that could not be readily carry away. The entire arrangement had to be replaced at company expense.[62]

In 1945 Nichols looked back on this policy of beautification through the use of art objects placed about the subdivisions. While he worried that the company may have done too much in some instances, he still believed that the more than five hundred thousand dollars the company had spent for such work was worth the cost. He concluded, "We feel this gives a lot of character and interest to the whole Country Club District, and we are still buying for the future adornment of our properties although vandalism has been pretty discouraging."

The Kansas City developer's impact upon his colleagues across the country extended beyond imitation by his immediate competitors. As an example, the influence of Nichols and similar developers on the thinking of landscape architects can be gained from a chapter entitled "Land Subdivision for Residential Purposes" in the first textbook for the profession, published in 1917. The writers sought to make practicing landscape architects aware of what developers were doing or attempting to do across the country. The chapter portrayed a partnership between the real estate developer and the landscape architect that helped make the project work. The real estate man was the one "who knows what the public expects in residential land, what the public will pay, what other land is being sold in competition, and how a selling campaign may be managed." The landscape architect was to bring to the equation "the technical skill and the experience to produce from the land the maximum of salable utility and beauty at the least cost."[63]

Like Nichols, the authors strongly supported the new zoning

62. Scrapbook 7:164–66; *Country Club District Bulletin*, December 15, 1920, 2; caption, *Kansas City Star*, December 14, 1924, 4B.

63. Nichols, "Mistakes We Have Made in Community Development," 7; Henry V. Hubbard and Theodora Kimball, *An Introduction to the Study of Landscape Design*, 275–94.

laws that were just coming into effect in New York City and else-where. The writers held that such laws were necessary to make sure the town or city grew properly without inefficient mixes of land use that would be detrimental to everyone in the long run. They indi-cated that the profession strongly supported the use of curvilinear streets and the matching of street plans to topography, just as Nich-ols had been doing since 1907.[64]

Beginning in 1916, Nichols vigorously advocated limiting the width of streets in purely residential sections to that sufficient for two vehicles to pass safely. The textbook writers adopted that same position one year later. Both Nichols and the writers admitted that the idea came from Charles Mulford Robinson in his *City Planning*. Further, the writers agreed completely regarding Nichols's favorite target—the sidewalk. They approved using a walk as narrow as four feet in streets that were not closely built up and even allowed for the omission of one or both sidewalks if the desired effect was strictly rural in tone. The Boston-based writers added another reason for having blocks run lengthwise from east to west to Nichols's prevail-ing-wind argument: they stated that because houses were usually oriented so that their length faced the street, north-south blocks did not allow the maximum number of rooms to benefit from the sun. They argued more for air and sunlight, while Nichols argued against too much wind.[65]

One of the areas in which Nichols's landscape thinking stands out even in the 1980s is the careful integration of shopping and service facilities into the residential landscape. Because he was able to con-trol such large areas, Nichols was able in most instances to insure that the store designs and physical arrangement would be compati-ble with his homebuilding. Only in an area adjacent to his Sixty-third and Brookside shops and on Main Street south of Fifty-first was he unable to prevent other developers from building stores without regard for his design plans. Indeed, the very size and scope

64. Hubbard and Kimball, *Introduction to the Study of Landscape Design*, 281–83; Nichols, "City Planning and Real Estate Development," 28–29.

65. Hubbard and Kimball, *Introduction to the Study of Landscape Design*, 282, 285–86, 289; Nichols, "City Planning," 281; Charles Mumford Robinson, *City Planning, with Special Reference to the Planning of Streets and Lots*.

of the Country Club District were probably its best protection against undue influence from developments not controlled by Nichols.

By comparison, one of the otherwise most successful planned subdivisions before World War I, Forest Hills Gardens in Queens, New York, is marred in the 1980s by uncontrolled urban commercial structures that reach its front gate. To illustrate, inside the gate in an open square one may even in 1988 dine in the local tea room, but only a few feet away stands a very garish McDonalds' storefront hawking Big Macs and fries. The contrast is unavoidable because the developers of Forest Hills could buy and control only so much land in an intensely competitive region; nonetheless, the lack of a gradual transition space between busy urban street and tree-shaded drives is woefully apparent.[66]

Thus, by 1917 Nichols's subdivision work was being nationally recognized as outstanding. Similar assessments done in the late 1920s and early 1930s offered the same evidence. Landscape architects realized that his ideas on streets, utilities, sidewalks, and plantings were important for them to use in enhancing the position of their profession throughout the United States. Certainly J. C. Nichols did not create all of the ideas he worked with, but he synthesized them in a way seldom found elsewhere in the United States prior to the 1930s. His company's landscape design work done between the Depression and his death in 1950 was essentially an extension of the patterns developed in this earlier time.[67]

66. This contrast is based on observations of Forest Hills Gardens by the author, July 2, 1988.

67. See, for example, Hubbard and Hubbard, *Our Cities To-Day and To-Morrow;* and *Housing America,* edited by the Editors of *Fortune.*

5

THE PROTECTION OF THE 1,000 ACRES RESTRICTED

J. C. Nichols often spoke of "protecting" his neighborhoods. Many of his 1908 advertisements used the phrase that provides the chapter title above. What was implied by *protection* in this instance was not the strong-arm tactics of organized criminals; rather, it was the shielding of property values in certain residential areas from depreciation through gradual encroachment by lesser property values in surrounding neighborhoods. Protection is provided for a subdivision by what are commonly called "deed restrictions," which are either made part of the deed or referred to in it as binding on the purchaser and on anyone to whom he might sell, lease, or assign the land in the future. Restrictions on the ways a buyer might use the purchased land were not new at the time of J. C. Nichols. They had been used in Kansas City since the 1850s, when Kersey Coates restricted construction in his Coates' Addition to all-brick buildings.

The actual heading of the above-mentioned advertisement read: "Have You Seen the Country Club District? 1,000 Acres Restricted for Those Who Want Protection." This was the first usage of the term *Country Club District* in J. C. Nichols Company advertising. The incorporation of the phrase *country club* in subdivision names became particularly prevalent during the 1920s across the United States. Nichols appears to be the first to have used it. In a 1913 brochure he extolled the virtues of his development with this concluding sentence: "In the Country Club District you are given the protection that goes with 'a thousand acres restricted.'" Thus, another important form of protection provided by Nichols was the large size of the controlled development, which went even further to help guarantee long-term value.[1]

1. Advertisement, *Kansas City Star,* September 6, 1908, 7C; Scrapbook 2:130. This discussion of the history and nature of real estate deed restrictions is based primarily on William B. Stoebuck, "Running Covenants: An Analytical Primer,"

There has been much legal confusion over deed restrictions. Some have wanted to consider them as part-and-parcel with the land and inseparable from the law of land titles, while other legal interpreters have differed to the point of saying that deed restrictions are simply "covenants" between buyer and seller and therefore are covered entirely by contract law. This view is supported by the fact that deed restrictions are often referred to as "restricted covenants." One of the more recent thorough studies of the problem concludes that a deed restriction is essentially a contract that "runs" with the land. The fact of its "running" with the land, literally attaching itself to the title of the real property, makes it more a feature of property law than of contract law.[2]

In English common law the concept of restrictive covenants, usually referred to in common-law courts as "real covenants," can be traced back to a case in 1583. The seller wanted to require the purchaser of a particular parcel of land to build a wall on it, but the purchaser later refused to build the wall. The seller sued to have his requirement or restriction on the use of the land enforced by the courts. In good legal fashion, the court found that the restriction had not been written properly and that the purchaser did not have to build the wall. What has been more important down through the centuries is that the court also stated that if the restriction had been written properly, the requirement to build the wall would have been enforceable.

The court laid down one other requirement for enforcement at the same time: if a deed restriction is to be enforceable, it must pertain to the way the land is held or used. If the thing or things required are not essential to the holding or using of the land, the court held that they could not be enforced. For example, a purchaser could be required to keep the improvements on the property painted and in good repair, but he could not be required to paint a portrait of the seller as a part of his right to the use of the land. The legal phrase used here is that the requirement must "touch and concern" the land in question.[3]

---

and Monchow, *Use of Deed Restrictions*.
   2. Stoebuck, "Running Covenants," 863–64.
   3. Ibid., 865–66.

What is remarkable about restrictive covenants is that they have been recognized and upheld at all in courts based on English common law. The underlying interpretation of real estate in English common law is that it is private property to be used or disposed of as seen fit by the current holder of title, except of course when land is publicly held, as by a government. Deed restrictions limited the use of the land and the ability of the title holder to sell to whomever he pleased. As late as 1916, courts in Ohio and other states did not consistently favor the enforcement of deed restrictions, for the reasons mentioned above. It was not that courts refused to enforce them entirely; rather, judges did not automatically favor restrictions. Subdividers argued that the use of deed restrictions was a positive benefit to the entire community and that individuals achieved this benefit by voluntarily giving up certain freedoms in the use or sale of their land so that a general stabilization in value of all surrounding land could occur.[4]

By the 1970s, one legal analyst believed that restrictive covenants or deed restrictions had come into a favored position with United States courts. J. C. Nichols's position in 1921 was vindicated. At that time he argued forcefully to a group of realtors, ". . . Every year we are planning and studying as to how we can impose upon that property more conditions, and more restrictions, and it has paid and it is paying." The point was that the restrictions made this particular land more salable rather than less so. A recent historian has chosen to interpret deed restrictions primarily as a forerunner of zoning and other public planning policies; while the point is well taken that restrictions were used by subdividers in the prezoning era, it must be noted that they are still used in subdivision and development planning in the last quarter of the twentieth century. This continued use comes in spite of extensive zoning and subdivision regulations in most United States metropolitan areas. Deed restrictions are still among the most formidable tools in a land developer's arsenal.[5]

4. Ibid., 885–86. See also the discussion following J. C. Nichols's speech entitled "Financial Effect of Good Planning in Land Subdivision," 107–8.

5. The analyst was Stoebuck, "Running Covenants," 886. Nichols, "Zoning," 38; Weiss, *Rise of the Community Builders*, 68–72.

Because J. C. Nichols was really a synthesizer in the development of deed restrictions as they apply to residential subdivisions, and because those restrictions are so universally applied in one form or another in 1980s subdivisions across the United States, it is important to look at the form of such restrictions before Nichols began to use them.

Just as J. C. Nichols announced he had obtained control of 1,000 acres for subdivision development in 1908, another developer, T. B. Potter, began to promote a similar project located south and east of Nichols's areas. Potter had moved to Kansas City from the West Coast in 1907 to continue his residential subdivision business. His proposed subdivision of Marlborough Heights at Seventy-sixth and Woodland comprised a full section of 640 acres. Potter had put restrictions scheduled to last for ten years on the subdivision lots requiring that homes built there cost at least $2,500 and that each structure had to be set back at least fifty feet from the lot line. Except for a ban on selling to blacks, few other restrictions were included in the deed. Restrictions were filed with each deed rather than with the plat to cover the entire subdivision. Marlborough Heights was intended to be an exclusive residence section, like Nichols's neighborhoods, but these restrictions were really very limited in practice and did not last long enough to provide much protection against changes after the restrictions lapsed.[6]

When Nichols started his development work on the Missouri side in Bismark Place, he was working with an existing subdivision. Restrictions could only be filed with each deed, as Potter had done with Marlborough. Although the filing of restrictions for the entire subdivision in advance of any sales became a basic Nichols technique for improvement in subdivision work, he did not begin to do this until the platting of Country Side Extension on October 24, 1908. The Country Side Extension restrictions were still comparatively simple requirements, which were to run for twenty years with no built-in plan for extension. No flats or apartment buildings were allowed; only single-family homes could be built on the lots.

6. T. B. Potter, Advertisement: "An Open Letter to the People of Kansas City," *Kansas City Star*, May 5, 1908, 6; Potter, Advertisement: "Third Open Letter to the People of Kansas City," *Kansas City Star*, May 7, 1908, 11.

The restrictions even specified the directions that particular houses were to face on certain lots. Houses had to cost a minimum of $5,000 and be set back not less than forty feet from the front lot line. Utility easements for electricity and telephone were reserved at the back of the lots. No sale to or occupancy by blacks was allowed.[7]

Early in 1909, the initial plat for Nichols's first truly elite subdivision, Sunset Hill, was filed by Ward Investment Company, for which Nichols was then a developing and sales agent. The building costs were raised to $10,000 in certain blocks. The effective length was extended to twenty-five years, and duplexes were permitted in one small section at the very entrance to the district. Otherwise, the restrictions for Sunset Hill were little changed from those prescribed for Country Side. In the spring of 1909 the plat was filed with restrictions for Rockhill Place on the extreme east side of the district. The restrictions were initially almost identical to those for Sunset Hill and Country Side Extension. Then, in August of that year, the Rockhill Place restrictions were modified in two distinctive ways: first, the revision included a regulation controlling the presence and location of outbuildings or garages; secondly, a clause was added that allowed the owners of a majority of the front feet in the subdivision to extend the life of the restrictions for another term by vote.[8]

Nichols once publicly credited Bouton with originating the idea of allowing the owners of a majority of the front feet in a subdivision to extend the life of the restrictions by referendum, but there is no record of any direct contact between the two prior to 1912. On another occasion, Nichols said that this feature was fairly common in subdivision restrictions prior to its use by his company. However, no one in Kansas City appears to have used it prior to his adoption of it in 1909.[9]

The issue of applying restrictions to land in advance of any development of that land was possibly responsible for the breakup of

7. "Book of Restrictions," 37; Plat Book B–15, 33.
8. Plat Book B–15, 47; "Book of Restrictions," 111–12.
9. The first comment concerning Bouton's input is from Nichols, "Financial Effect of Good Planning," 108–9. The second observation was made in Nichols, "A Developer's View of Deed Restrictions," 135.

Nichols and his first partners, the Reed brothers. He recounted to a journalist in 1923 that he had proposed to his partners that they set up the restrictions for a hundred-acre plot and apply them evenly to all lots regardless of when the lots were sold. Nichols said that his partners "ridiculed the possibility of success, so I went ahead alone." Actually, Nichols was never alone in the financial end of his developments until his financial backers were paid back with stock much later. One has to view this story with some skepticism because of the obvious effort to build up a myth of his own independent action, but the split over restrictions is plausible in that Nichols never filed any restrictions on entire plats while he was still with the Reeds.[10]

When the plat for Country Club Ridge was filed two years later, it provided for a twenty-five-year life for the restrictions with the option to renew. This was the first time the longer term had been used since the platting of Sunset Hill. Another clause stipulated that the covenants were to "run with the land," wording that intentionally emphasized the continuing nature of the restrictions. The Country Club District of Kansas City was probably "the first district in the United States where self-perpetuating restrictions were used."[11]

With the filing of the plat and deed restrictions for Mission Hills on the Kansas side in July 1914, the Nichols Company greatly broadened what they hoped to accomplish through deed restrictions in protecting both their own investment and those of the people who bought land from them. The company instituted a clause automatically extending the restrictions unless the owners of a majority of the front feet in the subdivision took action to change or revoke the original restrictions. This placed the burden of action on the owners who wanted to change the restrictions rather than on those who wished to keep them in force as they were; the restrictions thus became self-perpetuating in a positive way. The change to self-

10. Nichols, "When You Buy a Homesite You Make an Investment," 172.
11. Nichols made this somewhat immodest but true statement when he was chosen by the editors of a prestigious journal on land use to review a monograph on deed restrictions; see his "A Developer's View of Deed Restrictions," 135. See also "Book of Restrictions," 21.

perpetuating restrictions had other advantages. The new form nega-
ted any chance of the renewal period slipping by unnoticed, allowing the restrictions to lapse. Such restrictions would continue in
force even if the developer left the business or moved out of the
area. The new form also left open the possibility that the company
or the residents could change the restrictions to deal with new
situations that might not have been anticipated in the original
document. Such problems did later arise concerning garages, outside oil tanks, radio antennae, and sleeping porches. There was a
good deal of resistance to detached garages in the early years of the
automobile, and exterior oil tanks and radio antennae were considered eyesores. Sleeping porches over the front porch created problems when homeowners added them after initial construction. The
restrictions allowed porches, not rooms, to project toward the
street closer than the setback line. As newer houses included sleeping porches in the design from the beginning, this problem diminished over time.[12]

The self-perpetuating clause worked in a straightforward manner.
The restrictions were declared to be in effect for twenty-five years
from the date of the filing. Five years before the stated expiration
date, the homeowners' association notified property owners that
the owners of a majority of the front feet in the affected subdivision
had the right to change or eliminate the restrictions. If no action was
taken, the restrictions automatically renewed for another twenty-
five years at the end of the previous twenty-five years. The cycle was
unending without positive action by owners who wanted to change
the restrictions.[13]

Several items were purposefully omitted in the overall restrictions
but were included on the deed of each property when it was sold.
For the most part, they concerned the specific building to be done
on the lot. Items covered in the deed included additional minimum
cost levels, requirements for the direction a building was to front,
setbacks for the particular lot, requirements for free space on each

12. *Country Club District Bulletin* (hereafter cited as *CCD Bulletin*), March 1922,
2; Nichols, "A Developer's View of Deed Restrictions," 135–36.
13. "Book of Restrictions," 85–92.

side of the structures on the lot, and a requirement for the approval of plans before any construction on the lot.[14]

In 1916 several realtors questioned whether Nichols's ideas about self-perpetuating deed restrictions would be upheld in court. One Ohio developer argued that courts in his state seemed to favor deed restrictions that could not be changed and were thus perpetual. They tended to throw out plans for restrictions if the developers changed them at any time. Nichols did not have to contend with those interpretations in Missouri because courts there generally favored properly written restrictions at that time. He thought it was almost as important to be able to change restrictions or add to them as it was to make sure that restrictions remained in force.[15]

Beyond the addition of the self-perpetuating feature, the Mission Hills deed restrictions established what was called the Mission Hills Homes Company and bound every purchaser to be a member. This was the first true homes association founded by the Nichols Company along the pattern they later used in all their subdivisions. Briefly, the Homes Company was charged with maintaining vacant property; constructing and maintaining common sewers; providing electric street lighting; controlling plumbers' cuts in streets; maintaining streets and removing snow; maintaining shrubs and trees and all aspects of the public areas; taking care of all garbage and rubbish; maintaining street signs; paying taxes on streets and parks; and providing water, gas, electricity, and fire protection. With the advent of the Mission Hills Homes Company on the Kansas side, enforcement of the deed restrictions for the first time passed to the landowners themselves. This would not be done on the Missouri side until 1921, when the Country Club District Homes Association replaced the old Country Club District Improvement Association, a maintenance organization of homeowners that had been founded in 1909 with no role in the enforcement of restrictions.[16]

One measure of the impact of a developer's reputation and of the strengthening of restrictions can be taken from the J. C. Nichols Company's purchase in 1921 of a small, partially developed subdivi-

14. Ibid., 92.
15. Nichols, "Financial Effect of Good Planning," 110–11.
16. "Book of Restrictions," 17, 88–90.

sion named Westwood Park. This small subdivision was located directly north of the west edge of Sunset Hill and had the state line between Missouri and Kansas as its western border. Initially developed by L. R. Wright in 1913, Westwood had minimal restrictions placed on it when the plat was filed. Houses had to cost at least $2,500 ($500 less than the least expensive section in J. C. Nichols's territory at the time), and no billboards were allowed. Beyond this and the standard racial restriction, almost anything was allowed. Nichols was familiar with Wright because the latter had also been the developer of the Bowling Green subdivision adjacent to Nichols's land to the east. When Nichols purchased the unsold lots in Westwood Park, he doubled the minimum building cost and added many of the other restrictions he was using at the time. Company records indicate that during the first month of Nichols Company control, almost as many lots were sold as Wright had managed to sell in eight years. This example is strong support for Nichols's contention that a strengthening of restrictions paid off in more sales.[17]

With the filing of the plat for his company's Armour Hills subdivision in 1922, Nichols and his legal advisors arrived at a list of restrictions that would be the basis for such documents for the rest of his career. The format called for the designation and exemption of any lots to be reserved for nonresidential uses, such as church or shopping-center sites. Projected playground and park space was spelled out and exempted from the restrictions as well. All nonexempt lots were then restricted to single-family residential use. The self-perpetuating clause covered the entire area, while other clauses specified the placement of the structures on the lots, including the direction of the frontage; minimum building widths, in some instances; setback space from the street; maximum length for structural projections from the house; the required free yard space on the lot; and the placement of any outbuildings. The restrictions also indicated the minimum amount that could be spent in constructing the house on each lot. The deed restrictions prohibited ownership or tenancy by blacks, but white owners could otherwise sell or rent to whomever they wished. This new format also restricted enforce-

17. Plat Books B–17, 26, B–18, 19; Scrapbook 6:13.

ment rights to the J. C. Nichols Company, the present or future landowners in the subdivision through their legally established homeowners' association, and the homeowners in adjacent Nichols subdivisions. This clause was important because it meant that owners in the adjacent Nichols subdivisions could affect the quality of home maintenance or any other factors that might ultimately influence their own property values.[18]

In an important section of the adopted pattern of restrictions, Nichols's lawyers inserted a clause stating that enforcement would be by court injunction. This accompanied a clause stating that failure to enforce the restrictions was not to be construed as a waiver of the restrictions. With model restrictions for Missouri-side subdivisions in place after the filing of the Armour Hills document, the Nichols Company determined to bring their older subdivisions under uniform restrictions along these same lines and to institute homeowners' associations in each area. By May 1924, the legal legwork was completed. Nichols hosted a series of dinner meetings to which the residents of each previous subdivision were invited. Updated restrictions were proposed, along with an offer to organize separate homeowners' associations for Rockhill Park, Rockhill Place, Rockhill Heights, Country Side, South Country Side, Country Side Extension, Wornall Manor, Wornall Homestead, Country Club Ridge, and Country Club Heights. The landowners from three subdivisions that had not been developed by the Nichols Company, Cockins' Addition, Bowling Green, and Randall and Wheelocks' subdivision, also received invitations. This inclusion of the adjacent subdivisions was simply an extension of the Nichols Company efforts to give greater protection to their own purchasers. In the instance of Cockins' Addition, the restrictions initially filed with the plat were quite similar to those of Nichols's subdivisions at the time. He may well have influenced the owners in developing their restrictions from the start.[19]

The residents of Nichols's neighborhoods accepted the plan to

18. "Book of Restrictions," 1–8.
19. Ibid., 1–8. This did not include Bismark Place, where the ten-year restrictions by deed had already lapsed without renewal, much to the disappointment of Nichols. *CCD Bulletin*, 3; Plat Book B–16, 75–76.

extend the Armour Hills type of restrictions to the older subdivisions, doing so with enthusiasm in most cases. The majority of landowners saw this as an attempt to provide them with more property-value protection and to preserve the character of their neighborhoods for years to come. In one instance, however, a minority of the homeowners in the Wornall Homestead subdivision sued in court to prevent the action. They argued that the extension of these restrictions by majority vote should not be lawfully binding on all homeowners, and that the effort by the Nichols Company to extend the updated restrictions was an attempt to maintain their monopoly over the business property in the area. The case went all the way to the Missouri Supreme Court, which ruled in favor of Nichols and the majority of homeowners in Wornall Homestead.[20]

The degree to which the Armour Hills model came to serve as the standard for years to come can best be measured by an examination of the declaration of restrictions for Sagamore Hills, a planned upper-income subdivision on the south side of Mission Hills on the Kansas side. Filed October 19, 1937, it represents an example of the changes made in the form of the restrictions in the fifteen years between the filing of the Armour Hills restrictions and those for Sagamore Hills. The only substantive changes include the minimum building costs required for houses to be built on the affected lots. Actually, the dollar amounts are quite similar—$5,000, $6,000, and $7,500, depending on the lot. The main difference is that Sagamore Hills was intended for upper-income housing, whereas Armour Hills was definitely planned for middle-income families. By 1937, sufficient deflation had taken place in building costs to allow much more space to be obtained for the money than in 1922. When the first plat of Prairie Village was opened for public sale in 1941, the minimum building restriction was only $3,500, which denotes clearly that this new subdivision, ultimately the Kansas City version of Levittown, was intended by Nichols to be a middle-income neighborhood.[21]

20. Scrapbook 7:88.

21. "Declaration of Restrictions to Sagamore Hills," filed October 19, 1937, Register of Deeds Office, Johnson County Courthouse, Olathe, Kansas, Book 22 Misc., 105.

The difference in financial conditions between 1922 and 1937 is apparent in a restriction that specified blocks in Sagamore Hills where houses were required to have at least 60, or in some cases even 70, feet of frontage. In Armour Hills, some lots had had no minimum frontage required, while others had had 50 or 60 feet required. This means that in 1937 it was generally expected to get at least 10 feet more house width for the money than 15 years earlier. Additional restrictions in 1937 were minor: billboards and signs were prohibited except for "real estate for sale" signs, which could not exceed 5 square feet in total area, and above-ground oil-storage tanks were prohibited. Otherwise, the 1922 form appears to have fit the situation as well in 1937 as it had 15 years before.[22]

One form of restriction was kept on a strictly contractual basis rather than being included in a deed restriction: the Nichols Company's control over the design of homes to be built on the lots it sold. The use of architectural controls is one idea that can be documented to have been adopted by Nichols directly from the ideas and practices of Edward Bouton at Roland Park. There is no evidence of it prior to Nichols's first contact with Bouton in 1912, but during the next summer, Nichols wrote the Baltimore developer that he was trying to make this requirement a part of the sales contracts with new purchasers.

The Kansas City developer had floated the idea in discussions with some people who had already bought land from him. He told Bouton by letter that every one of them had objected to the idea on first hearing and said that they would not have bought land if that requirement had been part of the sale. Some, but by no means all, had come around to liking the protection it might provide them after they had reflected on the idea. This initial negative reaction may well be the reason that architectural review of plans never got into any Nichols deed restrictions. Many other high-income subdivisions, such as Guilford and Palos Verdes Estates near Los Angeles, inserted all the details about approval of plans directly in the restrictions. Nichols may very well have thought it would not be acceptable to enough land owners to get it inserted into old restrictions. The beauty of its inclusion in the sales contract is that it

22. Ibid.

was brought directly to the attention of the land purchaser at the proper time—the closing of the sale.[23]

With regard to the requirement for advance approval of building plans, Nichols had worked out a system by 1917 under which his salesmen, some of whom he had designated as "subdivision managers," were charged with keeping track of all construction in their subdivision. They were to check to see if the company had a copy of the blueprints and elevations on file for each house under construction. If such plans were not on file, the plans had obviously not been approved. They were to get the plans and review them to make sure they met all building restrictions. When problems arose, Nichols, who served as his own sales manager at this time, approached the homeowner to work out a solution.

The enforcement of this requirement became much more difficult when the land was sold by an outside real estate agent. These agents from other agencies usually were not aware of the necessity of review of plans, and the purchaser might complete the deal without ever knowing about the requirement. To prevent this, Nichols made the outside agents divide their commission with his own salesman who handled that subdivision, which discouraged much activity from an economic standpoint. Secondly, he did not allow the showing of his company's properties by outside salesmen without prior approval from the Nichols organization. What he most feared in these instances was the potential loss of control.[24]

Within a year, however, Nichols had changed his procedure for checking conformity with restrictions and the filing of building plans. Whereas he had formerly delegated this to salesmen, in the spring of 1918 he had a "grounds man" who had this duty as his full-time job. It seems that the salesmen just had not gotten the job done the way Nichols thought it had to be done. Whether he had restriction violations checked by his salesmen, by a "grounds man," or by himself, which he often did, on one point J. C. Nichols was adamant: he wanted someone who reported to him check building

23. Letter from Nichols to E. H. Bouton, dated July 30, 1913, in Roland Park Company Papers.
24. 1917 *Proceedings*, 120–22, 129. See also Nichols, "Suburban Subdivisions with Community Features," 19.

plans, not some highly respected, but ultimately uncontrollable, architectural jury. He would rather have the homeowners' association, made up of people with vested interest, make the decisions than have professionally trained architects rule on the acceptability of a given set of plans. On this issue, Nichols was unique among upper-income subdivision developers, for the others preferred architectural juries by professionals. Basically, Nichols trusted the tastes of his current residents more than those of outside professionals. This position lends credence to Robert Fishman's thesis that middle-class values were most influential in establishing the suburbs as "bourgeois utopias."[25]

Nichols believed that one tangible way tighter and longer restrictions with automatic renewal clauses could help his purchasers was the stability of property values such restrictions could create. This was particularly important given the banking community's practice of granting only five-year mortgages. When those mortgages came due after five years, the banks would be more likely to renew at favorable rates and for the same principal balance as the matured mortgages if the values of the neighborhood had remained steady or had improved. Though noted planner Henry Wright and J. C. Nichols would diverge in their ideas about land subdivision in the late 1920s, they agreed on the importance and meaning of deed restrictions in 1916. When Nichols expressed this view in a speech, Wright agreed completely: "It remains for our public to realize that he who exercises his independence in a way which will damage the value of his neighbor's property is just as much to be condemned as if he had actually taken from him some object of ascertained financial value."[26]

Nichols was almost always involved in speeches and discussions that dealt with the type of development he knew best—the subdivision of land and construction of houses for middle- and upper-income buyers. On two occasions, however, he took the oppor-

25. *Proceedings of the Second Annual Conference of the Developers of High Class Residential Property* (hereafter cited as 1918 *Proceedings*), 129; Richard Fowler, "J. C. Nichols," 330; "Restrictions Create Values in Country Club District," 39; Nichols, "A Developer's View of Deed Restrictions," 137; Fishman, *Bourgeois Utopias,* 13.

26. Nichols, "Financial Effect of Good Planning," 101, 116–17.

tunity to expound his views on the possible benefits of proper deed restrictions for working-class neighborhoods. In 1913 he was asked to submit an article on the subject to the American Academy of Political and Social Science. Entitled "Housing and the Real Estate Problem," his paper was reprinted in the *Annals* of that organization in January 1914. In it he argued that the protection of property values through the use of deed restrictions was possibly more important in working-class subdivisions than in upper-income areas. He stated that the land purchasers would have to be educated on this point, but that he believed restrictions could be drawn that would protect property values in all types of subdivisions.[27]

Ten years later Nichols found himself speaking to the Home Builders' and Subdividers' Division of the NAREB. He stated boldly, "In our subdivision, whether we are dealing with a man that has only a thousand dollars or fifteen hundred dollars, or even if it is only a one or two-room house, we are going to give him the God-given rights of protection that his family deserves." This met with applause from his listeners. Ironically, Nichols never sold that small a house to anyone in that financial condition after 1905. When he did have the opportunity in 1903 and 1904, no restrictions at all were applied to the property. Neither Nichols nor any of his listeners ever really put those ideas to the test of the market in inexpensive subdivisions. The theory remained untested in the private sector.[28]

As the housing decline of the late 1920s slumped into the depression of the 1930s, Nichols and his lawyers decided that foreclosures on mortgages might well become more common. By 1930 his company had begun to make the restrictions and conformity to them a prior right to any mortgage that might be on the land or its improvements. To do this initially required that the original landowners from whom Nichols was buying the undeveloped land had to lift their mortgages at least temporarily to allow the placement of restrictions on totally unencumbered land. Usually, Nichols got this written into the contract so that when a plat was filed, the owners would suspend their mortgage on record. The restrictions,

27. Nichols, "Housing and the Real Estate Problem."
28. Nichols, "Home Building and Subdividing Department."

which Nichols had convinced them would benefit the salability of their land, were then placed on the land in question without any other claims upon it legally. The next step was to replace the mortgage of the owners. Then, even if the original owners foreclosed on Nichols, which some of them tried to do in the 1930s, the restrictions would still be in place.[29]

Nichols was a pioneer in developing deed restrictions in the Kansas City real estate market. His impact on that market over the twenty-five years primarily covered by this study can be seen by the fact that many of the subdivisions surrounding his areas adopted quite similar restrictions as time went on. Whether Nichols invented the restrictions he instituted or only followed examples of similar subdivisions elsewhere in the United States cannot be resolved easily. While it is difficult to determine what he knew of other subdivisions and their restrictions at a given time, it is possible to identify the types of restrictions that were in use by a specified date. For example, developers of Riverside, near Chicago, utilized rudimentary deed restrictions as early as 1871. With the advice of Frederick Law Olmsted, the developers stipulated that land was to be sold "only to an absolute settler who will agree to build immediately or within one year from the time of purchase, a home costing at least three thousand dollars, to be located thirty feet back from the front of the lot line, which thirty feet must be retained as an open court or dooryard." With the exception of the requirement to build within one year, Nichols used all these restrictions and added little to them in his first lot sales in Bismark Place.[30]

Not only was the Olmsted landscape architecture firm the consultant for Riverside; it was, in the years to follow, consultant for many other subdivision projects. Most of these were undertaken after the retirement of Frederick Law Olmsted, Sr., in 1895. Fortunately, the records of the company were preserved long after the death of the founder. In 1926 another landscape architect used those records to

29. "Restrictions Create Values in Country Club District," 38; Nichols, "A Developer's View of Deed Restrictions," 140.

30. See Plat Book B–16, 75–76; Plat Book B–17, 65; Plat Book B–20, 43; and Plat Book B–20, 78, for examples of similar restrictions. Monchow, *Use of Deed Restrictions*, 3.

compile a listing of the most important aspects of deed restrictions used in most of the subdivisions for which the company was consultant. The results give some idea of the development of restrictions prior to Nichols's first platted subdivision in 1907.

The first Olmsted subdivision for which the company recorded its suggested restrictions after Riverside in 1869 was on Cushing's Island near Casco Bay, Maine. The plat was filed in 1883 for a subdivision covering two hundred acres. Builders were required to construct houses within two years after purchasing a lot; the location of the house on the lot had to be approved in advance by the company engineer; and no stores, saloons, amusement houses, or hotels were allowed to be constructed in this subdivision near the Maine resorts. Finally, houses had to cost a minimum of $2,000.

A better precedent with which to compare Roland Park and Nichols's Country Club District was begun in 1884. Brookline Hills subdivision, in the Olmsted firm's hometown in Massachusetts, consisted of 165 acres and was a modern development in the sense that indoor plumbing and central sewers were required. No privies, cesspools, or manure pits were allowed. It was reserved for single-family residences costing at least $4,000, with no buildings in the subdivision to be used for trade or manufacturing. House height, setbacks, and required free space on the side lines were specified for the life of the restrictions, to 1920.[31]

The Olmsted Company developed four other subdivisions prior to the firm's involvement with the second phase of Roland Park development in 1897. Most of the restrictions were similar to the earlier two developments. The differences included specification of maximum fence height, the institution of an assessment for maintenance of roads and alleys in one instance, general statements about the style of houses to be built (usually specified as needing to be "rural"), and minimum building costs ranging from $3,000 to $6,000.[32]

---

31. Fein, *Frederick Law Olmsted*, 165; Hubbard, "Land Subdivision Restrictions," 53–56.

32. Ibid., 55–56. The four subdivisions were Sudbrook, Baltimore County, Maryland; Lake Wauconda, Perry Park, Colorado (the recreational subdivision); Aspinwall Hill, Brookline, Massachusetts; and Newton Boulevard Subdivision, Newton, Massachusetts.

Roland Park was begun with the advice of landscape architect George Kessler. Initial restrictions were fairly minimal, allowing no places of business except on space reserved for such use by the company; only one dwelling per lot, with minimum building costs ranging from $2,000 to $5,000, depending on the lot; and setbacks varying from thirty to forty feet, again depending on the location. Whether Kessler suggested these restrictions or Bouton instituted them on his own is not clear. With the beginning of the long relationship between the Olmsted firm and the Roland Park development in 1897, restrictions began to be more elaborate. Under the guidance of the Olmsteds, the Roland Park Company introduced a nuisance clause prohibiting general nuisances and swine. The company began to place an assessment of not more than twenty-five cents per front foot per year on landowners to pay for maintenance of streets, street lighting, and sewers. Beginning with the fifth section of development after the turn of the century, the restrictions were altered so that changes could be made at specified intervals by approval of two-thirds of the owners of the front feet in the subdivision. In this same section of the development, the effective life of the restrictions was extended through 1960, and stables and houses with wood exteriors were excluded.[33]

Another extension of Roland Park began in 1908. Named Guilford, it probably had the most extensive set of restrictions of any subdivision in the United States to that time. The tendency in Roland Park was toward inclusion of more detail in the restrictions, while J. C. Nichols's restrictions tended to leave more latitude to the company and the homeowners' associations. Table 5-1 summarizes the similarities and differences between the Roland Park/Guilford restrictions and the ones developed by Nichols's staff in 1922 as a pattern for future developments, including the Armour Hills subdivision.

The fact that Nichols always retained much more flexibility in the wording of his restrictions than did Bouton in Roland Park/Guilford appears to be an extension of the personalities of the two men as much as anything else. Nichols was outgoing and gregarious;

33. "From the District's Archives," July 1931, 4–5; Hubbard, "Land Subdivision Regulations," 55–56.

TABLE 5-1

A COMPARISON OF DEED RESTRICTIONS BETWEEN
ROLAND PARK/GUILFORD SUBDIVISION AND
ARMOUR HILLS SUBDIVISION

Category	Roland Park/Guilford 1921	Nichols's Armour Hills 1921
Nuisances Prohibited:	Businesses, manufacturing and public buildings (except in approved locations), livestock, poultry, swine, and cattle (except for draft animals used during initial development), occupancy by blacks (except as servants), and dark coal smoke.	Ownership or tenancy by blacks prohibited.
Land Uses:	Private residences only. Private garages allowed only where specified. Business, public and park areas specified.	Church lots and shopping center sites exempted. All other lots for private residence only.
Setbacks:	Houses restricted by lot. All structures (except garages) required to be at least ten feet in front of lot back line. Free-standing garages required to be set back at least one hundred feet from front lot line.	Houses restricted by lot. Outbuildings required to be located within specified bounds for each lot.
Minimum Free Space:	Minimum free space specified. Maximum projections from house indicated.	Minimum free space specified
Maximum Widths:	Houses and blocks of houses required to be no wider than 250 feet.	No maximum. Minimum widths indicated for certain blocks.
Plans Approval:	Company approval of plans required before start of construction. Items required to be in plans when submitted included elevations, materials, placement of structures on the lot and the grading of the lot.	Company approval of floor plans and lot plans needed before construction began. This approval was part of the sales contract instead of in the deed restrictions. No invariable standards.

TABLE 5-1 (continued)

Category	Roland Park/Guilford 1921	Nichols's Armour Hills 1921
Right to Modify:	Nuisance clauses not to be altered at any time. Other clauses were renewable at specified dates by two-thirds affirmative vote of owners.	Twenty-five year length. Automatic renewal five years before termination unless owners of majority of front feet vote to change or terminate.
Maintenance Charges:	Annual charge of twenty cents per 100 square feet of lot area. Proceeds to be used for lighting and maintaining public areas, maintenance of storm sewers and vacant lots, garbage collection, police and fire protection, enforcement of restrictions, tax payments or any other assessments.	Annual charge of ten cents per front foot levied—part of sales contract. Proceeds to be used for public areas, storm sewers & vacant lots, for collecting trash, snow removal and for enforcement of restrictions.
Streets & Parks:	Rights to use streets and parks granted to owners with title remaining with company. Company allowed to convey title to streets and parks to any public agency or to another corporation.	Not specified.
Sanitary Sewers:	Company promised to build a sanitary sewer system for the subdivision. Assessed annual charge of ten cents per 100 square feet of lot area. Company retained right to dispose of sewer system to a public agency or a private corporation with provision that the corporation could not increase fees.	Not specified.

Source: Deed restrictions in *Guilford: Information for Buyers, Owners and Architects,* 19–29, and in "Armour Hills Subdivision," "Book of Restrictions."

he also did not hesitate to confront people with whom he had a grievance. There is evidence of a voluminous correspondence with homeowners concerning their property and adherence to deed restrictions. Bouton was a much more private man who had left Kansas City under a financial cloud in 1891 and seldom went back. In numerous conversations recorded as part of the *Proceedings* of the Developers' Conferences, he appears to have been a man who could stick to principle regardless of the arguments of others. His dealings with his homeowners were never, by his own admission, nearly as congenial as those of Nichols. This type of man was much more likely to record all conditions so that discussions or arguments could be settled summarily.[34]

A comparison of Nichols's restrictions with those that preceded his work shows that his innovation lay in the provision for extension of the restrictions. He correctly claimed to be the first to use the device automatically extending the restrictions unless the owners of a majority of the front feet in a given subdivision voted five years before the expiration date to change, delete, or remove them. Nowhere in the literature is this claim challenged. Nichols added a few other things in his deed restrictions that were not included in the Guilford restrictions, including specifications for the orientation of the houses toward the street, the designation of minimum width for homes on certain lots, and the prohibition of exposed oil-storage tanks for heating systems. Such omissions in the Guilford restrictions are minor. Overall, the Guilford listing was far more complete.[35]

When students of the last half of the twentieth century run across the term *deed restrictions,* race restrictions probably come first to mind. However, deed restrictions have covered many aspects of owning and using land and improvements. Almost always the briefest section of a set of restrictions was the one that prohibited sale and/or occupancy by blacks, and at times other minorities as well. Given the importance of the civil rights movement in United States history and the injustice of denying people the right to buy or live in

34. Fowler, "J. C. Nichols," 330.
35. Nichols, "A Developer's View of Deed Restrictions," 135; "Declaration of Restrictions for Sagamore Hills," 405.

a certain area simply because of their race, it is understandable that this brief clause in most sets of deed restrictions would draw the greatest attention.

State courts were the first arenas in which cases concerning race restriction were argued. One of the earliest was a case that would have directly affected J. C. Nichols. In 1918 the Missouri Supreme Court upheld a restriction of another subdivider that prohibited the sale, lease, or rental of the property in question to a black person during the twenty-five-year life of the restrictions. The final opinion spoke directly to the point:

> It is the rule that an absolute restriction in the power of alienation in the conveyance of a fee simple title is void, but it is entirely within the right and power of the grantor to impose a condition or restraint upon the power of alienation in certain cases to certain persons, or for a certain time, or for certain purposes. The condition in the deed under consideration does not come within the rule prohibiting restraints upon alienation.[36]

The term *alienation* in this instance means "sale." The Missouri opinion was widely cited in the 1920s as a precedent for restricting the sale of real property to members of specified minority groups. This is the position that J. C. Nichols took in all deed restrictions written by his company from 1908 forward: no sales to blacks were allowed or even considered. Other state courts held that restrictions against the sale of property were invalid but that restrictions against occupancy by members of minority groups were allowable. California courts were often cited in this regard. They differed with the Missouri opinion that selective restraints on sales were permissible, but the difference was more academic than substantive because the effect was the same—minorities were effectively barred from properties by deed restrictions.[37]

Thus for nearly two generations the clauses, when properly written, were upheld by the highest courts in the land. Racial discrimination by government action through a districting system similar to

36. *Koehler* v. *Rowland*, quoted in Monchow, *Use of Deed Restrictions*, 49–50.

37. *Los Angeles Investment Co.* v. *Gary*, and *Janss Investment Co.* v. *Walden*, both quoted in Monchow, *Use of Deed Restrictions*, 50.

zoning was disallowed by the U.S. Supreme Court in a 1917 case. The court ruled that such action by the state constituted a direct violation of the Fourteenth Amendment "preventing state interference with property rights except by due process of law." While the high court maintained that the state could not thus discriminate, only eight years later it allowed a racially restrictive clause drafted by white owners that prohibited the sale of real property to blacks in a given block of Washington, D.C. The plaintiffs had argued that the racially restrictive clause was unconstitutional because it violated the restraints of the Fifth, Thirteenth, and Fourteenth Amendments. The relevant portions of these amendments have to do with the right to hold property unless the right is taken or prohibited by due process of law (Fifth and Fourteenth) and with the right to act as a free person in American society (Thirteenth). The U.S. Supreme Court ruled narrowly that this argument of unconstitutionality was invalid because the amendments were intended as restraints on action by the state governments or their subsidiary powers, the cities and counties. "Individual invasion of individual rights is not the subject matter of the amendment," said the majority of justices. The opinion went on to uphold the right of contracts to control how property may be sold or used.[38]

The racially restrictive covenants were continually upheld until a 1948 U.S. Supreme Court case. In *Shelley* v. *Kraemer*, the Court began removing the various elements of discrimination that had evolved since the U.S. Supreme Court decision allowing racial segregation in rail transportation in the *Plessy* v. *Ferguson* case of 1896. The Court ruled in *Shelley* v. *Kraemer* that racially restrictive covenants or deed restrictions were unconstitutional and therefore unenforceable. This decision did not mean that such clauses had to be removed from existing statements of deed restrictions or that future declarations of restrictions might not have the clause inserted; the Court opinion simply held that such restrictions were unenforceable in a court of law. It took more than two decades after *Shelley* v. *Kraemer* for the effects of racially biased deed restrictions to abate.[39]

38. *Buchanan* v. *Wharley*, and *Corrigan* v. *Buckley*, quoted in Monchow, *Use of Deed Restrictions*, 47–48.

39. *Shelley* v. *Kraemer*, cited in George Lefcoe, *Land Development Law: Cases and Materials*, 479.

Somewhat more difficult to determine is the point at which sub-dividers began to believe it necessary to institute written clauses exercising racial restrictions. They were considered unnecessary through the era of the Civil War and Reconstruction because of other legal and social limitations placed on blacks. Upper-income areas protected themselves by pricing the housing stock out of the market of black families. Middle-income and working-class families were probably most worried about possible interracial neighborhoods.[40]

Racial segregation had its roots in Kansas City early in the city's development. It is clear by mapping residential patterns in Kansas City, Missouri, in 1913 that blacks were confined to certain areas of the city. Only one quite small black neighborhood existed within thirty blocks of J. C. Nichols's expanding subdivisions. The average black family income in that year was so low that the possibility of buying a J. C. Nichols house and lot costing a minimum of $3.500 was out of the question. Average annual income for black males was less than $483, and black women earned an average of only slightly over $200 per year. Only about 800 of 23,566 black people in Kansas City owned real property. The per capita wealth of blacks was given as $80.61. In Chicago in 1904, blacks worked as strike-breakers for a wage of $2.25 per day. This pay level resulted in approximately $700 per year, a maximum for unskilled workers, which included most Chicago blacks. Yet, in Kansas City, Nichols deemed it necessary to exclude blacks specifically from purchase or occupancy as early as 1908 with the Country Side subdivision deed restrictions. The Kansas City developer was certainly acting within the accepted white position when he inserted deed restrictions excluding sales to blacks. The national trend at the turn of the century was strongly in the direction of having written regulations on the subject rather than relying on unwritten tradition.[41]

40. C. Vann Woodward, *The Strange Career of Jim Crow.* Also see Allan H. Spear, *Black Chicago: The Making of a Negro Ghetto,* 21–23.

41. *Social Prospectus of Kansas City, Missouri;* Spear, *Black Chicago,* 37. See comments of Joel Williamson in his *The Origins of Segregation,* vi, vii.

Nationally, there appear to have been some written restrictions against ownership or occupancy by blacks prior to the start of the twentieth century, but the evidence is by inference only. In a 1929 study of the deed restrictions of 84 subdivisions, including some by the same developers, fewer than half (40 of the 84) have explicit racial restrictions. Of the 40 surveyed that have such restrictions, the 2 earliest were Bouton's Guilford (1908) and Nichols's Sunset Hill (1909). According to the study, Roland Park did not have express written racial restrictions in its earlier phases. This lack of a written statement notwithstanding, Bouton made his position about selling to minorities abundantly clear during the meetings of the High Class Developers' Conference in 1917 and 1919. In these sessions he was adamantly opposed to selling to Jews and Catholics, let alone blacks. His racial prejudice appears to have continued since his childhood in Kansas City. It is generally recognized in the historical community that racial segregation laws increased markedly during the last decade of the nineteenth century and the first decade of the twentieth. With regard to deed restrictions, de facto racial segregation in housing seemingly preceded the legal statement, so that racial restrictions simply put in writing what had been accepted practice for decades.[42]

Apparently Bouton did not even think it necessary to write down such a restriction against blacks in the 1890s. That any black person might put together enough money to buy into his property was probably unimaginable for him. Furthermore, if the occasion did arise, there was little to keep him from saying with impunity that he did not sell to blacks. After the turn of the century, as more rights were being advanced on behalf of immigrants and other minorities, the practice moved from an informal outright rejection to a more formalized (and legalized) statement in written restrictions.[43]

The possibility of a black family's purchase of a home in Roland Park, Forest Hills, or the Country Club District remained remote throughout the 1920s on the basis of price alone. Of much more

42. Monchow, *Use of Deed Restrictions*, 50; Williamson, *Origins of Segregation*, vi; 1917 *Proceedings*, B52–54; *Proceedings of the Third Annual Conference of Developers of High Class Residential Property*, 565–80 (hereafter 1919 *Proceedings*).
43. Spear, *Black Chicago*, 24–25.

immediate concern to these "high class" developers was the very real possibility that they might be faced with a potential sale to a Jew or, in the west coast subdivisions, to an Oriental. The developers discussed these possibilities at some length, with Nichols taking the lead.

The Kansas City developer raised the question at the 1917 conference of "selling Jewish people," as he put it. Hugh Prather in Highland Park near Dallas indicated that he had sold to two or three Jews, but he had "absolutely picked them. They are the best Jews in town and I would just as soon have them as anybody else." Other developers, including Emerson Chaille of Brendonwood near Indianapolis, William Demarest of Forest Hills, and E. H. Bouton of Roland Park, all clearly stated that they discriminated against Jews in residential sales and had no plans to change policies.[44]

Nichols explained to the group of developers that it had been his policy as well not to sell to Jews, but that four or five Jewish families had bought land or houses on his property through other real estate companies. He was beginning to get some pressure from Jewish leaders on the subject: "Within the last week one of the most prominent Jews in town came to my office and gave me the worst going over I ever had in my life, and it developed into a very bitter situation right here in Kansas City, and we are right on the fence; we do not know what to do." Demarest and Bouton interrupted Nichols's narrative to urge the Kansas City developer to resist the pressure. They thought it would be good public relations in the non-Jewish community because of "their being down on you." Thereafter, Nichols was ready to drop the subject, but it was clear that most of the developers present had no qualms about refusing to sell to Jews. They accepted it as a given that none would sell to blacks; Nichols, for example, never raised that question at all.[45]

Racial restrictions and policies were not considered in as much detail in the 1918 developers' conference, but discrimination in a broad sense was discussed, with Demarest of Forest Hills leading the others. At Forest Hills, Demarest employed a woman who worked as an investigator of potential purchasers before the sales were finalized. She looked into their work, their church affiliation,

44. 1917 *Proceedings*, B52–B53.
45. Ibid., B54.

their salary, and their history as good tenants or homeowners where they presently lived. Demarest believed that his approved purchasers actually appreciated this type of character and economic investigation because when they were allowed to purchase, they knew that they and their neighbors had been approved on the same standards. The investigation process also yielded new prospects among those who had served as references for the potential buyers. In one instance the investigator learned from a business associate of the possibility that a potential buyer's wife was a mulatto or part black. The business associate "would not care to have her as a neighbor." On learning of this, Demarest canceled the pending contract with the prospect and promptly sold a homesite to the associate who had testified against the first prospect.[46]

At another point in the 1918 discussion, Demarest explained that his company at Forest Hills had probably canceled a little more than one-fifth of total sales of $1,500,000. Most cancellations were made because the buyer turned out not to be able to buy, but Demarest was careful to point out that when they discovered the contract was made with a Jewish family, the contract was always canceled as well. In 1919, Nichols again raised what the developers must have thought of as "the Jewish problem." In response to Nichols's question "Shall we sell to Jews?" King Thompson, developer of the Upper Arlington suburb near Columbus, Ohio, responded with a flat "No!"

Nichols did not respond to these ideas at this particular conference, but he did put forth a clear statement of his consciousness of class at one juncture. The Country Club District developer explained to the group that he had proposed to hire a new salesman and had floated the idea with some of his current salesmen. One responded, "I think he will make as good a salesman as we have in the organization, but he is not of the type or class that we have among us now." On the basis of this observation Nichols determined not to hire the man he had proposed. He commented to the other developers present that he "felt proud they felt that way." Several other developers at the same conference, including Henry Kissell of Springfield, Ohio (a later national president of the realtors'

46. 1918 *Proceedings*, 122–24.

association), Paul Harsch of Toledo, Ohio, Hugh Prather of Highland Park, and Robert Jemison of Birmingham, Alabama (another
future NAREB president), all indicated that they excluded or discouraged Jewish purchases. Once again, William Demarest of Forest Hills was the most straightforward in his prejudice—he simply
told Jewish men who wished to purchase that they could not buy
the property. Nichols asked him, "Has it precipitated any attack on
you of any kind?" Demarest replied, "No. Of course, this would not
be true in New York." By "New York" in this instance Demarest
meant "in Manhattan."[47]

Nichols then explained his changing position on the subject:

> In Kansas City the situation has become very acute on the Jewish
> question. We have some fine Jewish families, in [World War I] work,
> and some of them are good friends of mine on the different charitable
> institutions or organizations. Some of them are on the boards of direc-
> tors of different charitable institutions, and they waited on me in behalf
> of the good people of the race and brought it to a straight out issue.
>
> I had taken the position that we would not sell a Jew, but we are now
> selling Jews, and I offered to sell any of the members of this committee
> that came to me, but they stated I had taken 1700 acres of the best
> residential section of the town and had put up a barrier against the race,
> and was making Kansas City a poor place for a Jew to live, and as a result
> of that they were being excluded from some of the best clubs, and they
> pointed out a number of people we had sold that were not anything like
> as desirable citizens; and personally it is getting very much under my
> skin, by George, it is so unAmerican, and undemocratic, and so unfair
> to exclude a man on account of his nationality, regardless of what he is
> himself.[48]

Such wavering on the part of one of their number brought several
of the other subdividers to comment negatively on Nichols's willingness to sell to Jews after his change of heart. Bouton of Roland
Park told the others, "I think it is a perfectly ghastly mistake." From
his point of view the biggest question was whether the other prop-

47. Ibid., 477–78, 142; 1919 *Proceedings*, 565.
48. Ibid., 571–72.

erty owners in the district would accept the idea of a Jewish neighbor. Nichols did not enter the discussion further and, as chairman, changed the topic as soon as he could. These conversations demonstrate that at least Nichols was having to deal with the question of the legitimacy of informal racial restrictions that had existed in fact though not in writing. That he was ahead of the other developers in making this change with regard to Jews seems rather clear.

The comments of many of the developers on reasons for not selling to Jews and for not allowing their residents to do so are instructive with regard to their overall prejudices. King Thompson of Upper Arlington commented, "The danger is of Jews congregating with Jews and going together." Prather of Highland Park said that was not true of the Jews he had sold. He noted, "This particular bunch of Jews don't congregate with Jews; they go with Gentiles more than Jews." Thompson retorted, "Then, they are not Jews." All of this got to be too much for Demarest, who brought forth his ultimate example: he had one homeowner who was convinced that he wanted to sell his house to a Jew. Demarest could not dissuade him. "So his next door neighbor came in there and told him that if he sold his house to a Jew that [the neighbor] would put a negro in his house as a tenant, and [the neighbor], went to the Jew and told him the same thing." Prather responded, "Your restriction would not allow that." Thompson, who was all for discrimination, interjected, "You can't restrict against Negroes at all." "You bet I can do it," shot back Demarest.

Trying to bring a tone of moderation and common sense to the conversation, Harsch of Ottawa Hills observed, "You know, Mr. Demarest, that no Negro would come in and live there in that locality." Defensively, Demarest came back, "He would put them in as tenants." Bouton observed dryly, "At any rate he would indulge in that effort." Prather, who would sell to Jews in Highland Park, gave a matter-of-fact response: "If he did [rent to a black] in Dallas, the next morning he would be hanging from a flag pole somewhere."[49]

The discussions of racial restrictions in 1917–1919 were the forerunners of more intense conversations among realtors during the

49. Ibid., 574, 577, 578–80.

civil rights struggle of the 1950s, 1960s, and 1970s. By that time, discrimination against Jews had diminished, though it had not been eliminated entirely, and the major question was selling to blacks. The Nichols Company was not in the forefront of change in this second round of opening up their neighborhoods to new minorities. Nichols ultimately feared anything that would threaten the overall level of values in his subdivisions compared to competitive subdivisions. In a very real sense, the Great Depression did not have this effect because all property values went down due to the lack of a market. What Nichols had seen happen elsewhere in Kansas City and around the country was the decline in value in formerly substantial neighborhoods.[50]

He had good reason to fear such a change. On occasion courts used such declining values as a reason to throw out the restrictions entirely. This concept, which came to be called the "change of neighborhood" doctrine, came into play "when the neighborhood in which the burden of a covenant that inhibits land use has so changed that a court ought (under one theory) to declare the covenant terminated or at least (under a second theory) ought to refuse to enforce it." Certain guidelines were normally used by courts to determine if such a change had taken place. The judges looked to see if the changes in land use were "physical and substantial" and attempted to be sure that the changes had produced land uses that were contrary to the restrictions. They checked to see if the changes were general over the entire subdivision or in just a few parcels. The final determination was whether the changes were so marked that the original benefits the restrictions were supposed to provide were no longer possible.[51]

When a court declared a change in neighborhood had taken place, the restrictions that were applied to maintain the character of the old neighborhood were no longer usable, either because the court terminated them or because it simply refused to enforce them.

50. For a rather thorough examination of the development of the J. C. Nichols Company during the post-J. C. Nichols era since 1950, see Wenske, "Fulfilling a Vision," C-1 through C-7. See particularly Nichols, "When You Buy a Home Site," 38–39; and Kinkead, "This Is the Town That Jess Built."

51. Stoebuck, "Running Covenants," 882–83.

The beginnings of such changes were always minor in nature, but if a restriction violation was allowed to go unchallenged, the door was opened for further violations and more difficulty in enforcing the restrictions because of the previous laxity. Nichols recognized this even though relatively few court cases had been decided using the change-of-neighborhood concept during his early years of development. The developer had his salesmen constantly on the lookout for restriction violations. After 1918 he had his grounds man look not only for houses going up without approved plans, but also for any restriction violations. This was the most effective type of "protection" he offered his buyers through the mechanism of deed restrictions. Ironically, Nichols used the change-of-neighborhood doctrine to his advantage in getting the courts to rule against an offensive brickyard near his subdivisions in 1920.[52]

In the post–World War II environment of 1947, Nichols expressed the importance of homogeneous neighborhoods with stable property values in this way to a *Time* magazine reporter: "When you rear children in a good neighborhood, they will go out and fight communism." The effect of this view, according to the reporter, was that "again and again [Nichols] has proved that his well-integrated city within a city (comprising the richest tenth of Kansas City's residential area) paid off: profits to merchants; the good life to residents." The irony of the use of the term *well-integrated* to apply to a racially segregated section was apparently lost on the reporter. The impact of racial restrictions in the Country Club District is dealt with more fully in Chapter 10. Suffice it to say that the area remained de facto segregated with regard to blacks and whites until well into the 1960s.[53]

Many land developers since 1908 have relied on a sound plan for their subdivisions, and most have reinforced the plan over time with some sort of deed restrictions. Nichols initially used good land planning and minimal restrictions, but he discovered quickly (by 1908) that more restrictions were necessary and that continued enforcement was essential. Nichols intended to continue in the planned residential development business for years to come. He

52. 1917 *Proceedings*, 48–49; 1919 *Proceedings*, 129.
53. *Time*, November 1, 1947; Nichols Personal Scrapbook 3.

foresaw the difficulties of restriction enforcement in the older, al-
ready-developed subdivisions. To avoid tying up his staff on a continuing basis in a less economically productive activity, he adapted
the existing format of the neighborhood associations into the concept of mandatory homeowners' associations. These organizations
had vigilance against restriction violations as their first priority, and
they also helped the firm ease out of the troublesome role of enforcing the restrictions. Deed restrictions thus served as the most effective mechanism for protecting property values while also hardening
the segregated nature of the residential city.

6

THE ESSENCE OF PLANNING FOR PERMANENCE

The Homeowners' Associations

J. C. Nichols thoughtfully observed the nine other real estate developers seated about the table. They were winding down a series of meetings in the late winter of 1919 about the future of their life's work—the development of high-cost subdivisions. Outside a window in the meeting room he could see just a hint of spring buds forming on the Birmingham, Alabama, fruit trees. A sobering thought had occurred to him as the subdividers prepared to leave. He wondered out loud to the gathering whether his subdivisions would endure as he had hoped if his company went out of business. There had been a precedent in another part of Kansas City:

> Hyde Park had a neighborhood of the most prominent people in town and in a few years, but in a few years they were all married and gone. The organization was out of existence, they stopped their neighborhood affairs, and the organizations are not functioning at all. I think it is entirely possible that my Mission Hills may go out of existence in some years.[1]

The developer of Mission Hills was right in many of his prophecies and predictions over the years, but he was quite wrong on this one. What was more important in this instance was his subsequent observation to the other developers that he was thinking about ways to transfer enforcement of restrictions and approval of building plans to the existing and future landowners in his subdivisions. The Mission Hills owners' group had the power to enforce restrictions from the beginning, but not the right to approve building plans.[2]

1. 1919 *Proceedings*, 707–8.
2. Ibid.

As he mused with his fellows, Nichols knew the problems facing their industry. The Great War was over, inflation ran rampant, and "HCL" or "the high cost of living" was a new phrase that worried people. Builders and people wanting to build were scared off by prices for materials and for wages that they had not seen since the 1880s, if they could remember that decade. Nichols himself appears to have been wondering in 1919 and early 1920 whether this type of work was what he wanted to do for the rest of his life, and whether he should stay in his present location. In 1917 he had expressed to this same group that he was thinking about what would happen to him and to his salesmen when they had sold out all the land he had accumulated under his control. He was thinking of possibly starting developments in Tulsa or Wichita or even of building a railroad in order to have something new to do. This last idea seems to have been inspired by the example of the Van Swearingens of Cleveland, who had developed Shaker Heights, acquired the Nickel Plate Railway along the way, and started putting their rail empire together with much publicity in 1916. By the spring of 1920 Nichols appears to have resolved the problem in his own mind. He told the nearly one thousand people who attended a series of three dinners for residents and lot owners of different sections of his developments "that he had definitely decided to continue the development of the Country Club District throughout his life."[3]

The period of 1919–1920 was a significant turning point for Nichols and his company. He determined to continue expansion by acquiring more land (for the Crestwood development). The Brookside Shopping Center, which had been in the planning stages since 1915, was actually begun. He initiated a whole new series of actions designed to boost neighborhood activities. A group of female residents organized the Women's Council of the Country Club Improvement Association. Finally, late in 1920 Nichols began to formulate the first true homeowners' association in his Missouri-side properties.[4]

Two earlier organizations in the Kansas City area had paved the

3. 1917 *Proceedings*, 239–41. A contemporary account of the Van Swearingens' activities was in "City Builders and Railroad Kings." Scrapbook 5:70–71.
4. Scrapbook 5:78.

way for the new Missouri-side homes association. The Country Club District Improvement Association was a voluntary association of lot owners. Nichols called its first meeting in a hall in Westport on December 5, 1909. The second pioneer group was the Mission Hills Homes Company, formed in an unincorporated part of Johnson County, Kansas, in 1914 to handle services normally supplied by municipalities. The precedents for homes associations go back far earlier than either of the two organizations Nichols set up. Probably the first such organization was formed in London in 1743 to control the use of and to pay for the maintenance of Leicester Square. The earl of Leicester created the park in the middle of a projected terraced residential square. As problems arose over the use and maintenance of the park in the square, the landowners banded together to form the association.[5]

Grammercy Park in New York City was probably the first instance of a North American association organized to administer property along the lines of the Leicester Square experience. The physical layout and purpose of the property was much like that of Leicester Square. The first attempt at control began in 1831, when the developer, one Samuel Ruggles, put up an eight-foot fence around the central park and supplied each of the residents with a key to the gate. Restricted access did not solve the continuing problems of maintenance. Ruggles then created a board of trustees to administer the use and maintenance of the park for the benefit of the owners of the sixty-six surrounding plots of land. Though not a homeowners' association as such, the Grammercy Park arrangement has stood the test of time and remained in effect in the 1970s.[6]

The first American instance of homeowners actually organizing for this type of group effort was at Louisburg Square near the State House and Boston Common. It was begun in 1844 for the same purpose as at Leicester Square and Grammercy Park—to control and maintain a central park area for the surrounding owners. It comprises the oldest continually active homeowners' association in the United States in the 1980s. Llewellyn Park in West Orange, New

5. Scrapbook 2:193; "Book of Restrictions," 85–90; "Some Information About Your Homes Association," n.p.

6. "Some Information About Your Homes Association," n.p.

Jersey, featured a homeowners' association organized in the 1850s to save the development after the Panic of 1857 had financially embarrassed founder Llewellyn Haskell. As has been noted, this association continues its activities into the 1980s. Like Louisburg Square, its purpose was and is to radically protect the privacy of the owners as well as to maintain the open spaces, including the Ramble. It is an example of a homeowners' association that was at least partially supported by the developer.

Louisburg Square was never large enough to influence strongly the area around it. Indeed, the fact that it consists only of four series of row houses facing one another about the small park area, which is, in turn, surrounded by an iron fence and "no trespassing" signs within cobblestone streets, gives a current onlooker a curious sense of disgust. Nothing within the common area seems important enough to warrant the prohibitions stated on signs every ten feet. The housing group is just one block from the Common, so the need for open space is not acute. The row houses do not have any front or rear yard space, as do nearby row houses. The result is the preservation of something that hardly seems worth preserving. These observations are based on a visit by the author to Louisburg Square on June 30, 1988. Only approximately forty houses are involved. At the time of observation, fully ten of them were vacant or undergoing renovation. Parking was at a premium, with additional signs informing passersby that vehicles could be parked on the cobblestone square only with a special permit. The effect was one of regulation run rampant.[7]

One possible inspiration for developer-organized homeowners' associations was the village improvement society, many of which had sprung up in New England and elsewhere across the country about the time of the Civil War. These were voluntary associations with the vague goal "to make the town or village seem more town or villagelike." Usually made up of the ministers, lawyers, and other leading citizens of the town, these groups lobbied with the local officials for various improvements, ranging from the reconstruction of the town center to make it more beautiful and efficient to the suggestion that fences be limited or eliminated in the residential

7. Ibid.; Swift, "Llewellyn Park," 328.

sections. Sometimes they proposed painting all the houses on one street the same color. In a few extreme instances they volunteered to have their houses moved to establish a uniform setback line where none had existed. They were the parks advocates, the road improvement supporters, and the tree planters.[8]

In the long run these voluntary associations accomplished very few of their goals. They blamed this lack of civic responsiveness on collusion between politicians and the contractors and construction people who would have to carry out the proposed projects. The reformers thought that more money went for payoffs than for actual work done. While there was certainly enough evidence to support this criticism in many communities, the reformers stopped at that point and tried to change the political system, proposing such things as town commissions and managers. The reformers never really understood that their ideas were little more than their personal views of how the world should be ordered and that it was impossible for them to impose these personal views on the quite heterogeneous society of their small towns. The key to the way in which these societies served as examples for later homeowners' associations lies in their initial goal: they had a view of what they wanted their town or village to be. They wanted to control and shape their immediate living environment in ways that proved unacceptable to most of their neighbors.[9]

Withdrawal seemed to be the only available solution to reformers who believed they had failed. Some simply withdrew into the confines of their homes and yards, creating an island of controlled living for themselves in an uncontrollable world. Others grouped together in neighborhoods hedged about by protective deed restrictions or established separately governed suburbs or semirural villages of like-minded people. As a group, they made up a significant potential market for someone who would put this type of subdivision together.[10]

Bouton at Roland Park and Nichols near Kansas City went about

8. The most comprehensive recent source on these organizations is Handlin, *The American Home*, 91–116.

9. Ibid., 113–16.

10. Ibid., 114–15.

creating the ideal neighborhood to sell to this type of person. These developers were planning an environment that was apolitical; party affiliation entered the picture only indirectly, as it was attached to class. The directors of homes associations did not run on party platforms. Indeed, the organizations had as their goals the upholding of the deed restrictions first and the development of activities to stimulate neighborliness second.

The oldest continuously active homeowners' association founded by a developer for the purpose of sustaining the goals of his development plan is the Roland Park Civic League. Founded before 1895 on a voluntary basis, the association took on many different functions. It helped support the independent fire department of the district and maintained a fire-alarm system for the community as a whole. League officers informed the members of the leaders' actions and of upcoming activities, lobbied assiduously with the company for the improvement of sidewalks, and oversaw the collection of rubbish and garbage.[11]

In 1907 the Civic League, along with one of its subsidiaries, the Oakland Club (Oakland was one of the later subdivisions of Roland Park), clashed with the Roland Park Company when the latter notified residents that it was going to have to raise water rates. Extensive correspondence documents the discussion between Bouton as president of the company and a joint committee of the organizations charged with conducting the negotiations on their behalf. The company "won" and the rates were raised, but shortly thereafter Bouton began to develop a plan to transfer control of the company's maintenance and utility activities to a homeowner-dominated corporation.[12]

The Civic League had incorporated itself as an organization totally separate from the company in that year. This was the first test

11. Report from E. H. Bouton, treasurer, Roland Park Civic League, to the membership, July 6, 1897; Report from E. H. Bouton to the Roland Park Civic League, August 1, 1899; Letter from E. H. Bouton to E. A. Robbins, chairman, Advisory Committee, Roland Park; letter from Bouton to Robbins, June 25, 1900; all taken from the Roland Park Papers.

12. Letter from E. H. Bouton to the Joint Committee of the Roland Park Civic League and the Oakland Club, December 30, 1907, Roland Park Papers.

of the strength of their independence. Among the responsibilities stated in its charter were the

> maintenance of an educational, moral, social and beneficial organiza-
> tion . . . for the promotion of friendly social intercourse . . . taking
> action from time to time on matters affecting the property interests of
> the members in Roland Park, for the purpose of assisting in the mainte-
> nance of a volunteer fire department in Roland Park, and, in general,
> for the purpose of fostering the common good and welfare of the mem-
> bers of said corporation.[13]

The new corporation opened its membership to all residents or property owners over the age of twenty-one. Both men and women were encouraged to join. The new maintenance corporation mentioned above was chartered as the Roland Park Roads and Maintenance Corporation on July 26, 1909. In the charter, the Roland Park Company transferred control of the following to the new organization: the roadbeds of streets, the sewer system, the right to collect, disburse, and administer the maintenance funds, and the right to waive or enforce restrictions in a given area. Ten residents served on the Board of Directors of the Roads and Maintenance Corporation; the residents of the various areas of Roland Park nominated seven members through their area leagues, while the continuing Roland Park Company nominated three members. The umbrella organization, the Roland Park Civic League Board of Directors, then ratified the elections annually.

In 1918 Bouton as president of the development company could report that from his standpoint this arrangement was working quite well. It made the residents responsible for negotiating with the utilities, which had by then all been transferred to municipal or public-ownership firms. Bouton believed that this brought about better relations between his company and the residents because they were not constantly squabbling over small matters like utility service and rates.[14]

13. William R. Dorsey, "Roland Park: A Modern Suburb," 10.
14. Ibid.; "Deed and Agreement between the Roland Park Company and the Roland Park Roads and Maintenance Corporation," Roland Park Papers.

The impulse that had led to the creation of the village improvement societies was similarly at work in some of America's cities.
Kansas City was no exception; indeed, at the turn of the century it
was one of the outstanding examples of a city influenced by reformers using neighborhood organizations. The highest achievement of
the reform impulse in Kansas City prior to the twentieth century
was the approval of the parks and boulevards plan in the early 1890s.
Under the plan, the parks were supposed to provide the working
masses with playground and breathing space, while the boulevards
and parkways were intended to help create protective homesites for
the well-to-do.[15]

Shortly after the turn of the century, it became clear that the
influx of manufacturing and foreign laborers was forcing the decline
of the most desirable neighborhoods near the downtown section.
Quality Hill, Merriam Place, and Independence Boulevard all lost
their attractiveness to the wealthy, who were, of course, most able to
choose their homesites. The Hyde Park section and Nelson's Rockhill District had begun to attract these disillusioned but well-
endowed families further southward. The Country Club with its
golf course and polo field beyond Brush Creek lured the tired
reformer, the harried lawyer, and the prosperous businessman alike
to more private pleasures. J. C. Nichols was in the right place at the
right time to give these people what they needed most—a place to
live in a neighborhood that conformed to their ideas of morality and
order.

The 1920s saw another brief flurry of political reform with the
adoption of the city manager plan of government. When this new
system was subverted by the city manager, Hugh McElroy, and the
city boss, Tom Pendergast, two men who lived among the former
reformers in the Country Club District, those reformers did little to
overcome the subversion. The good life in the Country Club District made the furor seem far, far away for most of its residents.
Active opposition came very late in the Pendergast era when "improvement projects" such as sewers and drainage ditches, unwanted
and unneeded by the affluent Country Club District residents, were
foisted on the neighborhoods. One resident, Dr. Logan Clenden-

15. 1918 *Proceedings*, 266–68.

ning, became so provoked that he tried to destroy an air compressor for a drill with an ax. This type of personal reaction was extremely rare in Kansas City or the Country Club District, though. The park and boulevard plan had been strongly supported by area improvement associations, and groups had formed in some sections of the city to pressure the city council and other officials for improvements in those sections. These were usually issue-oriented pressure groups that did not long survive the resolution of the issue at hand.[16]

Nichols used this model in 1905 when he and his financial backers, H. F. Hall and E. W. Shields, organized the Westport and South Side Improvement Association. Its main goal was to get rid of "the menace of the old Westport dummy line," which passed through their property on its way to the little community of Dodson. The menacing aspect of the steam railway was its smoke and noise. The association, led by Nichols and Shields, succeeded by early 1906 in raising a subsidy to pay the Metropolitan Street Railway Company to take over and electrify the line. This improvement association appears to have been abandoned after this successful campaign.[17]

Drawing on his personal experience and that of other associations he had observed, Nichols embarked on his first homeowners' association in 1910. The organizational meeting was held in Morton's Hall, a sometime dance hall at Main Street and Westport Road. He had notified all his lot owners of the meeting, which would have included all owners of land purchased from his company and located between 51st and 63rd streets from Holmes to the Kansas state line. The new group was named the Country Club District Improvement Association. Those present who wanted to band together for mutual service and protection signed the following agreement:

The undersigned, in consideration of the purchase and as owners of Lot _____ in Block _____ of [name of subdivision], an addition in Kansas City, Jackson county, Missouri, hereby agrees, during our ownership and until assumed by subsequent purchaser, to pay an assess-

16. *Report of the Board of Commissioners of Parks and Boulevards*, 14; Reddig, *Tom's Town*, 142–43; Wilson, *City Beautiful Movement*, 66–67, 80, 84, 120, 123, 129–30.
17. "Proposal for a Brush Creek Parkway," *Kansas City Star*, January 14, 1906, 1.

ment of not to exceed ten (10) cents per front foot per annum, upon said real estate above described, on the first day of July each year, for the general maintenance and beautifying of said Addition. The property owners of said Addition at a meeting called for that purpose, to select by a majority of votes cast, three of their number to constitute a committee to levy and expend any and all amounts paid under this agreement.[18]

This was a voluntary association. To help make it work, Nichols committed his company to pay the same assessment on unsold lots in all the subdivisions affected as would be required of members.

By October 1910, Nichols was able to notify property owners that the Police Protection Committee of the association had arranged, through the good offices of their area alderman, to have a policeman stationed in the district around the clock. The police located their post at the Kansas City Country Club house, and the officer on duty could be reached by telephone from anywhere in the district. Even though the Country Club District was not legally in the city limits until 1911, the city supplied a motorcycle, which was said to enable the officer to reach any point in the entire Country Club District within two or three minutes.[19]

The same letter also announced that the Garbage Committee of the association had "finally arranged that there shall be a collection of garbage in the Country Club District." The wagon would stop at each house. Owners were requested to make the pickup convenient for the garbage man by providing a garbage can that would always be kept in the same place. Nichols noted that if this were done to help the garbage man, the service should be able to continue. Such service was necessary because the Country Club District was not yet inside the city limits. City officials were apparently willing to help in the provision of police protection beyond the legal limits, but they did not offer the same assistance in garbage collection. Nichols quite possibly viewed the creation of the Improvement Association as something of a stopgap measure until the annexation question could be settled, for the association's responsibilities were largely

18. Scrapbook 1:164, 193.
19. Letter from J. C. Nichols to E. T. Wilder, October 19, 1910; Scrapbook 1:165.

those that would be taken over by the city when annexation was declared valid. The election had already been held and contested when the organizational meeting occurred.[20]

The next significant step toward homeow er organization came in 1914 when Nichols incorporated what he called the Mission Hills Homes Company. In this instance there was a definite need for carefully specified responsibilities for the organization, for no possibility existed of attaching this subdivision to an adjacent city in the near future. The closest city was Kansas City, Missouri; the closest incorporated place in Johnson County, Kansas, was Merriam, located several miles to the west. The Mission Hills Homes Company would have to do everything a city government would normally do. Nichols wished to use a homes association instead of a political subdivision such as a village because he wanted to retain as much control for himself and his residents as possible. He influenced the homes associations greatly during the early years.[21]

Chartered on August 18, 1914, by the J. C. Nichols Company and organized on November 4 of the same year, the Mission Hills Homes Company had extensive powers on paper. It was authorized to maintain vacant property, and it hired contractors to construct and maintain common sewers, street lighting, street signs, and the streets themselves. The officials of the association acted on requests for plumbers' cuts in the existing streets and arranged for snow removal and the maintenance of trees, shrubs, and grounds in public areas. The directors of each association were charged with enforcing deed restrictions, arranging for water, gas, electricity, garbage collection, and fire protection, and paying taxes on the public areas of Johnson County in behalf of all the residents of the subdivision. Membership in the Homes Company was automatic upon purchase of land, which was a new feature for Nichols and for Kansas City. It was also a distinguishing characteristic between this developing type of homeowners' association and the old model of the village or neighborhood association. Everyone in the subdivision was in-

20. Scrapbook 1:164.
21. Kansas did not then recognize not-for-profit organizations as legal entities unless they were incorporated, hence the name Mission Hills Homes Company. "Book of Restrictions," 85.

One of the most welcomed services provided first by the company and then by the homes associations was winter snow removal. Prior to the 1920s this was done almost exclusively with mule-drawn and homemade equipment as shown here. The plows consisted of reinforced wooden V's that could be attached to mule teams and pulled throughout the district. The city of Kansas City did not then supply snow removal in residential areas; this service proved to be a major selling point with many prospective buyers, even though as time went on they paid for it themselves through homes association assessments. KC54n19.

volved and had the same privileges and restraints. It is little wonder that Nichols's initial broadside announcement of Mission Hills referred to its "ideal city government." The advertisement in the *Kansas City Star* explained: "Not incorporated as a town, but a simple form of local government, giving quick and effective execution for community needs. Snow cleaned from walks in winter, all vacant and public property kept clean, garbage removed, streets lighted, restrictions enforced, etc." Nichols developed and retained the homeowners' association concept not only because he wanted his residents to do things his way in maintaining community standards, but also because he was afraid that if the subdivision were part of a larger village or town organization, the political unit would not be sufficiently responsive to the needs of his residents.[22]

On the surface, Mission Hills seemed to embody all that was

22. Ibid., 88–90; J. C. Nichols Co. advertisement, *Kansas City Star*, September 17, 1916.

desirable in residential living. The small community had lots of space, a required congenial architectural style, and a local government that took care of physical needs without becoming political. What a new resident might or might not have seen was that it also had a benevolent despot in the person of J. C. Nichols who would make sure everything stayed that way.

Residents paid an annual assessment levied at the rate of one mill per year per square foot to support the Homes Company's responsibilities. If this amount should prove inadequate, it was possible to raise the assessment to a maximum of two mills per square foot if two-thirds of the homeowners concurred. Nichols adapted this aspect of the Mission Hills Association from Bouton's Roland Park experience. There the assessments had been by the square foot rather than the front foot, which Nichols had used with the Improvement Association. Bouton had found over the years that initial assessments were often too little in later years, hence the possibility of raising the assessment. Even the use of a two-thirds vote came from the Roland Park example and from bond elections. In almost every other instance, Nichols used a simple-majority vote. This was the first time that Nichols assigned responsibility for the enforcement of restrictions to the homeowners. Again, this was probably because of the influence of Bouton, for the Baltimore subdivider had assigned this responsibility in his most developed portions to the Roads and Maintenance Corporation when that entity was organized in 1910.[23]

The Mission Hills pattern for homes associations had much to commend it for use on the Missouri side as well, but Nichols had a different situation there from what existed in his company's Kansas property. First, the association had not been begun at the start of development in Missouri. Second, after the approval of annexation, the Kansas City, Missouri, city government carried out a number of the municipal functions necessarily performed by the Homes Company in Kansas. Between 1914 and 1919, nothing was done to transfer the Mission Hills pattern to Missouri. By 1917 Nichols was confiding to his fellow developers that he knew he was going to have to do something because it was becoming increasingly difficult to

23. "Book of Restrictions," 92.

work with the original Country Club District Improvement Association as it continued to grow. At the same meeting Bouton indicated to the group that his company had no direct connection with the Roland Park Civic League. They shared responsibility for naming directors to the Roads and Maintenance Corporation, but Bouton did not have any other control over the league. This desire for separation from the homes association was something that Nichols never seemed to understand in Bouton. For his own part, the Missouri developer always tried to maintain as much personal involvement in the homeowners' activities as possible. To him, the relinquishment of control that Bouton seemed to covet would be abhorrent in the Kansas City setting. Nichols had too much of his own ego invested in his work to sit back and let his homeowners assume total direction of his subdivisions.[24]

While Nichols was determining whether to stay in development work in Kansas City in 1919–1920, he acted to remedy some of the problems he saw in the improvement association. Less than two months after returning from the 1919 Developers' Conference, where he had expressed his doubts about continuing in the business, Nichols inaugurated the *Country Club District Bulletin*, a four-page printed newsletter sent monthly to all landowners and residents of the district. As the year progressed, he organized a Women's Community Council as an adjunct of the improvement association to create and carry out programs for children and families in the district. In September he hired a young woman to be the community secretary; she was to assist the Women's Community Council in carrying out the programs they had planned.[25]

The Women's Community Council made itself a driving force in stimulating neighborhood activities in 1919 and 1920. During the 1919 Christmas season, the women sponsored a house-to-house Christmas caroling party for all interested residents and recommended that electric lights be used on Christmas trees because of the fire danger with candles. They published their concerns about auto-

24. 1917 *Proceedings*, B62.
25. *Country Club District Bulletin* (hereafter *CCD Bulletin*), April 15, 1919, 2–4; May 15, 1919, 4; September 1, 1919, 2, 4. Nichols gave credit for the idea of hiring a community secretary to Demarest of Forest Hills.

mobile speeding and the use of cut-outs on automobiles and motor-cycles. One group of women became involved in the selection of safe sites for snow sledding. Of premier importance to these emanci-pated women, "the servant problem" became the motivation for the establishment of an "employment exchange" through which Country Club District women might locate domestic help. "The servant problem" was the society matrons' euphemism for the diminished number of young women who were willing to work as domestics following World War I.

Another area took up many hours of Women's Council time. They had shared great apprehension about properly raising their children. As a result of this concern, the auxiliary of the home-owners' association hired a summer activity director for boys' base-ball leagues, arranged for the use of a private swimming pool by the boys, and developed playground programs. They sponsored a mother-daughter banquet and talks for women and their daughters on topics such as "What women and girls are doing in the modern world." The Women's Community Council was quite active at the start of the 1920s, but it tended to be less of a force as the decade went on. One important reason for the change was the organization of smaller homes associations in other areas of the district.[26]

Nichols's company founded the first true Missouri-side home-owners' association, the Country Club District Homes Association, on July 5, 1921. It was limited geographically to the area just south of the Country Club grounds (now Loose Park). The homes associa-tion agreement empowered the organization to do most of the things previously performed in Kansas by the Mission Hills Homes Company.[27]

Interestingly, even though the area covered was inside the city limits of Kansas City, Missouri, the association acquired some authority that would normally have been assumed by the city. For example, the Board of Directors was to arrange for snow removal

26. *CCD Bulletin,* September 1, 1919, 2; December 15, 1919, 1; February 1, 1920, 2; April 1, 1920, 2; May 10, 1920, 2; July 1, 1920, 1–2; November 15, 1920, 2; February 20, 1921, 2; May 15, 1921, 1–2; June 15, 1921, 2; August 15, 1921, 3; December 15, 1921, 1.
27. "Book of Restrictions," 17.

from streets and sidewalks, care for street trees, provide additional street lights where needed, arrange for collection of rubbish and garbage, and maintain playgrounds and public areas. The fact that the association was charged with these responsibilities implies that the municipal authorities were not providing an acceptable level of service. As a result of the association agreement, which each new purchaser was required to endorse, such services were provided at the highest level possible at a cost of one mill per square foot per year for each square foot of the lot area within 150 feet of the street front. The rate dropped to one-half mill per square foot per year on the lot area that lay more than 150 feet from the lot frontage. Total annual cost for a 100-foot by 150-foot lot, a common size in this part of the district, was $150 per year. The association was prohibited from operating with a deficit budget. The powers and rate of assessment could be changed by an affirmative vote of the owners of two-thirds of the land included in the Homes Association area.[28]

The Country Club District Homes Association was the first attempt to establish a homes association of the Mission Hills type in an existing residential section. The effort was obviously successful, for soon afterward Nichols decided to go through a much more extensive procedure to establish residential associations in his other partially developed Missouri-side subdivisions. The Nichols Company made a second attempt to establish a homes association in a partially developed area in the spring of 1922 with the Crestwood Addition, which had been initially platted in 1919. The flatness of the real estate market had led Nichols to withhold marketing the property until the spring of 1920. The declaration of restrictions was filed April 24, 1920, with sales commencing in May. By July, so many lots had been sold that a second part of Crestwood had to be prepared for sale ahead of schedule. Nichols sold almost all of the lots in Crestwood by late 1921.[29]

On April 24, 1922, Nichols had his legal department file the charter of the Crestwood Homes Association, entrusting to it powers quite similar to those given the Country Club District Homes Association the previous year. Some additional clauses had

28. Ibid., 17–20.
29. Jackson County Plat Book B–19, 57, 82–83.

to be inserted to cover the administration and maintenance of the interior parks, which had been built into the Crestwood design following the example of Guilford near Roland Park in Maryland. On the same day as the filing of the Crestwood Homes Association agreement, the Nichols Company filed an almost identical document for the Westwood subdivision, which had been purchased as a partially developed section a few years earlier. It, too, followed the Country Club District Association format. There was only a two-month gap between the date of filing of the restrictions for Westwood and the filing of its homes association agreement; this indicates a move on the part of the company toward establishing a homes association at the very beginning of a particular development.[30]

It was far easier to establish such associations in sections as the land was sold. In that way new residents bought their land with the understanding that they were also buying into the homes associations for the area. As Nichols had found with sewers in 1911, it was easier to get people to accept higher costs as part of the initial deal than to present them with the added cost after they had closed the deal. Nichols was never able, for example, to get a homes association going in the Sunset Hill subdivision. The fact that it was not his land and that he had a somewhat contentious relationship with Mrs. Ward (later Mrs. A. Ross Hill), who did own the land, may have contributed to this failure. The key to the associations' effectiveness was the willingness of all landowners, including the developing landowner, to accept the maintenance assessments from the beginning. Whatever the cause, no homes associations were ever formed in areas developed and sold by Nichols for the Ward estate. Ironically, Nichols's own home for the last thirty years of his life was in Sunset Hill, where he could not get a homes association going.[31]

Between 1922 and 1926 Kansas City in general and the Country Club District in particular experienced a tremendous spurt in land subdivision and homebuilding. This was part of the growth spurt in housing then occurring across the United States. Because of his experience with the Mission Hills Homes Company and the Coun-

30. "Book of Restrictions," 49–50, 166.
31. "The Homes Association Handbook—ULI Technical Bulletin #50—Highlights of the Findings and Recommendations," 4.

try Club District Homes Association, Nichols was ready to apply this mode of continued maintenance and restrictions enforcement to the new areas he developed during this boom. The first instance in which the restrictions and the homes association agreement were both filed at the start of development was the opening of the Armour Hills subdivision in the summer of 1922. Destined to be the second largest homes association in terms of total members, the Armour Hills association benefited from legal planning that was later to become the standard procedure for the Nichols Company in new development areas. This planning hinged on the concept of filing restrictions and homes associations agreements at the same time, before any significant sales had been made.[32]

Once this pattern was worked out, the establishment of associations proceeded in the older developed areas. This was done in conjunction with an effort to get these subdivision landowners to accept the self-perpetuating clauses for restrictions that Nichols had been using since Mission Hills in 1914. Nichols hosted dinners at the Mission Hills Country Club for landowners in the Wornall Manor, Wornall Homestead, and Country Club Ridge subdivisions to organize the homes associations in each instance. Previously, he had worked with some landowners to send letters to the other owners stating that the Nichols Company had assumed responsibility for many of the services to be performed by the proposed homes associations at no cost to the residents. The letters noted that such free services "certainly cannot be continued, and we should not expect it."[33]

The effort was successful, partly because approval required an affirmation of only the owners of a simple majority of the front feet in the areas. Even at this late date, some sixteen years after initial development of most of the sections taken into homes associations in 1924, the Nichols Company owned many scattered vacant lots, making it a major landowner in each location. Another reason for the successful campaign to organize landowners was that many could see the positive effect such organizations were having in the newer developments where the associations had been formed a few

32. "Book of Restrictions," 1–9.
33. *CCD Bulletin*, May 15, 1924, 3; Scrapbook 7:148.

years earlier. The example of Mission Hills was ten years old by this time, and that association had stood the test of time well in helping to preserve property values. As a result, most homeowners did not have to be coerced. Those who objected could move; few did so. Three more homes associations were formed during 1926 in the Armour Fields, Romanelli Gardens, and Stratford Gardens subdivisions. The Nichols Company formed the Fieldston Homes Association in what is today Fairway, Kansas, in 1927, and during that year the company's lawyers drafted the Oak Meyer Gardens Homes Association agreement as well. Oak Meyer Gardens turned out to be the last such organization formed before the onset of the Great Depression.[34]

During the expansive 1920s the Nichols Company set up a total of fourteen such homes associations. The first established in the 1930s was the Indian Hills Association, in the southern end of the elite Mission Hills section on the Kansas side, in 1932. In all, only four associations were formed in the 1930s, all of which were in Kansas and formed part of or were adjacent to Mission Hills. Thus it can be seen that a significant slowdown in homes association development coincided with the slowdown in housing demand of the late 1920s and early 1930s. During the 1930s the Fieldston, Fairway, and Mission Woods homes associations organized, while the Prairie Village association, destined to be the largest, did not organize until 1947. The longer waiting period for Prairie Village, which began to be sold in 1941, was occasioned by two factors: first, World War II intervened to prevent sales for more than four years; second, the Nichols Company always retained control over a homes association area as trustee for the residents until there was a sufficient base of homeowners to provide their own direction. When such activity resumed, the pattern followed was the one established as early as 1921 with the Country Club District Homes Association agreement. In this area, as with restrictions, the period of innovation was over before the onset of the Depression.[35]

34. Scrapbook 7:154; "The Homes Association Handbook," 4.

35. The three associations formed in the 1930s besides Indian Hills (1932) were Tomahawk Road (1935), Mission Woods (1937), and Fairway (1938). "The Homes Association Handbook," 4.

Nichols's ideas about the importance and functions of mandatory homeowners' associations served as the model for many subsequent developments across the country. Ridgewood in Springfield, Ohio, was one of the developments similar to Nichols's Country Club District and frankly modeled after it. Begun in 1913 after Harry S. Kissell had visited both Roland Park and Kansas City, Ridgewood was intended to be an upper-income community in a relatively small town. It initially consisted of only 160 acres.[36]

One of the earliest efforts of Kissell's company was the formation of an owners and residents' association to plan and carry out community activities. Like Bouton's Roland Park Country Day and Gilman schools in Baltimore and Nichols's Sunset Hill and Pembroke Country Day schools in Kansas City, Kissell urged his lot purchasers to form a private school that would serve the elite of the entire city. By 1924, Kissell believed that the activities of the owners' association and the development of the private school had been the two biggest factors in the success of his company's subdivision work.[37]

River Oaks subdivision in Houston, Texas, was a later development that benefited more from Nichols's later refinements in the areas of restrictions and homes associations than had Kissell. In 1924 Hugh Potter visited Kansas City as well as other subdivisions across the United States and in Europe to begin planning for River Oaks. Potter decided to follow the Nichols pattern of mandatory membership for all property owners. As in Kansas City, the River Oaks Association maintenance department took care of streets, trash removal, tree care, and garbage collection. The organization also provided a type of handyman service in which a homemaker could call the office and ask for help, at additional cost, in washing windows, mowing the lawn, painting walls, or any other service necessary for the maintenance of the home. Potter added this last service to the normal responsibilities that Nichols usually assigned to homeowners associations. Like the old Country Club District Improvement Association before annexation, the River Oaks organization found it necessary to organize its own fire department to

36. Brown Burleigh, "Ridgewood Development at Springfield."
37. Ibid., 16; H. S. Kissell, "Community Features for Subdivisions."

supplement the coverage available from the city of Houston. Nichols dropped this service from the list of those offered by homeowners associations as soon as possible after annexation into the city.[38]

Homeowners' associations began to take root in various upper-income subdivisions during the 1920s. Palos Verdes Estates, the most carefully designed new high-income U.S. subdivision of the 1920s excepting Nichols's own work, was begun in 1923. Frederick Law Olmsted, Jr., served as the consulting landscape architect and later moved to the site for his retirement. Olmsted had been involved in the planning for the later plats of Roland Park and had visited Nichols in Kansas City, so it is not surprising that the restrictions and homes association plans for Palos Verdes reflect those contacts. The property owner organization was called the Palos Verdes Homeowners' Association. Like its namesakes in Kansas City, this association had the power to interpret and enforce restrictions and to collect maintenance fees for general upkeep of the common areas of the property. It organized community activities, published a *Palos Verdes Bulletin,* and held title to all street, golf course, shore, and park land. This last responsibility was a step beyond Nichols, who never vested land ownership of public or country club areas in the homes associations. Nichols preferred to retain control through title in the public areas and board influence at the country clubs. This left the homes associations responsible for maintenance and improvements.[39]

Homeowners' associations have continued as important cogs in the wheel of control exercised by the Nichols Company over their residential developments into the 1980s. The associations' role in maintaining the high levels of property values cannot be overestimated. They carry out maintenance and improvements on behalf of other homeowners and the Nichols Company that many residents would not do themselves even if they were required to do so. The relationship between the associations and the company has occasionally been less than cordial, but the closeness of goals between

38. Don Riddle, "Homes to Last for All Time: The Story of Houston's River Oaks."

39. "New City . . . Planned for 1960 . . . and After: Palos Verdes Estates."

the groups and the firm is too great to permit lengthy or permanent breaks in communication. More recently, condominium owners' associations have followed the example of the Nichols associations as they strive to maintain common areas and to mediate the problems that are inherent in the cooperative nature of condominium living.

7

NICHOLS AND THE HOMEBUILDING INDUSTRY

At the end of the Depression decade, the J. C. Nichols Company architect offered his views on home design to a reporter for the *National Real Estate Journal.* Edward Tanner had been with the company since 1919 and had witnessed all but four of the company's biggest years in the homebuilding business. The architect told the reporter that in the years since the inception of the Depression, American families had come to expect houses with more extensive mechanical features than before, but with smaller rooms and somewhat less distinguished workmanship in the construction details. "The best way to describe this change is to say that today we try to build a highly livable hundred-year house, whereas ten years ago, we were trying to build sturdy two-hundred year houses," he told the reporter.[1]

It can be argued that construction standards were effectively lowered after World War I when the higher cost of materials and labor forced housing construction costs to increase along with most other items in the United States. There is, however, validity in Tanner's statement due to the changes brought about by the economic disruption of the Great Depression. Whether Tanner was accurate in his assessment of the durability of pre-Depression houses in J. C. Nichols's subdivisions cannot yet be determined. The oldest extant Nichols houses are but eighty-five years old in 1990 and thus have not reached even the century mark proposed for the later houses. What is apparent is that the pre-1930s house was built of more substantial materials, even if it was less well adapted to the technological desires of the buying public than the post-1935 house.

One commentator has stated that houses become worn out when they "have physically outlasted the interest of people in maintaining them." The continued desirability of the neighborhood has been one factor that historically has had much to do with retaining the

1. "Problems in Designing Houses for Today's Buyers."

interest of residents in the maintenance of their homes. Nichols worked to stabilize neighborhoods *and* to build houses that people would want to live in for more than one generation.[2]

The effect of consciously changing from a planned house life of two hundred years to one of one hundred years for the units the Nichols Company built was most noticeable in the scaling down of earlier styles to meet the deflated prices of the late 1930s. Homes built in the latter period generally offered smaller bedrooms and reduced living area on the main floors. The company abandoned the spread-out, one-floor bungalow plan and the broad-fronted Georgian and Italianate villa styles for what was in vogue nationally toward the end of the 1920s building boom. Effectively, the 1930s styles look ahead to the limited styles of suburban subdivisions in post–World War II America more than they look back to the more spacious homes of the 1910s and 1920s. The house plans illustrated in the 1939 magazine article were attributed to the Nichols architectural department. The very fact that the house plans used by the company in the late 1930s were reproduced in the national real estate magazine demonstrates the potential impact of Nichols Company architectural ideas on nationwide building practices.[3]

The period under study in this chapter terminates with the economic cataclysm of 1929–1930, when land subdivision and homebuilding effectively ground to a halt both nationwide and in J. C. Nichols's home territory. The types of housing constructed by the company during the expansive years from 1905 through 1929 have much to say about the type of housing Americans often wanted but found difficult to obtain in the suburban explosion following World War II. Nichols and his building department were in the forefront, constructing no less than 1,500 houses between 1905 and 1930, which amounted to approximately 27 percent of the total homes built on Nichols's subdivisions during that period. The other homes built after the Nichols Company began to review and approve house

2. Edward T. Price, "The Matter of Housing: Notes on the Longevity of American Dwellings."

3. Lester Walker, *American Shelter: An Illustrated Encyclopedia of the American Home,* 186–91, 200, 201; Mary Mix Foley, *The American House,* 220–21; "Houses Designed and Built by the J. C. Nichols Companies."

plans totaled about 5,000 homes. That record put the Nichols Company among the leaders in total house output both in Kansas City and across the nation.[4]

The questions raised by Tanner's comment that prior to 1930 the company had been building two-hundred-year houses are significant in regard to Nichols's lasting impact on the land-subdivision and homebuilding business in the United States. What type of housing styles appealed to Nichols's upper-middle and upper-income clientele? How much did he dictate style to the market, and, conversely, how much did market determine the styles and sizes of houses built by the Nichols Company? At what point did the technological innovation of the 1920s intervene sufficiently to create more of a one-hundred-year house life than one designed to last twice as long? Did the company build model homes as examples or as sales tools?

J. C. Nichols's move into land planning in 1905 initially involved little more than a continuation of a building program he had started two years before in Kansas City, Kansas. In 1903–1904 he had supervised construction and had done most of the selling for small workers' homes that were designed to sell for under $1,000, including land. The Kansas homes did not feature indoor plumbing, and they generally enclosed less than 1,000 square feet of living space. They were built sturdily enough, however, that they lasted into the 1980s in the neighborhood north and west of the intersection of Thirteenth Street and Quindaro Boulevard.[5]

On the Missouri side, south of Brush Creek, Nichols immediately started to build speculation houses that he planned to sell for more than twice the price of the Kansas bungalows. The Missouri houses were mostly two-story structures and often included basements and attics. His advertising in this early period indicated that he was striving to attract upwardly mobile middle-class couples and small families. In Kansas, Nichols and his first salesman, J. C. Taylor, mostly sold house-and-lot combinations, with only occasional

---

4. "Home Building Operations of the Nichols Company"; "King Developments"; "Kansas City Realtors Build 2000 Homes."

5. The California Park subdivision has several of Nichols's original houses still in place; author's observation, June 1984.

vacant lot sales. In Bismark Place on the Missouri side, they built houses only on some strategic lots in order to stimulate land sales.[6]

Nichols and his new bride, Jessie Miller, the daughter of a banker in his hometown of Olathe, Kansas, moved into the first house built on the new subdivision site at 3030 Walnut Street. The house is shown in the background of the photograph on page 73, behind the original grocery and drug store built by Nichols along the old "dummy" carline (now Brookside). Not only was it their first model house to show potential customers, but they were also the model residents—young, upwardly mobile college graduates out to make their fortune in the city. That first house still stands atop the hill mentioned in Nichols's earliest advertising, although the street address is now 3028 Walnut instead of 3030. The neighborhood was not covered by the company's automatically extending restrictions and has not held up in the same way as have the other areas. Mixed land uses such as apartment houses and vacant lots are nearby. The house itself has been maintained moderately well and shows signs that it might well, with care, indeed be a "two-hundred-year house" as described by architect Tanner.[7]

The first Missouri-side house designs were strictly "builders' vernacular." This meant that Nichols relied heavily on the wood-framed, two-story dwelling style with a front peaked roof, an overall boxlike effect, and a stone basement. If one wanted to be generous and assign a true architectural style to these sturdy dwellings, they could be considered Georgian Revival, with their foursquare fronts and hipped roofs. The similarity of the exteriors of Nichols's earliest houses to those being erected at the same time by other realtors like A. J. King and Fletcher Cowherd and by other individual builders indicates that Nichols was striving less for architectural significance than for customer acceptance.[8]

As salaries and earnings of middle- to upper-income Americans began to advance following the turn of the century, the percentage

6. Reed, Nichols & Co. advertisements, *Kansas City Star,* April 9, 1905, 18; April 30, 1905, 19; May 28, 1905, 19.

7. Observations by author, August 23, 1988.

8. Builders' vernacular architecture in Kansas City is discussed in *Kansas City: A Place in Time,* 186–88. Examples of Georgian Revival houses on a grander scale are in Foley, *American House,* 192–93.

of their income required to pay for housing declined somewhat. The average cost of new houses increased at a slower rate than did income for this population group until the start of World War I. Though he did not know it in 1905, Nichols had at least ten years of comparatively stable economic conditions in which to establish himself as a major provider of homes and homesites to the growing Kansas City population. The brief banking panic of 1907 had relatively little impact in the Midwest compared to its major effect in the financial markets of the East and West coasts. This ten-year "window" was all the time Nichols needed to become fully established.[9]

During the earliest years of house construction on the Missouri side, there is no evidence that the young developer used an architect to design any of the speculative houses he had his men build in his subdivisions. The general plan, financing possibilities, and some of the interior detailing of the "builder vernacular" houses are revealed in classified advertisements:

> $50 cash and small monthly payments will buy a beautiful new six-room home in the best location on South Side; choice ground; will take $2,200; others ask $2,750 to $3,000.[10]

> South Side Cottages: Great Bargain—most desirable location in whole city; four or five rooms; new and attractive; $60 cash and small monthly payment; prices reduced from $1,800 and $1,450 to $1,600 and $1,300 . . . .[11]

> Only $2,350; Others ask $3,000 for such houses; six rooms, elegantly furnished, bathroom, reception hall, furnace, large closets, fine porches and large beautiful lot.[12]

In 1906, the company offered five- and six-room houses (two- and three-bedroom units with living room, dining room, and kitchen) that also featured pantries, two porches, three-foot corn-

---

9. Wright, *Moralism and the Model Home*, 81–83, 238. This is supported by inference in Doucet and Weaver, "Material Culture," Table 4, 577.

10. Reed, Nichols & Co. advertisement, *Kansas City Star*, June 25, 1905.

11. Ibid., August 13, 1905.

12. Ibid., October 15, 1905.

ices as exterior support and decoration, and interiors with white enamel and weathered oak finishes on the woodwork. The painted and stained woodwork implies that pine or sweet gum was used throughout since hardwoods would have been finished with a natural varnish. Such simple houses could be built quickly from materials readily available in Kansas City. The foundations were built using rock quarried at the site during basement excavation. Kansas City rests on limestone formations that lie close to the surface and occasionally outcrop from the many hillsides; the facts that the stone was free and so near at hand accounted for its use more than any other reasons. The rubble-stone basements and foundations were more labor-intensive to construct than the concrete-block basement walls and foundations that came into use in many areas in the 1890s. If the stone had to be excavated anyway, as it did for Kansas City basements, then reusing it in foundations and basement walls did not add as much to the overall labor costs in Kansas City as later students of housing construction have estimated. William Rockhill Nelson had done much to popularize the use of limestone as a building material in his own home just north of Nichols's subdivisions across Brush Creek.[13]

Frame construction on such stone foundations was quite common in Kansas City, for a similarly practical reason: the city's role as a rail center meant that it was a hub for the lumber industry, which shipped pine and hardwoods out of Arkansas and the South into Kansas City en route to northern and western markets. The metropolis was headquarters for three lumber retailers—Long-Bell, Foster, and Sutherland—as well as several other wholesale timber dealers. Wood was a comparatively cheap and available commodity in Kansas City.

Another contributing factor toward the popularity of frame construction in Kansas City was the availability of paints and varnishes directly from manufacturers. Two large paint-manufacturing firms—Cook and Campbell—were in their initial stages of growth at the time Nichols was getting started. At the outset, these sources made materials cheaper and easier to get. In the next few years Nich-

13. Ibid., May 10, 1906; June 22, 1906; and September 8, 1906. Doucet and Weaver, "Material Culture," 568.

ols and other homebuilders would make the local market sufficient to sustain these companies and to maintain relatively low prices for their materials.

Until 1907, Nichols operated as a subdivider and speculative builder much like many others in the Kansas City housing market. The house plans for his "bungalows" and "cottages," as he referred to his houses in advertising during the years 1905–1907, were drawn from the workmen's knowledge and the many available plan books of the period. An examination of one collection of these mail-order plans reveals that four- and five-bedroom models were most often given as examples in 1900. The plan book offered potential cost figures for construction based on labor and material costs in the New York City market, but noted that such costs would be lower in other parts of the country. The smallest plan in this book from 1900 included 1,484 square feet on the two main floors, while the largest plan enclosed over 2,600 square feet on the same two floors. Using estimates of construction costs per square foot in 1900 (the estimates were derived in 1985), the cost of constructing the two houses in Kansas City was projected to be $2,226 for the smaller house and $3,900 for the largest house. The plan book estimated that the smaller house would cost $3,770 to build in New York City, while the larger was figured to cost $5,000 there.[14]

In 1910 the average cost of all new housing in Kansas City, Missouri, according to building permit information, was just over $2,600. It remained within $300 of that amount over the next eight years until the post–World War I inflationary pressures pushed average house construction costs up dramatically. Nichols's announced prices during the 1905–1907 period placed his activities in the mid-price range for single-family houses built during that period.[15]

14. Gwendolyn Wright outlines the types and availability of plan books and the speculative builders' reliance upon them in *Morality and the Model Home*, 21–40. Some of the turn-of-the-century plan books have been republished in the 1980s. Dover Books has republished *The Architecture of Country Houses*, by Andrew Jackson Downing. *Victorian Cottage Residences: Craftsman Homes*, by Gustav Stickley, gives details of some of the best arts-and-crafts style house plans. The specific collection on which this analysis is based is R. W. Shoppell, *Turn-of-the-Century Houses, Cottages, Villas*, 61–120.

15. "Chart Showing Building Activities," 51.

It was unusual for a speculative builder/subdivider like Nichols to work with an architect; it was even more unusual for architects like the Kansas City firm of Wilder and Wight to become involved in designing such unmistakably middle-class houses. While a few architects such as Frank Lloyd Wright and his associates might be willing to lend their names to domestic architecture, most members of the profession considered such work to be demeaning and not worth their attention. Architectural historian Gwendolyn Wright has written extensively on the divergent goals of builders, who also used the title *architect* in directories and advertisements, and the building designers, who coveted the title *architect* exclusively for themselves. The builder/architect erected houses using the house plans that could be obtained by mail order or in plan books. The trained architects generally eschewed the "model home" concept and argued that each house needed to be individually designed for the particular owner.[16]

Other national trends tended to create more demand for Nichols's land and houses at that time. Professional educators spent a good deal of time developing home economics programs to train young ladies in what was called "domestic science." Few of the young women who enrolled in these programs actually became wives of the purchasers of Nichols's homes in the early years. Classes in home economics were primarily offered at the state agricultural colleges, which attracted future farm wives more than potential urban home-makers at the turn of the century. Nichols benefited more from the increased attention to home life and kitchen design that came out of these programs than from the sale of homes to their graduates.[17]

Growing architectural interest in residential design was another developing trend that Nichols incorporated directly into his developments as early as 1907. Frank Lloyd Wright created a certain amount of excitement in Chicago and across the Midwest at the turn of the century with his "prairie school" designs for large, low houses with open interior plans, which were popularized through the

16. Wright, *Moralism and the Model Home*, 46–78 (see particularly 69–78 for the differences that separated the two groups); Handlin, *American Home*, 401, 415; Wright, *Building the Dream*, 158–64.
17. Handlin, *American Home*, 305–30.

Ladies' Home Journal. Prior to this time, only the truly wealthy could afford to plan and build custom-designed homes. Just after the turn of the century, the development of business middle-management positions with sufficient income to meet financial requirements created a new group of potential customers for true architects like Wright. The included the small, but growing, segment of the population making more than $10,000 per year. Nichols began in 1907 to target members of that group in Kansas City. The availability of precut houses from Sears, Roebuck also stimulated middle-class interest in the idea of building a home of their own, although these were hardly distinctive architectural designs.[18]

A third influence on the times came to be called the arts and crafts movement. This effort grew out of British and American calls for simplicity in furniture design as well as housing detail, favoring sturdy houses with exposed construction details such as half-timbering and minimal exterior decoration. Such houses were supposed to appeal to and be available for middle- and lower-middle-income people, but unfortunately both the furniture designs and the home plans of the arts and crafts movement were too expensive for people of average or below-average income. The primary boon to Nichols from this movement was that the arts and crafts effort called for a wider usage of the owner-occupied, single-family home in an urban setting than had previously been the case.[19]

Housing design and prices in Nichols's neighborhoods changed significantly in 1907 when he sold a block of land to a local architectural firm, Wilder and Wight. The architects bought almost five acres on the extreme east side of Nichols's developments, next to the streetcar tracks near Fifty-fifth Street, and announced plans for nine homes on the tract. As part of the deal, Nichols had to convince the county road department to macadamize Fifty-fifth Street west from the architects' land to the Country Club location. This would enhance values all along the route.[20]

The architects planned to build homes for their own use and to

18. Robert C. Twombley, "Saving the Family: Middle Class Attraction to Wright's Prairie House, 1901–1909."

19. Handlin, *American Home*, 436–50.

20. *Kansas City Star,* September 15, 1907, 13A.

offer "especially designed bungalows" for sale to others in the price range of $5,000 to $10,000 per home and lot. By April 1908, the firm had at least one seven-room house to offer for sale at $5,900. The effect of the architects' involvement was significant: this was the highest advertised price for any house in Nichols's subdivisions to that time. From this point on, Nichols worked closely with local architects in the building his company did and recommended those architects to lot purchasers who wished to build.[21]

The year 1907 was pivotal for Nichols in other ways besides the move toward architect-prepared designs. It was also the year in which he agreed with lawyer/landowner Hugh Ward to develop what they agreed to call the Sunset Hill subdivision, which was to surround the Kansas City Country Club grounds (now Loose Park) on three sides. This agreement brought him into direct contact with local landscape architect George Kessler, who was primarily engaged in the planning and construction of Kansas City's extensive park and boulevard system. As a consequence, Kessler had regular contact with professional architects such as Wilder and Wight. Kessler may well have helped influence Nichols toward cooperating with architects rather than continuing to rely upon stock plans.

Nichols's association with Ward definitely turned Nichols toward serving the more affluent potential customers. While some of Nichols's earliest advertising for the Missouri-side lots indicates that he wanted to create a "high class" environment in his subdivisions, all through the first three years of his work he referred to his speculative houses as "bungalows" or "cottages" while emphasizing their low price. These descriptions appeared in advertisements throughout 1905 and 1906 even though the houses being offered were mostly two-story structures. Following the agreement with Wilder and Wight in September 1907, his terminology in advertisements rapidly gave way to description of "homes" and "homesites." Nichols did not use "bungalow" again in advertising until the early 1920s. From late 1907 until the involvement of the United States in World War I, Nichols's concentration was on upper-middle- and upper-income "homes," not on middle-income "cottages" such as were portrayed in the plan books.

21. Reed, Nichols & Co. advertisement, *Kansas City Star,* April 23, 1908.

The arrangement with the architectural firm also marked the first public announcement of Nichols's plans for the creation of a planned residential community as opposed to a collection of similarly styled houses in a row on small lots in unrelated subdivisions. The developer announced in the fall of 1907 that even more expensive houses were planned for Fifty-fifth Street leading from the streetcar line to the Kansas City Country Club. Landscaping and fountains were included in the land-planning design.[22]

Planning for residential suburbs as a whole was just coming into vogue among the architectural profession across the nation. Up to this point architects had usually opted for the large building contract or for designing the huge baronial mansion. Some were beginning to think that if they could be involved in planning whole neighborhoods, the use of their professional skills might still be justified as they supervised the uplifting of architectural taste over a wider area. Herbert Croly, editor of *Architectural Record,* certainly supported this possibility as early as 1902. Wilder and Wight may have seen Nichols's burgeoning planning schemes as just such a way for them to have influence.[23]

Whether they were that far-sighted is not documented. It did turn out to be profitable for the firm, if for no other reason than they soon received contracts for other homes in the area, including one of the largest homes built in Kansas City up to that time. E. W. Shields, a grain dealer and financial backer of Nichols, hired the firm in 1909 to design his villa, the Oaklands, constructed four blocks northeast of the architects' area.[24]

Significantly, Nichols worked extensively with architects from this point, although he probably had not used them at all before. Company advertisements were full of house-and-lot offerings prior to 1908; many fewer such advertisements appeared between 1908 and the end of 1914. The increased involvement with architects indicates that the company did much less building on its own behalf during 1908–1914. The appeal was for land sales during this period. One of the main reasons Nichols seems to have been willing to

22. *Kansas City Star,* September 15, 1907, 13A.
23. Wright, *Moralism and the Model Home,* 274–78.
24. *Kansas City,* 144. See also *Kansas City: A Place in Time,* 242.

involve architects was his desire to attract upper-income buyers to his neighborhoods; this type of land purchaser was accustomed to employing architects for individualized homes. Nichols again demonstrated his desire to bring the leaders of Kansas City to his development by turning over much of the homebuilding direction to local architects.

One example points up this change in emphasis. In October 1909, the Nichols organization advertised that it had a house and lot for sale for $7,750. This speculative venture featured a south front with a cream-colored stucco finish alternated with a brown-shingle exterior. The interior portions were decorated with a heavy oak finish, including oak flooring. The eight rooms included a living room, a dining room with beamed ceiling, a breakfast room (which was just coming into use in American houses at that time), and a kitchen with "built-in refrigerator," all on the first floor. The second level had four bedrooms, one of which had a fireplace, making it "suitable for family living," and a bathroom in white enamel with a tiled floor. The attic consisted of a billiard room and the servants' quarters. The house came complete with a cemented basement, a combination furnace (for heat or fan circulation only), and a sodded yard. A much higher income was required for people to afford such houses compared to the $2,500 houses Nichols had offered only three years before.[25]

Not surprisingly, Nichols found it necessary on the same day he advertised the $7,750 house to insert another advertisement denying that the Country Club District was strictly for the wealthy. He noted that his land prices were less than those asked for residential lots in other prestigious sections of the city. This was true in that the same page offered lots in a "no restrictions" subdivision at $45 per front foot. Other realtors offered lots in varying locations for between $25 and $40 per front foot. Nichols asked for $18 to $22 per front foot in Wornall Manor subdivision at the time.[26]

Nichols offered package financing to those who hired his crews

<hr />

25. J. C. Nichols Co. advertisement, *Kansas City Star,* October 10, 1909, 19C.

26. Ibid., October 3, 1909, 15C; October 10, 1909, 19C. Advertisements of Homer Reed Investment Company and H. W. Cunningham Realty Company, *Kansas City Star,* October 10, 1909, 19C.

to construct their homes. This meant a 50 percent first mortgage on house and lot, with principal due in five years and interest payable semiannually. A 30 percent to 40 percent second mortgage was payable monthly like an amortized mortgage within the same five-year term. A 10 percent to 20 percent down payment was required. Assuming the most favorable terms for the purchaser—i.e., 10 percent down payment with a 50 percent first mortgage at 5 percent interest and a 40 percent second mortgage at 5 percent—the payments would have been as follows for the 1906 house at $2,350 and the 1909 house at $7,750:

TABLE 7-1

FORMULATION OF HOUSE PAYMENTS
FOR TYPICAL NICHOLS HOUSES

	1906–$2,350	1909–$7,750
Down payment	$ 235	$ 775
50 percent first mortgage	$1,058	$3,875
Semi-annual interest	$ 32	$ 97
Monthly principal + Interest on second mortgage	$ 19	$ 60
Total payments over five years	$2,753	$9,220

(Figures do not include payments for taxes and insurance, which were not usually made a part of mortgage payments at that time.)

If the five-year total payment is divided by sixty months (the number of months in the five-year term), the average monthly payment would have been $46 for the $2,350 house and $154 for the $7,750 house. This translates to $551 as the average annual payment for the $2,350 house and $1,844 for the $7,750 house. Neither of these figures includes the cost of the land, which at $18 per front foot (Nichols's minimum in 1909) would have amounted to another

$900 (or $15 per month) for the minimum-width lot of fifty front feet.

These figures demonstrate that the statement concerning the availability of lots for other than "wealthy people" may have been accurate to a certain extent, but the cost of placing a $3,000 house (Nichols's minimum building restriction at that time) on those lots was prohibitive for all but a small percentage of the wage-earning population in the United States in 1909. It has been estimated that less than 6 percent of all industrial wage earners in the United States were earning more than $1,000 per year in 1904, and there was only small improvement in these wages between 1904 and 1909. It was impossible with wages of less than $1,000 annually to save the required $500, plus interest, per year, to pay off a combined first and second mortgage of $2,500 in the five years allowed. Indeed, it would have been very difficult to do that on an income of less than $1,500 per year. This figure would have prevented all but 2 percent of Kansas wage earners in 1907 from paying for a $3,000 house.[27]

These costs effectively limited the actual homebuilders in Nichols's neighborhoods to professionals, successful business owners, and capitalists who had sufficient incomes or assets to afford the stiff requirements of lending institutions for home mortgages. The fact that Nichols offered his land for less money per front foot did not determine who ultimately lived in the houses he and other builders erected in his subdivisions; rather, occupancy was controlled by the cost of house construction and the lending policies of available sources of money.

Nichols was not the most expensive builder and subdivider in Kansas City at the time. For example, only two years later, in 1911, a speculative builder/"architect" named Madory built a house for an insurance man in the Hyde Park section, some twenty blocks closer to downtown, at 3659 Campbell Street. The building permit was taken out for $10,000 on a two-story house with basement and attic. It had three rooms and an enclosed porch on the first floor, three bedrooms (one with a fireplace) and two baths on the second

27. Frank H. Streighthoff, *The Distribution of Incomes in the United States,* 121, 137.

floor, and a billiard room and servants' quarters in the attic. The building permit probably underestimated actual costs since property taxes would be based on the permit amount. The rooms were large, but almost all of the woodwork was enameled pine rather than the more expensive hardwoods. The exterior was brick veneer on the first floor and stucco on the upper floors. In short, features of the $7,750 Nichols house of 1909 (which included the price of the lot) and of the $10,800 Madory house of 1911 (not including the price of the lot) were quite comparable.[28]

A significant market existed in 1909–1910 for this type of home in the $10,000 price range. Kansas City's older elite neighborhoods were changing. Upper-income and upper-middle-income families were leaving the Quality Hill/Merriam Place sections and the old Near East Side along Eighth and Ninth streets. Their old, large homes were either being razed to permit other land use or divided up for rental space to lower-income individuals and families. Kansas City's meat packers and the garment district were expanding, and hundreds of working-class families from rural America and recent European immigrants poured in annually between 1900 and 1915. For the most part, they found housing in these vacated older homes and formerly elite apartments near the downtown and West Bottoms industrial areas. Kansas City became a classic example of the filtering process in housing during that period.[29]

Nichols was ever alert to the concerns of upper-middle-income parents for the quality of life available to their offspring. His company presented its subdivisions as a bright alternative to the older deteriorating neighborhoods in which houses were squeezed onto narrow lots with small yards: "Children's lives are affected by the atmosphere in which they are reared. Build a home in the beautiful Country Club District and insure a healthy growth for your boys

28. The author is familiar with the 3659 Campbell house because he and his family lived in it for three years, from 1979 until 1982.

29. Naysmith, "Quality Hill," 34. *Filtering* occurs when less-affluent residents of a city find available housing almost exclusively in older homes formerly occupied by more wealthy owners or tenants. These latter groups create the openings by moving to newer, seemingly more desirable neighborhoods of homes and/or apartments.

and girls—give them the advantages of out-of-door life, pure fresh air, desirable associations and beautiful surroundings." Obviously a believer in the truth of environmental determinism, this developer wanted his potential buyers to consider prestige and protection (in all meanings) as well as price.[30]

"The most notably discerning people in Kansas City have chosen home sites in the Country Club District" was the direct message of one of Nichols's advertisements during this period when he was heavily emphasizing the social appeal of his subdivisions. These "notably discerning people" included, another advertisement proclaimed, "some official in nearly every bank and large business house in Kansas City." Not only would the children have "better" friendships; one could improve one's own contacts merely by buying land and building a home in Nichols's country. Nichols's success with this sort of advertising meant that over time, the wealthy of Kansas City did begin to cluster in the Country Club District. The city had always been segregated to a significant degree by race and class; Nichols's ability to attract the affluent land buyer and home-builder simply made that segregation more intense.[31]

While the bulk of the available homesites in Nichols's initial 1,000 acres were designated for middle- and especially upper-middle-income families through the minimum price restriction, almost half of the total land in that 1,000 acres was restricted to homesites for the truly wealthy. The Sunset Hill district surrounding three sides of the Country Club had minimum restrictions of $15,000 to $25,000, depending on the particular area. The down payments of $1,500 to $2,500 needed for such houses (assuming the normal requirement of 10 percent down) required financial accumulations beyond the reach of most people at the time.

According to a September 1910 Nichols advertisement, the company had sold over 100 lots with such high cost restrictions by that time. Further, it was indicated that 13 homes were already built or under construction in the exclusive subdivision, at an average cost of $35,000.[32]

30. J. C. Nichols Co. advertisement, *Kansas City Star*, March 19, 1910, 2A.
31. Ibid., April 24, 1910, 8A; June 15, 1910, 7A.
32. Ibid., September 25, 1910, 2A.

Again, assuming a 10 percent down payment and a 50 percent first mortgage with five-year term and 5 percent interest, the costs for such houses can readily be projected as follows:

TABLE 7-2

TYPICAL PAYMENT STRUCTURE FOR $35,000 HOME

Down payment (10 percent)	$ 3,500
Mortgage principal (due in five years)	$17,500
Semiannual interest	$ 394
Second mortgage (principal + interest payable monthly)	$ 290
Total payment in five years	$42,340
Average monthly payment	$ 706

Payments of $706 per month are prohibitive for a large portion of the population in 1990, even with inflated wages and with both husband and wife gainfully employed. Almost all the lots in Sunset Hill consisted of at least 100 front feet and sold at $20 or more per front foot. This meant that the land cost at least $2,000, which nearly equaled the entire cost of the type of houses the company was offering in 1906.

One of the larger homes built in Sunset Hill during the summer of 1910 was designed by the first female architect to work actively in the Kansas City market. Mary Rockwell planned a house at Fifty-second and Belleview for her father, grain merchant Bertrand Rockwell. She had already designed and built a smaller home for herself in the more modestly priced section nearer the streetcar tracks on the east side of the development in 1908. Prior to that she had studied architecture in Paris and Chicago. She had returned to Kansas City just as Nichols was getting his development underway, but found that no architectural firm, including Wilder and Wight, would put a woman on its staff; she was eventually accepted, however, by the firm of Howe, Hoit, and Cutler. Still later, she married, acquired a

A side view of the Rockwell mansion at 52nd and Belleview illustrates the use of mixed materials for exterior finish. KC54n18.

partner, and set up her own firm of (Mary Rockwell) Hook and (Mac) Remington. Her later residential designs in the Country Club District tended toward the more traditional Italian and English styles that were in vogue. They were certainly less massive than the Fifty-second and Belleview home of her father. She is but one example of the variety of outside architects who did several designs in different parts of the Country Club District after 1907.[33]

The house at Fifty-second and Belleview was Mary Rockwell's early masterpiece. Cost figures for the house are not available. Measuring 86 feet by 40 feet around the exterior, it had a basement, two full stories, and a large attic. The two main floors had 6,800 square feet by themselves. The house featured a large reception hall (26 by 30 feet) and a separate small hall behind which was the enclosed staircase to the second floor. Seven bedrooms, each of which had access to a large screened-in sleeping porch, comprised the second level, along with bathroom facilities. The young architect designed a 40 by 46 feet studio for her own use in the attic, with a 14–feet-high window overlooking the Brush Creek valley and allowing plenty of north light. The Rockwell home, which probably cost more than

33. "A Home of Her Own Designing," *Kansas City Star,* July 10, 1908, 8A; *Kansas City: A Place in Time,* 251; *Kansas City,* 164.

the $35,000 average spent on the thirteen homes built in Sunset Hill before the coming of the sewers, is an example of the early small mansions that have become the trademark of this section of J. C. Nichols's subdivisions.[34]

The major importance to Nichols of the Rockwell house at Fifty-second and Belleview was that it demonstrated that people were willing to put up expensive homes in his subdivisions even before the sewer situation was fully worked out. Its massive form helped to underline the point of an October 1911 Nichols Company advertisement that spoke of "Permanence—That's the Spirit upon which the Country Club District was conceived and upon which every detail of it has been developed, established and protected." Landscape planning and deed restrictions could only go so far in carrying out Nichols's protection scheme for his subdivisions; it took the physical presence of some truly large homes like Rockwell's to demonstrate the solidity of the property values he promised to his purchasers.[35]

While Nichols was able to sell a large number of lots between 1905 and 1911, the major hindrance to actual homebuilding on these lots was that the Country Club District and other areas were not officially annexed into Kansas City, Missouri, until 1911. The fact that the subdivisions lay outside the legal limits of Kansas City prior to that date meant that the new homes could not be attached to the city's sewer system. Kansas City followed the practice of piping city water into outlying areas, partly because this could be done fairly inexpensively, but the situation was quite different with sewers. Not only would larger pipes have to be laid, but lift stations would also have to be built because of the uneven terrain. It was too expensive for the Kansas City municipal services to provide sewer connections until it was forced to do so by annexation election. Prior to the ratification of the annexation in 1911, Nichols compensated for the "inconvenience" of the lack of city sewers in two ways: septic tanks were placed behind each house in the less expensive subdivisions on the east side of the 1,000 acres of development; and

34. *Kansas City: A Place in Time*, 251.
35. J. C. Nichols Co. advertisements, *Kansas City Star*, October 29, 1911, 7A; April 10, 1910, 20B.

he began to construct his own sewer system in the more expensive Sunset Hill section, where he generally was able to charge higher prices for the land.[36]

Politically, Nichols fought this battle in another arena. As soon as he gained control of the 1,000 acres in 1908, he began to agitate for annexation by the city. The election was held in 1909 with a close but favorable outcome for Nichols. The voters had approved annexation, but the election was immediately challenged in the courts by conservative forces in the original city limits who did not want to help subsidize development in the new sections. The challenge kept the new sewers tied up until the Missouri Appeals Court overruled the objections to annexation in 1911. The decision came none too soon for Nichols in that a competing subdivision directly south of his area was in the process of building a sewer for its medium-priced sections. This development would compete directly with the parts of Nichols's area that had suffered most from septic tank overflow prior to that time.[37]

Aside from the blatant aspects of the sewer problem, there was a growing consciousness of the necessity for good sanitary sewers because of the impact of the home economics and public health movements on a national scale. This is a prime example of rising consumer expectations. If Nichols had been developing just twenty years before, during the land boom of the late 1880s, there would have been much less concern about the problem.

The move toward "strictly modern" houses with indoor plumbing for both fresh and waste water was a late nineteenth- and early twentieth-century phenomenon. Women led in the call for such modern conveniences because the extra work and general inconvenience of outside facilities and portable bathtubs fell mostly on them. Nichols learned early in his development career that the concerns of women were very important when he tried to make a sale. Good sanitary sewers were a must for extensive house construction to get underway in his subdivision.[38]

36. Scrapbook 1:138.

37. J. C. Nichols Co. advertisement, *Kansas City Star,* March 26, 1911, 8A; The Westmoreland Company advertisement, *Kansas City Star,* March 16, 1911, 11A.

38. Wright, *Building the Dream,* 102; Handlin, *American Home,* 455–71.

Up to the time of annexation, Nichols sold just over 1,000 lots in the acreage he was subdividing. Because of the sewer problems, only 200 homes had been built in scattered areas. Most of the houses had been built by the company for speculation and to attract potential buyers who wanted a more "built-up" feeling in the years 1905–1908. Then, the floodgates opened, for with annexation and the promise of new city-built sewers, no less than 50 houses were begun in the first month. By the end of July 1911, Nichols advertised that 300 houses were actually built and another 75 were under construction. In October of that year there were almost 100 "high class homes" under construction; 7 had been started during the last weeks of September alone. This was the point at which other builders and developers became heavily involved in the designing and building of houses on a custom basis in the Country Club District. They had to do so—there was no way for the Nichols Company to handle all these construction projects at once. Some builders and architects came to work almost exclusively in the Country Club District during the next twenty years. Clarence E. Shepherd, for example, designed more than 600 houses in Nichols's subdivisions between 1911 and 1930.[39]

The fall of 1912 and spring of 1913 proved to be the seasons Nichols was able to anchor and protect the property values of his neighborhoods more thoroughly by attracting wealthy land buyers who built fabulous mansions on both sides of his development. Actually the mansion-building trend dated from 1909–1910, when E. W. Shields had his large home built just east of the streetcar tracks and when Bertrand Rockwell indulged his daughter's architectural bent by buying on the west side of Sunset Hill. H. F. Hall, another early financial backer for Nichols, built a fourteen-room house, costing $50,000, almost next door to Shields in 1910.[40]

W. S. Dickey, an Independence, Missouri, clay-pipe manufacturer, announced plans in October 1912 for a huge residence just around the corner from Hall's and Shield's homes. The Dickey resi-

39. J. C. Nichols Co. advertisements, *Kansas City Star*, March 26, 1911, 8A; April 23, 1911, 8A; July 30, 1911, 3A; and October 1, 1911, 16B. *Kansas City*, 147; *Kansas City: A Place in Time*, 247.

40. *Kansas City*, 144; Scrapbook 1:156.

dence ultimately cost approximately $700,000 for its three full floors plus attic and basement. A local architect and an architect from New York who had previously designed the New York Stock exchange collaborated on the project. After World War I the east-side mansion grouping was completed with the Uriah Spray Epperson residence. Looking more like a Jacobin castle than a home for a packing-plant manager and investor, the Epperson domicile was so large that it could be readily converted into a men's dormitory for the University of Kansas City after the passing of its first owner. As the Dickey project was getting underway on the east side, Nichols was able to attract buyers who wanted to do impressive mansion building of their own between the recently surveyed Ward Parkway thoroughfare and the Kansas state line. Along both sides of Fifty-fifth Street between Ward Parkway and State Line Road, huge residences were under construction during the winter of 1912–1913.[41]

At the northwest corner of Fifty-fifth (then called Santa Fe Road), the owner of the city's traction lines was directing his own construction company in the building of a distinctive home. Bernard Corrigan hired Kansas City architect Louis Curtiss to design his mansion. The result had a Prairie School style roof line with arts and crafts style ornamentation. The architect used huge stained-glass windows to establish a thematic center for the somewhat blockish design, which cost an estimated $140,000 to construct.[42]

Next door to the west on Fifty-fifth, C. S. Keith, heir to a coal fortune, built an impressive Mediterranean-style home with five suites of bedrooms on the second floor. Keith was never very comfortable in the hotel-like structure, and in 1920 he sold it to J. C. Nichols, who used it as his own residence until his death in 1950. Nichols found the large dining rooms and palatial living room ideal for the entertaining his development work required. Mrs. Nichols oversaw the maintenance of the several acres of ground. The bedroom arrangement, each with its own bath, worked quite well for

41. *Kansas City Star*, October 27, 1912, 6A; *Kansas City: A Place in Time*, 241; *Kansas City*, 143.

42. *Kansas City*, 161; *Kansas City: A Place in Time*, 254.

The Keith mansion, which Nichols bought in 1920, served as a business residence in a remarkable number of ways. Employees and purchasers were enter-
tained at extensive (and expensive) garden parties behind the main edifice. Traveling dignitaries were often accommodated in the spacious second-floor bedroom
suites. The very presence of the house itself and the impeccable manner in which
it was maintained served as an example to other residents of Nichols's neighborhoods. There is no available evidence to suggest that the last situation might
also have worked to build resentment in residents who thought Nichols was living
too lavishly on income made from their home purchases. KC54n37.

the visiting dignitaries and real estate developers who wished to
evaluate Nichols's work or copy his ideas.[43]

To the south of the Corrigan-Sutherland mansion, M. B. Nelson,
vice-president and general manager of the Long-Bell Lumber Company, built another large home. It contained three floors to the
Corrigan's two and housed the servants in spacious quarters over the
three-vehicle garage. Much less innovative, the Nelson house was
designed to be more impressive than daring. From Nichols's point
of view, that was probably better than the architectural flights of
fancy that distinguished the streetcar magnate's abode.[44]

43. Scrapbook 4:44.
44. "Home with Glass Enclosed Bathtubs," *Kansas City Star*, December 21,
1913, 16B; Fred Simmons, "Kansas City's Largest Home, a Fabulous Mansion, To

The effect of all this mansion construction on both sides of the Country Club District was to create an image of prestige and stability in the midst of the Kansas City land-buying and homebuilding public. All around them they could see deteriorating neighborhoods and former homes of the wealthy being given over to transients and "light-housekeeping." The *Kansas City Star* was more than willing to give news space to the announcement of new home construction by the wealthy of the city. Since after 1912 most of those homes were going up in the Country Club District, the Nichols Company was the beneficiary of thousands of dollars of free advertising through these announcements. That the company was also one of the *Star's* most prolific paid advertisers (next to home remedies and the downtown department stores) probably did not hurt.

Not all houses going up in the "1,000 Acres Restricted" of the Country Club District were as large or traditional as the Nelson mansion. Nichols's construction department built a demonstration house out of hollow tile blocks, which were then stuccoed on the exterior, during the summer of 1913. Located at Brookside and Huntington Road, the house had plans calling for the use of steel I-beams for support—a practice just then coming into use in the city—and for Portland cement to be used for mortar. The plumbing and heating equipment were guaranteed "to give perfect satisfaction."[45]

Earlier in 1913, the president of one of the two music conservatories in Kansas City had built a home in Mission Hills, just south and west of the mansion-building area on Fifty-fifth Street. The most interesting aspect of the house design was the placement of the kitchen at the front of the house. Prior to this time, almost all kitchens were located at the rear of the house because of the heat, odors, and waste created in food preparation. With modern plumbing, electric and gas ranges, refrigeration, and the first electrical appliances, it was possible to think of locating kitchens anywhere in

Be Sold by Auction," *Kansas City Star,* January 31, 1951, 1A, 29A.

45. "The First Hollow Tile House," *Kansas City Star,* June 8, 1913, 6C; J. C. Nichols Co. advertisement, *Kansas City Star,* June 8, 1913, 15B. The increasing use of concrete and stucco, often with hollow tile, as residential building materials during this period is investigated in Handlin, *American Home,* 279–88.

the house. The new gadgets also allowed the kitchen to shrink in size; indeed, much of the popular home-design literature of the period concentrated on creating the most efficient (and smallest) kitchen possible. This led, as well, to a variety of location options within the house, which simply had not been possible when kitchens had to be large food-production areas.[46]

At the same time that the large homes and true mansions were going up on the extremities of the district, Nichols was opening up another neighborhood home site with minimum price restrictions for houses of only $3,000, $5,000, and $4,000. The advertised land prices by this time were $25 to $35 per front foot. This translated into lot prices of $1,500 to $2,100 for a sixty-foot frontage, which was the norm by this time. The fact that land prices were nearly amounting to half of the minimum required construction costs meant that only people of means would buy the land. The houses they built tended to be more expensive than the amount required.[47]

The year 1914 proved to be a good one for construction in the Country Club District, with the Nichols Company continuing to deemphasize its building activities. A new building technique, the use of hollow tile for structural walls, came into greater use, particularly in the custom-built homes in Nichols's subdivisions. During the 1920s this technique of replacing wood studs in the framing process would become more common for larger structures. After 1914, however, building activity fell off sharply in the district and across Kansas City. Shipping embargoes among the belligerents in Europe resulted in somewhat higher prices for some building materials, but general uneasiness about the possibility of American involvement was a greater factor in discouraging building in late 1914 and early 1915. In this way Nichols conformed to national trends as a land developer and homebuilder. His primary business was the selling of improved vacant land; when it was necessary to attract people by building houses on some of the vacant lots, he did so. This had been the case from 1908 through the conclusion of the annexa-

46. "A Kitchen at the Front of the House," *Kansas City Star,* January 12, 1913, 9C. The shrinking of the kitchen is discussed at length in Handlin, *American Home,* 422–23, and in Wright, *Building the Dream,* 169–70.

47. J. C. Nichols Co. advertisement, *Kansas City Star,* June 22, 1913, 8A.

tion fight in 1911. When individual buyers and other speculative builders indicated a willingness to start homebuilding in earnest in 1912–1914, Nichols slowed down the construction activity of his own firm. When World War I threatened to stop others, he turned his staff once again to the job of building houses to attract customers to a completed product—house and lot in finished form. "Community builders" across the country tended to follow a similar pattern.[48]

Nichols's company policy was to do more building when other builders and architects decreased their level of activity. This had been the case before 1907 when almost no one else was doing any building, and it continued to be true on a reduced scale until the construction explosion of 1911. After a modest business slump set in during 1914 when the situation in Europe worsened, Nichols reorganized his building department in early 1915 under his chief lieutenant, J. C. Taylor. They hired another man to superintend the actual construction on the site and to stimulate new construction throughout the district. The plan succeeded until the United States actually became involved in the Great War in 1917.[49]

Nichols and his construction planners determined to offer "the packaged house"—that is, house, lot, and financing all offered from a single source. This was little different from their previous practice except that they were better able to provide financing than at the start of the development. The provision of the "housing package" as early as 1915 is one of the aspects of Nichols's homebuilding activity that marks his company's efforts as distinctly modern. Nichols's financing people promised to handle the financing for the construction with a first deed of trust (or mortgage) set up for five years at 6 percent interest. Two points (2 percent of the mortgage amount) were charged for arranging the financing. Interest on this first deed of trust was payable semiannually by the buyer. The principle amount ballooned in five years. The company required a 10 percent down payment, with the balance on a second deed of trust at $70

48. "A Villa of Hollow Tile," *Kansas City Star,* June 7, 1914, 14B; "New Home of Charles Opel," *Kansas City Star,* December 6, 1914, 16A; Weiss, *Rise of the Community Builders,* 38–41.

49. "Home Building Operations of the Nichols Company," 61–62.

per month on principle and interest (also figured at 6 percent) until the balance was paid in full. The Nichols Company carried paper on the transaction itself and used it as collateral for loans on open notes from Commerce Trust Bank and other sources. As far as the buyer was concerned, the entire transaction was with the Nichols organization. This appears to have been a typical financing arrangement.[50]

For its speculative houses, the Nichols financial people set up sales contracts in a similar manner except that the cost of the land was usually included in the total cost of the contract to the buyer. Nichols's people usually put up non-custom-built houses in groups of two and threes. This was done in order to use the same crews at the same site for similar work on each house and to obtain economies of scale through volume buying of materials. Architects were commissioned to design these groups as companion houses during this period.[51]

In July 1915, the company advertised that it had completed or was working on 65 homes in the Country Club District. At the end of August the number under construction stood at 98, with a larger number already completed. This renewed vigor placed the Nichols Company among the largest home construction companies both locally and nationally. It continued as the largest land development company in the metropolitan area. Much of this building activity was centered in the area from Fifty-eighth to Sixty-second streets between Wornall Road and Penn Street. Nichols concentrated on medium-priced houses with an average selling price of $7,500. This meant, of course, that only upper-middle-class or independently wealthy families could buy the houses the company offered.[52]

While the emphasis was on such speculative construction because of the flatness of the custom building market, the company did not turn down a contract for construction when it appeared. In 1916 the Nichols building department entered a contract to build at 835 West Fifty-eighth Terrace a single-family home for an estimated

50. Scrapbook 3:135, 193.
51. Ibid., 128, 185.
52. J. C. Nichols Co. advertisement, *Kansas City Star,* July 11, 1915, 16B; Scrapbook 3:185–93.

$9,114. The contract guaranteed that costs would not go more than 10 percent over the estimate, not including the company's 10 percent overhead fee.

By the end of the summer of 1916, the Nichols Company building department had completed more than $750,000 worth of new houses since the reorganization in the spring of 1915. Another $500,000 worth were still under construction in September of the second year. To that date, almost 1,500 houses had been built in the district (compared with only 200 in March 1911).[53]

One of the new features in home construction at the time of the First World War was the expressed or implied home warranty. This was not something generally offered by speculative buyers of the day, but it became a natural outgrowth of the building done by long-term developers and homebuilders like the J. C. Nichols Company. At Forest Hills Gardens, a partially privately subsidized development in Queens, New York, the developer's construction company gave a written guarantee for their houses to be "storm tight" for one year. Additionally, heating was guaranteed in writing for one year, with plumbing guaranteed for two years. "But as a matter of fact," the developer explained to Nichols and a group of other developers in 1917, "we stand behind the thing [the house] forever."[54]

At that time Nichols supplied written guarantees of houses constructed by his company only when requested to do so by the purchaser. He never advertised the availability of such warranties. Because he had to maintain his reputation as a quality builder in order to attract customers for his land and houses, Nichols effectively guaranteed workmanship "forever" like the Forest Hills developer. The Roland Park Company followed similar policies during that same period. Nichols and his fellow "high class" developers viewed warranties as a necessary evil brought about by their desire to stay in the same business and the same location over a period of some years. Past customers had to be satisfied with their houses, or they would discourage future purchasers. Thus, this form of consumer protection never quite became an important factor outside a small circle of developers until after World War II. The practice of offering new

53. Scrapbook 3:181–82.
54. 1917 *Proceedings*, B25.

home warranties was presented as an industry standard in the 1970s by the National Homebuilders' Association. Called HOW's or Home Owners' Warranties, they were being used in the 1980s as advertising points.[55]

Building cycles have always affected the housing business in the United States. Kansas City experienced a sustained building boom from 1905 almost until the entry of the United States into World War I in 1917. Although a building downturn occurred citywide in 1913 coinciding with a national recession, Nichols was able to run counter to the trend for that year, but even his company began to feel the decline in 1914. Partly as a result of the Nichols Company's reentry into the homebuilding business in a large way in 1915, the number of building starts for that year and for 1916 improved significantly over the 1914 housing start numbers in Kansas City.[56]

Actually, entry of the United States into the Great War in April 1917 had a delayed impact on residential land purchases even though it curtailed building in that year. Because the Armistice was signed nineteen months later, the country barely got fully mobilized before the conflict was over. The war's brief impact was greatest in the provision of services that were dependent upon manpower. Homebuilding, for example, ground to a halt in 1918, when the smallest number of new homes were begun since the height of the depression of the 1870s. At one point in 1918 the city's streetcar service was curtailed by manpower shortages to the extent that the Country Club District was being served by only one car running over one of the two available lines.[57]

Though the Nichols Company had as many as 100 homes under construction at any given time during the building seasons of 1915 and 1916, the firm completed only 17 speculative houses in 1918. The sales total (land and house) for these 17 sites was $232,000. Even with the reduced numbers of new houses under construction, which limited Nichols's building department's ability to employ the

55. Ibid., B42–B43.

56. Manuel Gottlieb, *Estimates of Residential Building, United States, 1840–1939*, 83; "Chart Showing Building Activities," n.p.

57. "Chart Showing Building Activities," n.p.; Gottlieb, *Estimates of Residential Building*, 83; Scrapbook 4:128; 1919 *Proceedings*, 218.

economies of large-scale construction, the company managed to make a healthy profit on the 17 house-and-lot combinations. Total profit on this activity was $48,000, with $17,000 coming from building department sources and the remainder derived from the sale of the lots. This developed an overall profit from building of just over 20 percent of the total sales.[58]

The two-to-one level of land profits over building profits points up the fact that the company historically made more money from its land sales than from its construction activity. The land being sold had cost Nichols $16,000; profits were thus almost 100 percent on the land transactions. In some instances before World War I, Nichols estimated that his profits from land sales had been as high as 400 to 500 percent.[59]

The profitability of building departments in companies that developed upper-income subdivisions varied across the nation. E. H. Bouton of Roland Park, who had been a homebuilder and subdivider most of his adult life, indicated to other subdividers in 1917 that he had ceased building in Roland Park and Guilford because "we can never build a high priced house and not lose money on it." By comparison, Nichols made his best margins on the most expensive houses he had built in 1918, while he calculated that his organization barely broke even on the houses in the $7,500 price range (his least expensive house built in that year).[60]

Immediately after the conclusion of World War I, the country experienced tremendous inflationary pressure on prices for building material and in the wage demands of organized labor, particularly in the building trades. The developer of Forest Hills Gardens in New York City estimated in early 1919 that the cost of building materials had escalated 68 percent above prewar levels. Labor costs had risen an estimated 32 percent. This translated into almost a 50 percent increase in the cost of house construction in 1919 over what it had been two years before.[61]

Nichols was quite concerned about both of these price rises, but

58. 1919 *Proceedings*, 78–86.
59. Ibid., 83–85; 1918 *Proceedings*, 416.
60. 1917 *Proceedings*, B55; 1919 *Proceedings*, 78–79.
61. 1917 *Proceedings*, 184–95.

he tended to vent his greatest wrath against the increases in wages being asked by the tradesmen. He told a meeting of real estate colleagues in 1919 that he believed that "labor is better paid today than ever before" because they had low taxes (under the recently imposed income tax system) and because the cost of goods they purchased for daily use had not increased in price as much as the cost of the construction materials Nichols had to buy. In the same meeting, Nichols remarked that building tradesmen should be happy enough just to have jobs immediately following the war. "The attitude at this time we know is to do everything in the world to give employment to labor. Yet labor all over the country is asking for higher prices." The ideas depressed and angered him: "I think it is the most inconsiderate thing I ever heard of."[62]

In this respect Nichols was a typical entrepreneur who saw himself doing his workmen a favor by providing a place to work. He could readily see that if he agreed to the increased wage demands, the higher payrolls would reduce his profit margin. In early 1919 people were not yet willing to pay the inflated prices for new houses that the higher costs demanded. As a result, they delayed their purchases. This led to Nichols's outburst about the "inconsiderate" workers who dared to ask for more money. Income taxes already increased his tax burden; he was not interested in having less income with which to pay those taxes.

Another thought lay in the back of Nichols's mind immediately following the war: could higher prices for home construction price people completely out of the single-family home market? He foresaw the possibility that the more well-to-do, who had been buying the lots, would move in greater numbers to apartment hotels than to custom-built or speculative homes in the Country Club District. "We must keep the single family residence popular," he told his fellow developers in 1919. They had to do this in order to make good their tremendous investment in undeveloped land.[63]

Nor was Nichols alone in fearing a decline in demand. Bouton at Roland Park had used the shortages of the war, which had increased demand for residential rental space in Baltimore, to force renters in

62. 1919 *Proceedings*, 161, 199–206.
63. Ibid., 226.

company-owned houses either to buy their residences or to move out. As compensation, he offered the tenants a reduced price, but at the same time he required them to take out a second mortgage that would mature in three years instead of the customary five. Bouton anticipated a continuing drop in demand for such houses. He wanted to get his Roland Park organization out of the rental market on speculatively built residences that had to be rented because they had not sold. A sale would free up working capital, which he wanted to put to other uses.[64]

In addition to his outcry against those whom he perceived as driving up the cost of such housing, Nichols used the 1919 meeting of other developers of such "high class" residential property to suggest other alternatives. He reasoned that if his potential buying public was likely to become more interested in living in apartment hotels, there had to be some way to profit from that as well. He was discovering in 1919 that he could generate significant income from the rental of commercial space on land his company already owned, income which might, in time, challenge the income he had made in the past from homebuilding and even from land sales. Nichols considered the possibilities of profiting from shops that could be built close enough to his affluent residents to gain a monopoly on their purchasing power. If he tied the rent on the shops to their growth by basing rent on a percentage of gross sales, he could profit by sales of land for apartment hotels, by sales of lots and houses in his single-family sections, and from the rents generated by increased sales in the shops themselves. Even if he lost the income from residential land sales, he might well be able to make up for it with shop-rent income and land sales for apartment sites near his proposed shopping centers.[65]

Construction was just beginning for his Brookside Shopping Center. His men were already scouring the city and checking land records for ownership of lots in a small subdivision called Country Club Plaza, which was in a promising location in the Brush Creek valley. Nichols's lawyers were striving to get a condemnation order for a stone quarry site that overlooked the valley and the proposed

64. Ibid., 22.
65. Ibid., 692.

subdivision site. He did not announce his grandiose plans for the shopping center at Country Club Plaza until 1922, but the ground-work was well underway when he spoke with the developers at the national meeting in February 1919. Thus he was working to renew interest in the single-family home and attempting to reduce its cost by lowering materials costs and wage demands. At the same time, he hedged his bets by acquiring land for a proposition that would produce income whether any more single-family homes were built or not. It proved to be an unnecessary precaution in the short run because the building boom of the first half of the 1920s outstripped all previous building periods nationally and locally in the produc-tion of single-family homes. For the longer term, this diversification away from homebuilding and subdividing provided just the type of continuing income the company needed to weather the Great De-pression after 1930.

Nichols's company policy was in part responsible for precipitating the 1920s building boom even before that decade got underway. By September 1919, he had his employees and other contractors at work on 157 different homes across the district from the streetcar tracks to Mission Hills. In November the development company opened Crestwood, a subdivision east of the car tracks along Fifty-fifth Street. Within another ten months, the company had more than $1,000,000 in homes under construction for both speculative purposes and private owners.[66]

While Nichols made most of his early money from land develop-ment and a good portion of his later money from shopping-center rents, he took great pride in the accomplishments of his homebuild-ing department. During the spring of 1920, one of his people sold five acres in Mission Hills to an oilman who was moving from Independence, Kansas, to the Kansas City area. Nichols's building department personnel so impressed the buyer, A. R. Jones, that the oilman contracted with the Nichols Company to build his home as well. Projected to cost well in excess of $100,000, the house com-prised the largest single building contract ever won by the Nichols building department. Prior to that time, the mansions in Sunset Hill, along Ward Parkway, and in Mission Hills had been designed

66. Scrapbook 4:197–99; Scrapbook 5:116.

The A. R. Jones mansion is shown shortly after completion in 1921. Note the three-car garage, one of the first in Kansas City. KC54n35.

by outside architects and built by other companies. With the Jones contract in hand, Nichols could prove to other millionaires that his company could build the very large homes just as well as anyone in the business. For this reason, the Jones contract was an important step in establishing the Nichols Company as a major homebuilder as well as the premier land developer in the city. According to the compiler of the company scrapbooks, the signing of this contract for construction was the proudest moment in Nichols's life to that point.[67]

As the building boom of the early 1920s gathered steam, some old terms used in the homebuilding business took on new meaning. Prior to 1920 when builders or even architects spoke of *model homes,* they were referring to the plans for homes that could be obtained from pattern books or even by mail order. With the opening of the Armour Hill subdivision in 1922 on land purchased from the meat-packing company, J. C. Nichols had his company build its first model home in the more modern sense. Erected as a comparatively small home in an area of bungalows, the model home at 117 West Sixty-fifth Terrace was unique: it was all electric. No wood or coal were necessary for heat, and natural gas pipes were eliminated.

67. Scrapbook 5:25–26.

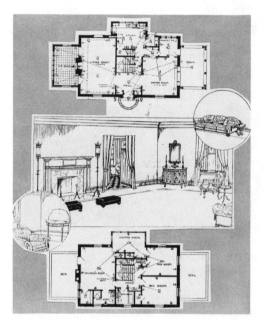

The floor plans and interior drawing of the "Electrical House" reveal a home designed for circulation of residents around a circular staircase. This early 1920s design did not include a main floor bath or powder room, which was more a 1930s innovation, but it did have two baths located on the second floor and, presumably, one on the third floor near the maid's quarters. Note the back staircase leading directly from third-floor rooms to the kitchen on the main floor. KC54n44.

The exterior view of the Electrical House demonstrates how it was planned as a home facing more than one street. The main entrance is covered by a canopy erected by the company to accommodate visitors waiting to view the model home. The signs indicate that the house was open daily for viewing. This exhibition was cosponsored by Kansas City Power and Light to spur the use of electricity in 1920s home construction plans. Note the elevated planter in the triangular parklet at 65th Terrace and Linden Road. The house and parklet served essentially as an entrance to the more moderately priced homes Nichols built in Armour Hills, his 1920s version of Prairie Village. KC54n45.

Thousands came to see the new phenomenon. Even as late as 1913, when the concept of a model home came to be placed in the context of a "model community" in a Chicago design competition, the aspect of model home as an idealization on paper was still the operating notion. Builders and developers put up houses in certain spots in advance of sales to attract buyers and other builders, but they did describe them as *model homes* until the 1920s.[68]

The house on Sixty-fifth Terrace was also unique in that it was furnished with drapes, rugs, and furniture, just as though someone lived there. The local power company, Kansas City Power and Light, had arranged with retailers to provide for display examples of every electrical gadget available. The electrical innovations included, among other things, underground wiring to the home, more than 200 outlets throughout the house, an intercom system, a built-in radio antenna, an illuminated house number on the exterior, and the most modern kitchen appliances, from refrigerator and range to dishwasher and ironing machine. Other appliances and gadgets on display throughout the model home included a vacuum cleaner, phonograph, electric player piano, sewing machine, mixer, percolator, toaster, waffle iron, grill curling iron, vibrator, hair dryer, milk warmer, and oscillating fans. Thus, the term *model home* came to mean for Kansas Citians an example of everything that was up-to-date. J. C. Nichols introduced the concept and used it repeatedly to highlight the possibilities for homes in his neighborhoods.[69]

The all-electric model home was a tremendous advertising success for the Nichols Company and Kansas City Power and Light. Over 30,000 people came to see the new features. Armour Hills subdivision sales boomed. Nichols's building department committed to putting up 30 new residences in the subdivision, including the all-electric house. Most were bungalows, but these were selling for over $10,000 after the war. When it came time to sell the model home early in 1923, it brought an astounding $36,500 in a neighborhood of relatively modest homes.[70]

68. Wright, *Moralism and the Model Home*, 1–4; Scrapbook 6:237–40.

69. Scrapbook 6:237–41; see also *Kansas City Star*, June 18, 1922, 16D, and November 5, 1922, 8A.

70. Scrapbook 6:159; *Kansas City Star*, January 14, 1923, 4F.

The 1924 model home was furnished by local stores to demonstrate to visitors how best to accent the most up-to-date 1920s suburban home. The use of stucco and heavy timbering was more common in the 1920s because it was more economical and yet still lent a air of stolidity to the more moderately priced house. KC54n49.

The living room interior of the 1924 model reveals the use of wall sconces for decorative lighting, less expensive mantelless fireplaces, hardwood floors, and a plaster ceiling trimmed with a picture rail. Hot-water heating by means of radiators was still in vogue to supplement heat from the working fireplace. KC54n51.

In 1924 the company put up another model home, or "exhibition home," as company advertising sometimes referred to them. This was a larger home than before in a more prestigious neighborhood. Built at 808 West Meyer Boulevard, the model home featured a Mediterranean style with brick veneer over concrete cinder blocks and a red tile roof. The lot size was a generous 125 feet of frontage. The house was oriented to face south. French doors opened from interior rooms on the front of the house onto a Mediterranean-style veranda, which ran the width of the house across the front. Before it had finished its run as "a home building example" for Nichols's potential buyers, more than 50,000 had people tracked through its comparatively elegant interior.[71]

Nichols's building department erected other model homes in 1925, but possibly its most interesting and innovative example of the genre was constructed during the summer of 1926 at 6512 Linden Road. Cosponsored by the Lehigh Portland Cement Company, this was an all-concrete house, one of only four such structures that the concrete company cosponsored across the United States during that record-breaking building year of 1926. It featured a basic structure of twelve-inch concrete walls, concrete-slab main floor, which eliminated the usual basement feature, and a reinforced concrete floor for the entire second story. Floor coverings included cement tile in the entry, living, and dining rooms. Linoleum covered the concrete in the rest of the house. The exterior was designed to have the appearance of an English cottage.[72]

This form of construction was not new in the 1920s. The architect-planner, Grosvenor Atterbury, had used similar construction techniques at Forest Hills Gardens as early as 1916. All-concrete construction was as daring in Kansas City in 1926, however, as the all-electric house had been four years before. Significantly, the technique was used widely in the East but seldom occurred in the Middle West even after these experiments, probably because lumber, brick, and stone were readily available at lesser cost. The wide-

71. Scrapbook 7:216; *Kansas City Star,* September 29, 1924, 1D.
72. Scrapbook 8:33, 77, 205–6, 253. These model homes were erected at 405 West Sixty-eighth Terrace and at 6532 Edgevale Road. The company constructed another traditional model home at 2105 Dartmouth Road in 1926.

The upstairs master bedroom (called "the owner's room" in the Electrical House plans) of the 1924 model home illustrates painted woodwork (as opposed to varnished hardwood trim on the main floor), a tiled master bath, and a single closet. It was still expected that women would do spring (and fall) cleaning, which would include a transfer of seasonal clothing to and from attic or basement storage, both of which were supplied liberally. Note the furnishing with twin beds for the owner and his wife. KC54n52.

The 1925 exhibition home had even more pronounced timbering to set off the plain stucco exterior. Located in newly opened Romanelli Gardens, directly west of Armour Hills, the house was adjacent to the extension of the Country Club carline, which ran in the median of Wornall Road at this point. A stairway to an elevated streetcar stop at Wornall and 69th can be seen dimly behind the opening to the screened porch at the right rear of the house. Note the outdoor floodlight fixture in the yard to light the home at night for advertising purposes. KC54n54.

spread use of concrete-slab floors was delayed in Kansas City until after World War II.[73]

Nichols used the bungalow style of home design widely in his Armour Hills development beginning in 1922. He planned a neighborhood of modestly priced homes in the $8,500 price range. As a building style, the bungalow was a catch-all for many types of designs for the smaller home. It seems to have originated in California about the turn of the century, and by 1905 speculative builders used it nationwide. Nichols called his earliest houses in the Country Club District (prior to 1908) bungalows. Typically the style was a one-story layout with a low-pitched roof and wood-framed siding. Story-and-a-half options sometimes appeared, and stucco was sometimes substituted for the wood siding, particularly in California and occasionally in the Kansas City examples. Space was used economically, for most bungalows had six rooms—living, dining, kitchen, and three bedrooms—although two-bedroom models were not uncommon.[74]

Nichols viewed the 1920s bungalow as a first home for the young married couple. It was not true middle-class housing even at that time, though. The $8,500 price tag meant that even with inflated wages, at most somewhat less than half the city's population could afford to buy such a residence. The restrictive financing options probably limited the availability of a J. C. Nichols bungalow to even fewer people than that in Kansas City. Another limiting factor was that in spite of its unpretentious appearance, the bungalow, whether built by Nichols or a contractor anywhere in the country, was probably "the least house for the most money." Because the style emphasized single-floor living, it required extensive foundation work, a large exterior wall area, and an expansive roof to cover the spread-out living area.[75]

In spite of the relatively expensive nature of an Armour Hills bungalow by the J. C. Nichols Company, this particular subdivision did more to make the company a "full-line" housing concern than

73. Handlin, *American Home*, 285–88.
74. Scrapbook 6:159–63; J. C. Nichols Co. advertisement, *Kansas City Star*, August 3, 1924, 1D.
75. Walker, *American Shelter*, 186–91.

Still another early 1920s model home gives evidence of different treatment for smaller homes. This house is quite com-
pact, with three main rooms on each floor, a screened-in
porch on one end, and a trellis area on the east side near the
kitchen and dining room. KC54n30.

The living room interior of the above home provides a modest approach to both
decorating and function. All woodwork, except the stair railing, is painted, which
indicates the use of less-expensive pine lumber. A painted fireplace mantle is included, but roll-up shades have been substituted for drapes; a smaller rug reveals
more of the hardwood floor; and, for the first time, central forced-air heating is
evident as opposed to hot-water radiators. Housing costs skyrocketed during the
1920s; this house is a Nichols Company response to HCL, or the High Cost of
Living, as it was called at the time. KC54n29.

At the other end of the scale from the small home shown in the previous two illustrations, this model home built in 1924 was much more sumptuous, partly as a result of its location on Meyer Boulevard. The broad front hinted at mansionlike proportions, but the house had no rear projections and was really quite narrow. Nonetheless, the Meyer location lent it more prestige, and the exterior design was intended to convey that message to any passer-by. KC54n48.

One of the homes built by the Nichols Company for its Ward Parkway Gold Coast had more than passing importance. Tom Pendergast was by World War I the undisputed boss of Kansas City's Democratic factions. By 1926 he would have his men in position to control the entire city government. After his fall in the late 1930s, some of his old supporters said that he had forgotten his roots—a charge that may seem to have some validity when one witnesses the home Pendergast had Nichols's construction department build for him. It was, and is, one of the truly impressive Ward Parkway mansions. Tom Pendergast doubtless felt he had come a long way from the old West Bottoms and stockyards district—maybe, thanks partially to Nichols, he had come too far. KC54n59.

Another Nichols-built house that seemed oddly out of place in the trendy Sunset Hill section was Walter Bixby's modernistic mansion on the Missouri side of State Line Road. While not placed so prominently as the Pendergast chateau, the Bixby structure stands out rather than blending into the surrounding neighborhood. Bixby, however, was president of the Kansas City Life Insurance Company and could afford whatever style he wished. Nichols architect Tanner designed it as tamely as he dared. KC54n57.

any other subdivision he created. Automobile companies were becoming full-line companies in the 1920s by offering everything from a Chevrolet to a Cadillac. Life insurance companies are considered "full-line" if they offer term, whole life, and health policies. Nichols became "full-line" in the land development and home-building businesses by offering lots from fifty-foot frontage to five acre tracts and houses from bungalows to mansions. To fulfill this range of options, the company built thirty bungalows in 1922 and several in succeeding years, while at the same time building some of the largest homes on Ward Parkway in what became Kansas City's "Gold Coast." Generally, however, Nichols preferred to leave the construction of smaller homes to independent builders. His profit margins were greater, at least in 1918, on the larger homes and mansions. He supported the "full-line" concept mostly by making available the type of building site and neighborhood that would cater to each level of home style and construction.[76]

76. Coleman and Neugarten, *Social Status in the City*; Scrapbooks 6:159 and 8:200.

During the last half of the 1920s, Nichols expanded the "full-line" in another direction. He had started selling land to builders for three-story walk-up apartment houses around the Country Club Plaza site within a month of the initial announcement of the center in 1922. Nichols and the C. E. Phillips Construction Company announced plans for a string of high-rise apartment buildings to be located just west of the developing Plaza shopping center in August 1925. Construction of more than $1,000,000 worth of buildings began after January 1, 1926. Shortly thereafter, Nichols sold land to McCandless Construction Company for the five high-rise apartment buildings that were built between 1926 and 1930 south of Brush Creek facing the Plaza. With these additions Nichols offered a complete line of housing, from bungalows to mansions to luxury apartments.[77]

One of the ironies of this period is that while inflation pushed up housing costs, the white-collar work force of the city was growing more rapidly than ever before. As the city population grew and the percentage of middle- to upper-middle-income families increased, the demand heightened for the Armour Hills type of house. By the middle of the decade, however, Kansas City's need for this type of residence slowed as a result of the huge building boom that had dominated the first half of the decade. The Wall Street crash and the Great Depression were still a few years away, but the western Missouri metropolis had absorbed about as much new housing as it could.

The homebuilding boom of the 1920s peaked in Kansas City and across the country in 1925. The local record, which stood until after World War II, was 3,645 single residences begun in 1925. That compares to 2,686 starts in 1924 and 2,185 starts in 1926. Nationally, the number of single-home starts in 1925 exceeded 1,000,000 for the only time in the decade. After that year, housing starts declined steadily, with only half that many starts in 1930 and only approximately 100,000 starts over the entire nation in the economic low year of 1933.[78]

---

77. *Kansas City Star,* May 28, 1922, 14D; "Into 1926 Apts., 1 Million," *Kansas City Star,* August 2, 1925, 1D; see also "The Outlying Apartment Hotel as a New Development in Urban Housing."

78. "Chart Showing Building Activities," n.p.; Gottlieb, *Estimates of Residential Building,* 83.

In Kansas City the number of housing starts ranged over the 2,000-per-year category every year between 1921 and 1927, when the total for single-family units fell to just under 1,000. By 1930 the building doldrums had really set in, with only 493 units started all year. Even this low figure declined further to a bottom of 109 units started in 1934. Clearly, the drop from 3,645 to less than one-seventh of that number between 1925 and 1930 demonstrates the onset of the Great Depression in a major way.[79]

As Nichols anticipated in 1919, the apartment construction business boomed during the 1920s; he had simply not counted on the corresponding boom in the single-family area. From the beginning of 1920 through 1929, a total of 19,231 building permits were issued for new single-family dwellings worth an aggregate of $71,227,600. The average cost per dwelling permit was $3,687. By way of comparison, during the decade 1910–1919 a total of 12,894 new single-family houses were issued permits in Kansas City for an aggregate of $34,239,871, an average of $2,655 per house. In part, the higher figures for 1920–1929 reflected the inflated prices being charged for new single units in that decade, but they also reflected the fact that Nichols and some other contractors were building more expensive homes, which raised the overall average. Building contractors usually underestimated actual building costs on the permits because the county government computed property taxes on those amounts. While Nichols was one of the largest-scale builders in Kansas City during this period, small builders erected the largest number of houses.[80]

Apartment construction moved ahead both nationally and locally during the 1920s as well. In Kansas City 15,152 new apartment units (not including 1,092 new duplex housing units) came on the market during the decade 1920–1929. The biggest year in apartment construction was 1924, when 2,239 units received permits. Interestingly, 1927 was the second-best year in the decade, with 2,135 new units. This indicates that apartment construction did not slump as badly in Kansas City after 1924–1925 as did the single-

79. "Chart Showing Building Activities," n.p.
80. Ibid., n.p.

family home market. By 1930, however, there were only 397 new units built; and in 1932 the apartment market hit rock bottom, with no new units built.[81]

While the absolute number of apartment buildings constructed in Kansas City began to dip sharply in 1928, the amount of apartment construction around the Country Club area remained high throughout 1929 and into the beginning of 1930. All five of the ten-story apartment hotels that stand on the south side of Brush Creek facing the Plaza to the north were built during 1928–1930. These were designed to be rented "only to the City's most exclusive families." Four of the high-rise apartment buildings located west of the Plaza (and named for poets and other writers) also opened in 1929. These apartment units invited residency primarily by adult couples with no children, although the latter were more excluded by design rather than regulation. The individual suites ranged from four to six rooms, with opening rents starting at $95 for a four-room efficiency unit with one bath to $235 per month for a six-room unit with two baths. Each had a kitchenette with an electric refrigerator and range. The buildings were designed so that all rooms faced the outside and did not directly face another wing of the same building. Some of the buildings had a large central dining room for residents, while others did not.[82]

With the addition of this style of apartment living for young married couples or for older couples whose children had left, the Nichols neighborhoods provided an even wider range of accommodations than ever before. Nichols did not build or own any of the large high-rise apartment buildings adjacent to the Plaza; he sold the ground to the developing companies and profited through his Plaza store rents from the increased density of population. In terms of income level, he was continuing to deal with upper-middle- and upper-income residents in these apartment situations.

The most exclusive high-rise apartment complex of all commenced with the announcement of plans, in 1926, for the construc-

81. Ibid., n.p.; *Kansas City Star,* February 10, 1929, 1D; January 6, 1929, 1D; January 5, 1930, 1D; January 4, 1931, 1D.
82. Scrapbook 10:67–68, 88; "The Outlying Apartment Hotel as a New Development in Urban Housing."

tion of the Walnuts. Designed as a three-building, ten-story, coop-
erative-plan apartment arrangement, the Walnuts was not finally
completed and opened until early 1930. Just as with the units
around the Plaza, Nichols was not directly involved in the development of this prestigious complex. He did not even own or control
the land on which the complex was built. Nevertheless, he supported the project because of the high-income anchor it would
provide in the middle of his other development areas and the prestige its presence would lend to the Plaza.[83]

The Walnuts was built on a ten-acre site on top of the bluff
overlooking the Country Club Plaza. Apartment units ranged from
five-room suites to nine-room plans under the standard layout. It
was possible, however, to obtain variations from the master scheme,
such as the reservation of two floors and the construction of a two-
story living room much like the opulent studio apartments that had
been so fashionable in New York City in the 1890s. The sheer
luxuriousness and exclusivity of the Walnuts attracted enough of the
city's most wealthy and socially prominent residents to shift the
mythical social center of the city to the doorstep of the complex
when it opened in 1930.[84]

As the new single-family home market contracted severely in
1930, Nichols used the forum of his *Country Club District Bulletin* to
reaffirm his faith in the essential qualities of such homes. Clearly he
also hoped to generate new interest in the residential style with the
following statement:

> It was natural that our liberty-loving forebears should hand down to us
> the tradition of home ownership. Fundamentally we are and must con-
> tinue to be a home owning people. Consistency demands it of us and
> those who come after. No matter how greatly the American attitude
> towards life may change, one thing is clear: the highest conception of
> the highest standard of living for which we as a people are distinguished
> implies a continuing devotion to family life based on the one-family
> house, occupied by its owner.[85]

83. *Kansas City Star,* May 23, 1926, 1D.
84. "Another Realtor Built Group"; Handlin, *American Home,* 377–85.
85. Nichols, "Country Club District Upholds American Traditions," 1.

This was not gushy prose issued in a cause Nichols knew was lost or rejected. He firmly held to the principles he expounded; yet he also hedged his bets. When the single-family home had been threatened at the end of the previous decade, he had planned for high-rise apartment buildings and shopping centers. As the 1920s wore on and residential building of all types tapered off, Nichols put even more energy into building up the Plaza area. The centerpiece for him was the Plaza Theatre, which was designed to be as ornate as any downtown theater so that his residents would not have to go downtown for nighttime entertainment. The goal was to keep his residents satisfied with stores, restaurants, and theaters under his control as much as possible.[86]

By the end of 1930, however, most single-family home construction had ceased. Land sales fell off noticeably, and even shopping center and apartment development slowed after the opening of the Walnuts. Nichols stopped publication of his *Country Club District Bulletin* as an economy measure. He even stopped the long-running lawn and garden contests. Many of his residents were too hard-pressed financially by the fall of 1930 to maintain their lawns and gardens.[87]

Early in 1931 the company opened a rental department for the first time. Since the Nichols Company carried the paper on homes it built, it did the foreclosing when that proved necessary. Repossessed homes were offered for rent as well as vacancies in the non-Nichols apartment complexes around the Plaza. Nichols did not have a direct financial interest in those complexes, but they needed to be occupied if the shops in his centers were going to generate the income he needed. This proved to be a most important step, for before the end of the Depression the Nichols Company had to rely almost entirely upon the shopping center percentage rents in order to stay in business.[88]

According to company architect-planner Tanner, the decline in house and land sales after 1930 brought about the demise of the

86. Scrapbook 7:51, 123; Scrapbook 8:57, 108; Scrapbook 9:85, 267; and Scrapbook 10:138.

87. *CCD Bulletin*, October 1930. This was the final issue of the publication.

88. Scrapbook 10:290–93; Scrapbook 11:24.

two-hundred-year house. One major distinction he made, however, was that the era of the one-hundred-year house was marked by
more dependence upon electrical innovation in appliances and the
like, which brought greater attention to the mechanical aspects of
housing. Additionally, the smaller-sized houses of the 1930s had
their precedents in some of the company-built offerings of the late
1920s.

By late 1940, for example, the Nichols Sunday newspaper advertisements called attention to two- and three-bedroom homes available in a new subdivision on the Missouri side that were priced in
the upper-$6,000 range, including land. The ad copy well illustrates
the appeal of the new subdivision of Armour Hills Garden and other
such houses and neighborhoods:

ESCAPE!

Escape from the old fashioned house, so carelessly planned that
housekeeping is drudgery to a brand-new home so thoughtfully
planned that housekeeping becomes mere play . . . and you have time
left over to do all the countless things you always wanted to do, but just
couldn't find the time.

Escape from the dingy kitchen, impossible to keep clean and orderly,
to a 1941 model.

Escape from the outmoded heating plant to a wonderful new gas
one, with thermostatic heat control and circulating air that keeps the
whole house ten degrees cooler in summer.

Escape to a fine community with every neighborhood convenience
. . . . Priced from $6,985.00. FHA long-term, low-interest plan.[89]

As the above indicates, Nichols was building and selling homes
on the Missouri side in late 1940, but the greatest amount of post-
Depression development took place on the Kansas side of the state
line. Early in 1940 the company had begun to push the Fairway
subdivision (platted in 1937) as "Kansas City's fastest growing,
closest in, new medium-priced homes community." These medium-
priced homes were available on FHA financing to qualified buyers,

89. *Kansas City Star,* December 15, 1940, 8D.

By early 1941, the company no longer felt that strictly "tasteful" signs and messages were essential, as is shown with their huge first birthday cake for Fairway. The little girl is dwarfed by the colossal plywood cake erected on Mission Road. Given the doldrums of the 1930s, during which the company was lucky to sell one hundred houses or lots over five years, let alone in just one year, the kitsch cake may be excused. One of the implications of this tremendous period of sales is that the FHA amortized mortgage combined with pent-up demand from the Depression might well have made the 1940s a boom decade from start to finish had not the war (which was already underway in Europe) intervened. KC54n60.

This postcard-style advertisement sums up the attractions of Fairway: it was economical, close to Nichols shopping at the Plaza, and close to both Kansas City downtowns, in Missouri and Kansas (Minnesota Avenue). The appeal to Kansas City, Kansas, workers was new for the Nichols Company; since 1905, their advertising had spent no time appealing to Kansas-side homebuyers. Both the lower cost and the proximity via Rainbow Boulevard made Fairway a potential homesite choice for "the other Kansas City." KC54n58.

This 1949 overview of Prairie Village graphically illustrates not only the growth of this single large development, but also the growth that extended through the entire lifetime of J. C. Nichols. From the Plaza behind the three Walnuts towers in the upper left-hand corner to the towers of Baptist Hospital in the upper right and back to Prairie Village, almost every lot in view was developed by the J. C. Nichols Company and its predecessors. More than 50,000 people lived in the neighborhoods by this time on both sides of the state line. There is literally no other contiguous development of this size by one developer in the United States. KC54n64.

which made them the most accessible housing Nichols had put on the market since 1908. By early 1941, the majority of lots in Fairway were sold, and plans were being made to open what would become Nichols's largest and most mass-market-oriented subdivision since the opening of the original Armour Hills in the early 1920s. Prairie Village became the prototype post–World War II suburb for Kansas City, but its origins are certainly prewar.[90]

90. Ibid., January 12, 1941, 6D.

"Live Better for Less"—the opening slogan for Prairie Village set the tone of many aspects of the development. The land was priced less ($17.50 per front foot for sixty- and sixty-five-foot frontages) than in any Nichols development since World War I. Building restrictions were also comparatively low at $3,500. This meant that it was theoretically possible to buy land and build a home in Prairie Village for less than $5,000—if a builder could be obtained for a $3,500 contract. The company advertisements estimated that a $6,000 minimum cost for house and lot was more realistic.[91]

By September 1941, the company had new homes ready for purchase on the FHA plan with payments of $39.16 per month for principal, interest, taxes, and insurance. These were two-bedroom houses that had a finished stairway to an unfinished second floor, which could become a third bedroom. An unfinished basement was usually included. This became the standard type of Prairie Village home built by the company during the 1940s. This move into virtually mass-produced housing at very competitive rates was really the first time the company had appealed to the moderate-priced housing market since its earliest offerings in 1905.[92]

The Prairie Village models were quite spartan by comparison with other Nichols homes, but they compared favorably with the first offerings of the Levitt firm in Hempstead Township, Long Island, in a 1947 subdivision the Levitts first named Island Trees. Soon renamed Levittown, the New York houses were also four-room units with an unfinished attic. Set on sixty-foot lots, the standard imitation Cape Cod style went up on a concrete slab and sold for $6,990 in the earliest versions, though prices soon rose to $7,990. Levitt's first units were only available on a rent-to-buy plan with monthly payments of $60.[93]

During the postwar era, Nichols again offered land at $17.50 per front foot as late as 1947. Housing-material costs pushed prices up to comparable levels with those at Levittown. By 1950 over 1,000 houses had sprouted in Prairie Village, almost two-thirds of which had been built by the Nichols firm. This is a comparatively small

91. Ibid., May 11, 1941, 6D.
92. Ibid., September 21, 1941, 6D; September 28, 1941, 8D.
93. Jackson, *Crabgrass Frontier*, 234–37.

In one of the last model homes offered before his death, J. C. Nichols joined with homebuilders across the country to capitalize on the remarkable popularity of a book and movie about custom-built homes. Eric Hodgins wrote what amounted to a humorous short story for the April 1946 issue of *Fortune Magazine* about a man and his wife who wanted to build a simple place in the country outside New York City for around $20,000 for house and lot. It wound up costing Hodgins's hero (named Mr. Blandings) something over $50,000. Nichols and the other developers decided that if they would each build the type of house generally described in the story for much less than Mr. Blandings reported it costing, the builders could cash in on the free publicity afforded by the movie's release in 1948 and prove to the home-buying public that it was not nearly as expensive to build as they had been led to believe. Entitled *Mr. Blandings Builds His Dream House,* the movie accomplished exactly what Nichols desired, in Kansas City at any rate. This photograph shows a portion of the crowd who came to see Mr. Blandings's dream house, actually built just off Ward Parkway south of Meyer Circle. KC54n63.

number by comparison with the thousands of houses put up by the Levitts, but Nichols did accomplish an integration of shopping and residence that fits together harmoniously in a way never approached in Levittown.[94]

The history of the Nichols Company's homebuilding efforts highlights the fact that the company was always primarily a land- and business-development firm. The periods during which the company

94. *Kansas City Star,* March 30, 1947, 8D.

engaged in extensive homebuilding were generally times when individual land buyers and investors were less than enthusiastic. In a sense, the company "primed the pump" with homebuilding activities at its inception, after each war, and toward the end of the Great Depression. After the founder's death in 1950, the company more often returned to the former practice of acquiring and developing land for homesites.

8

THE HEART OF THE PLANNED SUBDIVISION

The Shopping Center

The impact of retail businesses locating near his subdivisions had worried Nichols when he first started large developments in 1908. By 1919, automobiles were becoming commonplace, and wealthy people could drive several miles to shop where they wished. If the shops were well designed and sufficiently separated from the best residential sections, yet still relatively close by, shopping areas might work as an adjunct to his planned neighborhoods.

Nichols had gotten into retail business development by building filling stations for the automobiles his residents were driving to work and for leisure. He had invested sixty thousand dollars in four "artistically designed" filling stations located on the periphery of his subdivisions between 1914 and 1917. One of these is shown in the foreground of the illustration of the Plaza lights on p. 38; a somewhat later model appears as a backdrop to the Piggly Wiggly in the Romanelli shops on p. 253. In 1918, Nichols had realized a 60 percent profit from the rent on the small service stations.

When the annual meeting of the Developers of High Class Residential Property arrived in 1919, Nichols had mapped out his commercial strategy. He chose to test it with his colleagues at the end of their three days of meetings. The other subdividers were tired; they had been in the Birmingham, Alabama, hotel for almost the entire meeting, aside from one tour of the local member's subdivision, and nearly all they had done was talk. They wanted to go home, but Nichols, who had just regaled them with his concerns about whether the homeowners would maintain interest in their subdivisions, wanted to change the subject to retailing. They listened politely as he said, "I may be mistaken, but I don't think there is anything we have discussed that is more vital. I will tell you why. I think that because I believe before this year is over I will earn on that basis and will be worth a hundred thousand dollars more money on

One of Nichols's goals with his artistic filling stations was to disguise as much as possible the fact that the structure was what it was. This particular filling station could accomplish that fairly easily because the actual gasoline pump was basically like the old-style hand water pumps with a lever on the back for operating the pumping mechanism. Later pumps were larger and electrified, which made them a bit more difficult to hide. This particular model won a prize for most artistic filling station in the nation. KC54n25.

it than I am now. I am going to double the rent from what I was getting on a flat rate by going to rent by a percentage of gross sales."[1]

It did not work. The others were too tired and too afraid of business encroachment to be interested in encouraging or even in making money through such schemes. They thought Nichols was off on a tangent. But Nichols did not need the approval of these men to go ahead with his ideas of promoting retail trade by constructing buildings and charging rent as a percentage of gross sales. He had not needed their approval to sell to Jews, nor had he needed their support for his ideas of relatively independent homeowners' associations. Nichols was simply trying out ideas; he already knew what he was going to do in each case.[2]

While Nichols was ostensibly trying out his ideas for retail business development in 1919, he was actually an old hand at this. In addition to the filling stations he had mentioned to the subdividers,

1. 1919 *Proceedings*, 691–92.
2. In the discussion on selling to Jews, Nichols indicated that he was already doing so; see ibid., 572.

he was already landlord to several business establishments. As early as 1907 he had constructed buildings for a pharmacy and grocery near the streetcar stop for his subdivision (see illustration on p. 73). The Brookside shops, which opened within a year after this conference in 1919, had been in the planning stages since 1914. The announcement of a projected Country Club Plaza was still three years away; yet Nichols had started acquiring land for it in 1912.[3]

Nichols told the other developers in 1919 that he was about to embark on business ventures that would change his development style dramatically. His earlier question of whether he should stay in the development business would be answered partly by the decision to create more homeowner interest through activities and organizations. The other part of the answer was that he was going to vary his own activities by participating more in retail development. In retrospect, Nichols's decision was significant; many recent historians discuss Nichols as a shopping center developer much more than as a subdivider or land developer. The most recent study of national suburban development devotes equal space to Nichols's residential planning and his shopping center innovations. Kenneth Jackson introduces Nichols's retail experiences this way:

> Although the *Guinness Book of World Records* lists the Roland Park Shopping Center (1896) as the world's first shopping center, the first of the modern variety was Country Club Plaza in Kansas City. It was the effort of a single entrepreneur, Jesse Clyde Nichols, who put together a concentration of retail stores, and used leasing policy to determine the composition of stores in the concentration. By doing that, Nichols created the idea of the planned regional shopping center.[4]

When the *Kansas City Times* devoted an entire section of its Thanksgiving, 1984, edition to the Nichols Company, the writer spent at least as much time discussing the company's shopping cen-

3. J. C. Nichols Co. advertisement, *Kansas City Star*, July 14, 1907; Scrapbook 6:107.

4. *Crabgrass Frontier*, 258. Other recent historians have paid somewhat more attention to Nichols's development work, including Warner, *The Urban Wilderness*, 210, 222, and Wright, *Building the Dream*, 202–3.

ter work and the implications of changes in the Plaza in the 1980s as he did on residential planning. In an interview for the story, the current president of the J. C. Nichols Company, Lynn McCarthy, stated that control of the land around the Plaza area "is one way to control your destiny." The writer then commented, "That destiny takes in more than the Plaza. It takes in a personal and corporate dynasty of national prominence. It would be hard to imagine what Kansas City would be today without the influence of the J. C. Nichols Co."[5]

It may also be difficult to imagine that one shopping center could dominate a metropolitan area of over one million people in the 1980s. That the Plaza does so is testimony to the farsightedness of Nichols in the World War I era, when serious planning for the Plaza got underway. The degree to which natives and newcomers to Kansas City become attached to the Plaza is also a commentary on the quality and focus of life in Kansas City and the United States.

An emphasis on the consumption of goods bought in retail stores began to dominate American economic activity about the beginning of the twentieth century. It was a major factor in the growth of American cities in the late nineteenth and early twentieth centuries. Beginning with the 1920s, however, the trend was toward decentralized distribution of consumer goods, aided by the increasing use of automobiles and trucks. This in turn reflected the increasing suburbanization of single-family residences spinning out around American cities. Nichols was quick to see the trend in residential movement. He was not, however, the first to recognize or to take advantage of this ever-outward movement in residential choice by upper-middle and upper-income groups. He did study the growth of Kansas City sufficiently well to recognize not only the trend but the direction of the trend, and he put himself in the right place at the right time.[6]

In examining the possibilities of the retail trade moving out from the downtown center where it had been anchored since the 1850s,

5. Wenske, "Fulfilling a Vision," C–1 through C–7.
6. Nichols repeatedly stated that he had led the growth of the city to his site rather than following an established trend. See Al Dopking, "From a Tract Beside a Hog Lot Grew His District of 10,000 Homes," *Kansas City Star,* August 2, 1947.

As is clear from the wording on the sign above the fire-engine door, Nichols was not the contractor for the Brookside Fire and Police Station. One cannot help but believe, however, that he and his architectural staff had something to do with making the building look like a residence with a single-car garage. No other such mundane facility in Kansas City at that time showed this concern for style and decoration. KC54n24.

Nichols was more of a pioneer. Others in Kansas City saw the prospects of building small business establishments near the intersections of major streetcar lines, but no one before 1920 was thinking about a retail business center that would attempt to attract shoppers arriving by automobile.

Other developers moved along traditional lines not only in Kansas City but across the country as well. In fact, when the developer of much of the business property along Hollywood and Wilshire boulevards in the Los Angeles area spoke to the National Realtor Convention in 1930, he told them that 1919 was a good base year for measuring the growth of outlying business property in the Los Angeles area. Almost nothing had been done prior to that time, and most of the retail development near Beverly Hills occurred after 1925. Yet, by 1907, Nichols equaled the commercial floor space of the Roland Park shopping area merely by constructing his pharmacy and grocery in the streetcar tracks. By 1912, he was acquiring land for the site of the Plaza. And by 1915, he was working with noted city planner John Nolen on designs for the Brookside shops, which were planned as a neighborhood center.[7]

The early planning for the Sixty-third and Brookside location had been stimulated by the city's decision to locate an "artistically designed" combination police and fire station in the area in 1914. Nichols had sold the land to the city for this use. Just before he was able to announce the actual start of construction at the Brookside location, the Nichols Company opened another enterprise designed both to make money from the use of company-owned land and to emphasize the rural side of Nichols's residential developments. A riding academy complete with stable was announced in September 1919, to be located on the future Plaza site but well away from the section where the company had already determined the first Plaza buildings would be constructed. In conjunction with the riding academy announcement, the company laid out and publicized several riding trails going off into the undeveloped parts of Mission Hills.[8]

Although Nichols had drawings from planner Nolen in hand by 1915, he did not move immediately on the Brookside project. World War I intervened, and then came Nichols's period of self-doubt in early 1919 as the economic horizon looked cloudy indeed. By October 1919, however, all doubts had been erased, and construction commenced. Plans called for a total of eight shops in the initial phase, with an English Tudor, half-timbered exterior style. This made the Brookside shops appear remarkably similar to the Roland Park shops, built more than twenty years earlier. At the same time the company got underway at Brookside, it also began to expand the small shops where its retail business activity had begun in 1907. Renamed "The Colonial Shops," these buildings received additional shop space and renovated exteriors that emphasized the colonial architecture theme.[9]

7. Davies, *Real Estate*, 130, 173; Mason Case, "Outlying Business Districts." Drawings for the proposed Brookside shops, dated 1915, are in the John Nolen Papers.

8. Scrapbook 2 and Scrapbook 4.

9. Scrapbook 4; *CCD Bulletin*, September 1, 1919, 1.

Located approximately at the site of Seville Square on the Plaza of 1990, the riding academy was the second Nichols-built structure to go up on the site. Completed in 1920, it predates by two years the famous announcement of Spanish style for the Plaza, and yet it was just as clearly designed for that style as the Fire and Police Station was specifically designed for the mock-Tudor style of Brookside Center. This building was designed and constructed before Nichols traveled to Spain. KC54n28.

Some buildings at Sixty-third and Brookside were ready for occupancy in January 1920. One innovation for Nichols was the location of space for doctors' offices on the second floor of some of the shops. While this practice had been followed in some cities, with doctors relocating part or all of their practice to second-floor offices near streetcar intersections, few examples of this pattern had occurred in Kansas City prior to Nichols's Brookside Center. This opportunity to carry out part or all of their practice in close proximity to their more well-to-do patients appears to have been attractive to physicians. By April 1920, seven doctors had rented space in the Brookside shops. Some had moved their entire practice to the new location, while others divided their time between Brookside and their downtown offices.[10]

Nichols constructed a community hall on the second floor above the shops in one section away from the doctors' offices. This space was available for rent to music teachers, dance instructors, and other people providing the various "lessons" that suburban mothers believed their children should have to round out their education. At

10. Scrapbook 5:10–12.

The Brookside Shopping Center opened in 1920 with a drug store on the corner and a grocery as the tenant of the second ground-floor shop space down the street. Café tables can be seen under the street trees next to the drug store, which featured a complete fountain and sandwich shop. Canned goods are stacked in the windows of the grocery to the left of where the woman and the girl are standing. The second floor housed the Community Hall along with doctors' and dentists' offices. KC54n31.

The enclosed shelving and counter along the back wall of the interior of the Brook-side drug store stored the pharmaceutical portion of the business. The fountain and kitchen facilities were in back of the photographer when this picture was taken. Note the perfumes and cigars in the glass cases in the foreground, as well as the café tables along the windows. Drug stores were not simply drug stores even in the early 1920s. KC54n32.

The interior of the first grocery at Brookside reveals that it was not a "self-service" store but rather that clerks would wait on customers who came to the individual counters. The clerks would actually get the items from the shelves, sack or box them, and then carry them to the customer's vehicle. Note the refrigeration units behind the cash register area. Meat and other perishables were stored behind the glass doors. KC54n33.

The Community Hall above the Brookside shops was used for a variety of events and regular meetings such as Masonic lodges, church services for congregations organizing in order to build their own edifices in the district, women's groups, and others. This is a dance class with over thirty young ladies learning the social graces. Even kindergarten classes used the facility on a daily basis in the earliest years. Homes association dinners, with food catered by the Eastern Star organization, which met in the hall, were annual events in the building, as was the District Flower Show. This meant that the Brookside Shopping Center served as a community center as well throughout the 1920s and 1930s. KC54n34.

night, the space in the Community Hall was given over to meetings of Masonic lodges and Eastern Star chapters. The Nichols Company maintained the hall at its own expense and used it as the site of its annual district flower shows and other special events from time to time.[11]

The next retailing project upgraded a property the company had acquired at the future site of the Country Club Plaza. In 1917 Nichols's business property manager, George Tourtellot, Jr., succeeded in getting a nursery company, Chandler Floral, to relocate to Nichols property at the southwest corner of Forty-seventh and Main. They had been located since the founding of the company in 1909 on a site in the Hyde Park District at Main and Armour Boulevard. The first building housing the nursery had been a rather mundane structure with one distinction: apartments for renters were located on the second floor. These were the first apartments built by the Nichols Company in a location that would become by the middle 1920s the epitome of the term *high rent district* in Kansas City.[12]

In 1920 the Nichols Company for the first time converted a property on the Plaza site into a more functional building that would pay better rent. The company tore down the original Chandler Floral building and replaced it with a structure done in a Spanish architectural style. With the Colonial and Brookside shops the Nichols Company had already demonstrated its ideas about varying the architectural styles among its shopping centers. It is not surprising that a totally different style was going to be used at this new site. What is impressive is that the architectural theme for the Plaza had been determined a full two years before the formal announcement of the center was made in 1922. The rebuilt Chandlers' location was ready in time for Thanksgiving, 1920. That same fall the first restaurant in the Country Club District opened as the Country Club Coffee Shop in the Colonial shops. Its interior was designed to make it look like an old English coffee house. It would serve as the rallying point for various district activities such as Christmas carol parties during the early 1920s.[13]

11. Ibid., 13–15.
12. Scrapbook 4:1.
13. Scrapbook 5:113, 137.

The Country Club Plaza site, seen just before the first public announcement of plans for the shopping center was made. Chandler's Floral and Greenhouse is in the lower right center, along with two artistic filling stations. Another station and the riding academy are at upper left center. The Broadway bridge over Brush Creek is visible at left center, as is a vintage view of the creek itself before the Pendergast paving job of the mid-1930s. The paved road zigzagging from the bridge down to Chandler's and then exiting at lower right is Ward Parkway until it hits Main, which continues off to the left after intersecting with 47th Street, coming between Chandler's and the filling station in the lower right corner. KC54n41.

In 1921 the first section of the Crestwood shops was built in a modified colonial style at Fifty-fifth and Oak streets. The new location was four blocks straight south of the recently expanded Colonial shops. By the beginning of 1922 there were three groceries, two drug stores, two dry-cleaning shops, one bakery, two beauty shops, four clothing stores, one coffee shop, one shoe repair shop, and one florist in the Crestwood location. Because of the proximity of the two centers, the colonial style was retained for the newer center; in the 1950s the Colonial shops were remodeled again and lost their colonial styling altogether, although the name was retained. In one of the earliest promotions of the company, human-sized Easter bunnies were placed on the sidewalks and at intersections near the Crestwood shops at Eastertime in 1922. This was such an effective attention-getter that replicas of those first large bunnies were still being placed on sidewalks in the Plaza area in the 1980s.[14]

Ironically, the earliest part of the Plaza story had little to do with J. C. Nichols. A competing real estate entrepreneur platted the site in the sluggish Brush Creek valley just below the infamous Lyle Brickyard and Rock Quarry in 1911, laying the subdivision out in lots forty-eight feet wide. Though he advertised occasionally in the Kansas City papers, much of his sales efforts were directed toward mail order purchases. Given the dismal appearance of the site when a prospective buyer might visit, it is not surprising that he found it easier to market by description through the mail than by sales talk on site. On the plat map, subdivider George F. Law named the subdivision "Country Club Plaza," which gives him one continuing claim to fame in connection with some of the most highly priced retail property in the Kansas City region.[15]

Nichols appears to have gotten interested in the property during the following year, by which time lots had been sold to more than one hundred different purchasers. Nichols and his business property man, George Tourtellot, were faced with tracking down these mail-order buyers and offering to buy the property from them. Nichols stated in 1923 that this process had cost the company more than $1,000,000. The land thus acquired actually went beyond the boundaries of Law's Country Club Plaza subdivision to include a total of more than 6,000 front feet of land on the hillsides of the valley and extend to the east and west from the proposed main site. The land acquisition that hindered the project most, however, was as close to Nichols's original Bismark Place subdivision as it was to the Plaza. This plot was the site of the old Lyle Brickyard, which Nichols had successfully shut down through court action in 1920. Understandably, the brick and quarry owners were bitter toward Nichols and did not sell out to him immediately after the court action; he got control of the property only after two years of negotiation. A photograph of the original Plaza site with dust from the brickyard rock crusher in the background is reproduced on p. 119.[16]

14. Scrapbook 6:66, 206.
15. Ibid., 259, 276.
16. *CCD Bulletin,* June 1, 1923, 1; "Millions in New Shops," *Kansas City Star,*

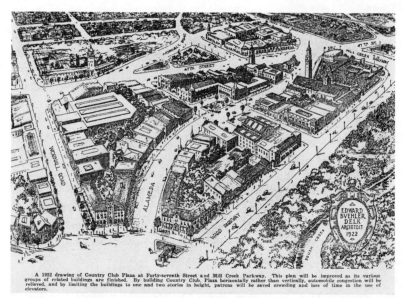

A 1922 drawing of Country Club Plaza at Forty-seventh Street and Mill Creek Parkway. This plan will be improved as its various groups of related buildings are finished. By building Country Club, Plaza horizontally rather than vertically, automobile congestion will be relieved, and by limiting the buildings to one and two stories in height, patrons will be saved crowding and loss of time in the use of elevators.

This reproduction of the original plan for the Plaza reveals that the general style has been closely adhered to over the years but that the actual buildings and even street arrangements have been altered as different opportunities presented themselves to the Nichols Company. Even from the beginning the Plaza was destined to change. KC54n42.

With all the pieces of land in place, Nichols announced his plans to Kansas City on Sunday, April 30, 1922. The *Star* cooperated by giving him almost a full page for a rendering of the proposed project as it might look in completed form. While few of the buildings actually ended up in the form imagined by architect Edward Buehler Delk in this first drawing, the street design, the "general Spanish type of architecture," and the use of towers to punctuate the otherwise low skyline of the development all remain part of the center into the 1980s. The drawing was immodestly captioned in capital letters: "A NEW BUSINESS DISTRICT, TO BE DEVELOPED BY J. C. NICHOLS AT FORTY-SEVENTH AND MILL CREEK PARKWAY, PROMISES A NEW STANDARD IN AMERICA FOR OUTLYING BUSINESS SECTIONS."[17]

April 30, 1922, 12D; *CCD Bulletin*, April-May 1922, 6.
    17. "Millions in New Shops."

The accompanying story began its explanation of the project this way: "An outlying business center planned in compliance with modern traffic demands, involving an ultimate expenditure of five million dollars and with all buildings in architectural harmony, is to be built by the J. C. Nichols Development Company on thirty acres of land west of Mill Creek at Forty-seventh street." Nichols planned for the Plaza to be attractive in both its architecture and its landscaping, to provide maximum convenience for the automobile-oriented shopper, and, of course, to make money. By the end of the 1920s, similar shopping areas adjacent to high-cost residential subdivisions were cropping up at River Oaks in Houston, Highland Park near Dallas, and Shaker Heights near Cleveland.[18]

One of the main reasons Nichols wanted the Lyle Brickyard site to be under his control before announcing the project was that his plans called for using it as a plot on which high-rise apartments could be built. Nichols recognized as early as 1922 that the Plaza would need greater population density within walking distance of retail shops than single-family homes alone would supply. He was constructing a captive market for his stores with his plans to surround the shopping area with apartments. Upper-middle-income (as opposed to strictly upper-income) apartments had their origin in late nineteenth-century Manhattan, New York. In Kansas City, apartment building construction was plentiful just before America's entry into World War I. In fact, the second-most-active year for apartment construction in Kansas City between 1910 and 1941 was 1916, with 226 buildings under construction. Apartments were not seen as proper living environments for young children as late as 1930, however. Nichols proposed these units for young married couples and for older couples, as well as for singles.[19]

The landscape plan called for the Plaza itself to have no buildings higher than two stories except for the decorative towers. Nichols did not want to spoil this effect with taller apartment buildings that would dwarf his masterpiece. He and his planners realized, however, that relatively tall buildings of nine stories could be built across

18. Ibid.; Riddle, "Homes to Last for All Time"; "Model Business Center."
19. Wright, *Building the Dream*, 135–51. Building statistics are taken from "Chart Showing Building Activities," n.p.

This 1926 photograph shows the low-rise apartment buildings (some of which have been removed by 1990 to make way for non–Nichols Company buildings) facing south on 47th Street. Nichols bought this land along with the land eventually covered by shops, but he sold the apartment land to developers who signed agreements to build apartments that would help raise the local population density in order to support the concentration of shops Nichols envisioned for the Plaza site. The edge of the riding academy riding oval is at lower left. KC54n54.

Brush Creek to the south of the Plaza if they were placed at the foot of the hillside that climbed sharply from the Brush Creek valley. The hillside would provide a visual backdrop to the tall buildings preventing them from overpowering the low-rise structures on the Plaza. Only in the 1980s did the company change its aversion to high-rise office buildings near the Plaza. While the historic center still retains a three-story maximum building height, new high-rises have been built around the edges by the Nichols Company. In the late 1980s construction was underway by other developers for building complexes including structures of more than twenty stories.[20]

The allocation of space for automobile traffic and parking in the main shopping area was critical from the beginning for Nichols. He normally tried to allot no more than 25 percent of the total land area in a subdivision to streets. With the Plaza he altered his thinking and had the planners include more than 50 percent of the space as street area. Nichols planned to be able to handle three to four times more traffic in the Plaza than could be handled on regular-width city streets. Part of this street area was given over to widening the exist-

20. "Millions in New Shops."

ing thoroughfares in order to allow diagonal parking on both sides of the street. Off-street parking was planned from the beginning as well.[21]

In an interview with a *Star* reporter, Nichols outlined the standards for shopping center planning he was instituting with this project. Whereas "planning" for most business sections across the country amounted to little more than lot-by-lot treatment by the individual owners, Nichols proposed to enforce uniform height and cornice lines to achieve something of "the orderly effect so generally praised in Paris and certain other European cities." Together with his architects, Edward Buehler Delk and Edward Tanner, Nichols spent about three years studying other outlying business centers, all of which were along streetcar or rail lines, to determine the best plan. One initial decision was to adopt architectural motifs derived from Spanish Renaissance and Baroque work "as the most adaptable and elastic for our purpose." They decided this before the new building was constructed in Spanish motif for Chandler Floral in 1920.

Planning called for a predominance of one-story shops to reduce traffic problems and entice customers who might not like climbing stairs or riding elevators. A few two-story buildings were planned "to give the necessary architectural accent." Nichols argued that his studies had shown that traffic congestion was directly related to the height of buildings because taller buildings accommodated more people, whether for work or for apartment residence. Then, too, one-story shops would provide "light, air and sunshine . . . to every shop window, thereby providing pleasant shopping conditions as well as good sanitation."

The provision of rear unloading docks and courts for all stores resulted in better traffic flow. No merchandise would be allowed to be unloaded at the front of a store. Forty-seventh Street was widened at company expense to the width of one hundred feet to provide diagonal parking, making the street as wide as any boulevard in the city. Actual paving width would be one hundred feet as well, making it the widest fully paved street in the entire city at the time. Nichols had sent Delk on tours of Spain, South America, and Mex-

21. Ibid.; "Joins Beauty and Business," *Kansas City Star*, April 30, 1922, 12D.

ico to collect architectural ideas for the center. The intended effect was the creation of "the feeling of an old market place of picturesque Spain [in] Kansas City." A major part of the planning toward this "feeling" was to require a particular color scheme for buildings, roofs, wrought iron work, and even awnings to protect the merchandise from the summer sun.[22]

Finally, in a rambling sentence characteristic of Nichols's rhetorical style, he laid out the truly revolutionary aspect of his plans: "It is our plan to provide for both exclusive and popular shops not only to serve Rockhill and other nearby property, becoming the general market of the Country Club District, to which this section becomes the gateway, but to also serve the general trade in Kansas City and tributary territory." He was proposing to attract the shopping traffic from residential areas well beyond the confines of his own development, which simply had not been done outside of central downtown shopping districts served by streetcars and interurban lines. The announcement gave no evidence of the traditional concern of retail shop owners: proximity to streetcar lines. Nichols did include the proposals for surrounding apartment construction as a means of augmenting the market capability of the immediate neighborhood. Furthermore, his shopping center was within a block of a streetcar stop. The developer chose to ignore this in his publicity, although he did build his first buildings as close to that streetcar stop as possible. Nichols liked to hedge his bets.[23]

Actual construction of the initial phase, scheduled to start in May 1922, did not in fact begin until November of that year. Nichols felt compelled to assure his homeowners in the residential districts that he was going to be as rigid in enforcing restrictions in the business plaza as he was in the neighborhoods. He told them by newsletter in November 1922 that sign design and placement would be strictly controlled. Outside advertising would be in good taste and sharply limited, compared even with the downtown shopping district. He further announced that the most up-to-date methods would be used: smoke-abatement would be practiced through the use of oil-

22. Scrapbook 7:100; "Joins Beauty and Business." All quotations are taken from the latter, which is an interview with Nichols.
23. "Joins Beauty and Business."

fired burners for heat, and automatic sprinkler systems were being installed to gain the best insurance ratings for the buildings, most of which the Nichols Company would continue to own. Overall, it was to be "The Country Club Plaza—America's paramount suburban business development! Through it, downtown shopping facilities will be brought to the very door of every Country Club District home."[24]

The first tenants moved into the initial building at the intersection of Forty-seventh and Mill Creek Parkway in March 1923. A children's photographer moved in first, closely followed by a furniture company. The latter occupied the largest space, which earned it the right to have the building called the Suydam Building after the name of their store. Other early tenants in this building included Mrs. Chisholm's, a millinery shop, a beauty shop, a baby shop, a dry cleaner, and a drug store. Service businesses seemed to sense more quickly than many retailers the advantage of being close to the affluent clientele of the Country Club District. Attesting to the concern of Nichols for adequate facilities for servicing autos, the Plaza Garage opened on April 11, 1923. It was built of red structural tile and stuccoed to conform in style with the other buildings.[25]

The second retail building, called the Triangle Building because of its shape, opened in June 1923 at Forty-seventh Street and Wyandotte. Shops included a branch of one of the pioneer mass food retailers, Piggly Wiggly. Their self-service method of selling groceries found quick acceptance in the 1920s. Another dry cleaner, a gift shop, a lingerie emporium, and a Western Union office completed the tenant list in the second structure. In these first groupings, it was not entirely clear how "utilitarian" shops were being segregated from the more "refined" variety. The company began the first building designed to emphasize the Spanish motif by the use of a tower in December 1923. The Tower Building, located between the Suydam Building and the Triangle Building facing south onto

24. "Millions in New Shops"; *CCD Bulletin,* November 1922, 1, and December 1923, 2, 8.
25. Scrapbook 7:49–51, 259.

The interior of a Piggly Wiggly self-service grocery was quite different from the type of grocery pictured at Brookside. The Piggly Wigglys were designed so that customers had to enter through the turnstile at lower left and then proceed through the entire store before coming to the checkout counter at center right. The only exit was the narrow aisle past the checkout point. The idea in a Piggly Wiggly was to force the customer to walk past every item of merchandise in the hope that they would pick up as much as possible. Note the lack of ceiling decoration and the decidedly mundane light fixtures. Most importantly, most Piggly Wigglys were planned for only one employee—the checkout clerk, who would stock shelves when the store was empty or after hours. The wire and wood racks atop the dividers were designed to keep people all going the same way and in view of the clerk as much as possible. Piggly Wigglys were not only the first self-service grocery stores, but were also among the first discount stores. They did not mark down prices; their prices were simply less because of the reduced overhead from the features mentioned. KC54n47.

Forty-seventh Street, featured an ornate seventy-foot tower in authentic Spanish style.[26]

A possibly more "refined" store opened in January 1924. Fred

26. Ibid., 50–51, 99.

Wolfermann had exclusive food stores located in the better parts of Kansas City. His Plaza store was housed in his own building, designed by his own architects. As opposed to the self-service merchandising pioneered by Piggly Wiggly, Fred Wolfermann offered personal service from clerks who called orders to stock boys through an in-store telephone system. When the customer entered, he or she read the list to one of the clerks, who called the stock boy, who then brought it to the counter where the bill was written, and finally the boxes were carried to the car. Home delivery was also available. If the waiting customer desired, purchases could be selected from the in-house bakery display cases or from the glass-doored coolers and meat counters in the in-house sausage shop. An announcement proclaimed that the new store would "carry just as complete a line of merchandise as is carried in their downtown store."[27]

Robinson's Shoes (a tenant, in name, of the Plaza until 1989 although under different ownership) opened their Plaza store on May 12, 1924. It featured a "Kiddie's Play Room," complete with toys to play with while Mother shopped for shoes. The store also contained space for a barber who specialized in children's haircuts. Robinson's, like Fred Wolfermann, had a downtown store. These two businesses were among the first downtown merchants to establish a suburban outlet in the entire city. An early instance of a downtown store closing that location entirely and moving to the suburban sections was the Wilkie Furniture Company, which moved to its own building on the Plaza in the general vicinity of Suydam Furniture in November 1925. A women's dress and accessory shop opened in the Tower Building on October 1, 1924. Other shops opening in the Tower Building in October were a Ford motorcar agency, another beauty parlor, a dressmaking shop, a hardware store, a radio equipment store, a stationery supplier, and an art gallery.[28]

Turnover in tenants always occurred in the various Nichols shopping centers as some businesses failed and others expanded. In some instances, the business might have been making enough money for its own purposes, but not enough to satisfy the Nichols Company,

27. Ibid., 123–24.
28. Ibid., 155; Scrapbook 8:64, 188; *CCD Bulletin,* October 1924, 6.

which might obtain a better share of profits from another tenant. If this were the case, the Nichols Company canceled the lease, with proper notice. In October 1924, Miss Houston's kindergarten moved from its temporary space in the meeting hall above the Brookside shops to the space vacated by the failed Colonial Shops Coffee Shop. The demise of the first restaurant did not mean that such shops could not survive in the Country Club District, for a restaurant in the Brookside shops and a tea room in Crestwood were both thriving at this time. Further, the former manager of the Mission Hills Country Club dining room opened his own restaurant on the Plaza in the Triangle Building facing Wyandotte Street. It offered lunch at reasonable prices and a carpeted "high-class dining room."[29]

By the end of 1924 a total of thirty-seven shops and filling stations were located at the Plaza, and six doctors had relocated part or all of their practice to second-floor locations. Brookside shops housed a total of twenty-five shops and four doctors' offices. The Crestwood shops included on that date twenty-four shops and one doctor's office. There were six shops in the Colonial area. The leading tenant was the Piggly Wiggly chain with three locations throughout the Country Club District. Nichols had intended to return to building other neighborhood shopping areas in 1923 after the Plaza was well underway, and the company announced plans for an Armour Shopping Center to be located at Sixty-ninth and Brookside. For a variety of reasons, including negative reactions from surrounding residents, this small center was never built. The land, which Nichols had reserved for shop space in the original plat, was subsequently replatted for residential use.[30]

By May 1925 the company was proceeding with another set of plans for shops at Gregory and Wornall Road. The Romanelli Garden shops were planned and built some five blocks straight south of the proposed Armour shops location. They were styled to resemble a French Provincial village. The first tenants in the Romanelli Center included still another Piggly Wiggly, plus a second grocery store, a pharmacy, a beauty and barber shop, and another cleaning and

29. Scrapbook 8:190, 212–13.
30. Scrapbook 7:214, 79.

This Piggly Wiggly was located in the Romanelli shops at Wornall and Gregory (71st Street). By the late 1920s the chain assumed the slogan "All Over the World" (see slogan under store name in window) to prove their growth. At one time there were more Piggly Wigglys in Nichols's shopping centers than any other tenant. Note the White Rose filling station with its tall prominent pumps, which instead of being hidden, as with the earliest stations, were by the late 1920s a fashionable part of the design of the stations. KC54n53.

dyeing establishment, along with an "artistic" Benzo-Gas filling station.[31]

One of the longest continuously running store promotions in the United States had its debut in December 1925. The Plaza merchants cooperated in putting up Christmas trees along the streets, hanging wreaths on their doors, using evergreen roping to enhance the lines of their buildings, and stringing "thousands of colored lights" along the roof lines. The lighting of the Plaza Lights on Thanksgiving night is now considered to officially open the Christmas season for all of Kansas City. An early view of the Plaza at Christmastime appears on p. 38.[32]

The single instance in which the Nichols Company developed a shopping center that was not immediately adjacent to a residential

31. *CCD Bulletin*, May 1925, 4; August 1925, 4; November 1925, 4. Scrapbook 8:63.
32. Scrapbook 8:104.

section also developed by the company occurred in October 1927 with the opening of the Sixty-third and Troost Center. Located four blocks straight east from the nearest Nichols subdivision at Sixty-third and Holmes, the center was later renamed "The Landing," was remade into an enclosed mall in the 1980s, and remains a Nichols Company property. The first Plaza building to be erected on the south side of Forty-seventh Street was completed in late 1927. Constructed at the southwest corner of Forty-seventh and Broadway, the first section of the Knabe Building extended halfway down Broadway toward a diagonal street originally named Alameda. The building faced east toward a then-undeveloped open square and housed a music studio.[33]

Construction began on the Plaza Theatre during the summer of 1928. Plans had originally been done for the building by Edward Buehler Delk, the architect Nichols had imported from the East to design the Plaza. For some undocumented reason, Delk did not complete the plans. Edward Tanner, who had been working for Nichols as an architect since 1919, completed them and supervised construction of the largest, most ornate movie house outside the downtown area. Also during that summer of 1928, an extension of the Knabe Building was completed. This part of the building had a large meeting hall on its second floor, which was used for some years to house special events for the entire Plaza area. It extended the frontage of the building along Broadway all the way to the corner with Alameda. To the south of that intersection, facing Brush Creek, the Ward Parkway Garage opened in June 1928 with two enclosed stories of parking space for 275 vehicles.[34]

Parking space was even further expanded that year with the addition of two off-street parking stations enclosed by decorative walls and extensive landscaping to disguise their purpose. One parking area was on the open space in front of the Knabe and Balcony buildings; the other was behind the Knabe Building, with entry off Forty-seventh Street. This latter station was later remade into a three-story parking structure, while a second story of parking was

33. Ibid., 85. Alameda Street was renamed Nichols Road after the founder's death in 1950.

34. *CCD Bulletin,* May 1925, 4; Scrapbook 9:194–95, 233–34.

similarly added to the area in front of the Knabe. The most interesting aspect of the enclosed garage on Ward Parkway and the fenced-in parking stations was that there were almost no structures around them at the time—these were parking spaces for buildings largely as yet unbuilt. It might be said that Nichols at times planned for cars even before planning for people.[35]

Part of the purpose of the landlocked Ward Parkway Garage became clear the following spring of 1929 when the company started construction of a two-and-a-half-story building just east of it facing the Parkway. This was planned as an office and shops building to house the headquarters of the Nichols Company. The company reserved for its own use on ground level only one small storefront in the middle of the block; the rest of the company space was on the second floor.

Nichols continued to buy land around the periphery of the Plaza when he had a chance to do so. In 1929 he was able to purchase a few acres on the north side of Forty-seventh Street between Madison and Summit that had been owned by a man who had a small stone-cutting business. Nichols bought the land primarily to control the edges of his development. After acquiring it, he built a filling station for Standard Oil on the site. The Plaza Bank of Commerce opened its doors on the Plaza in 1930 at the northeast corner of Alameda and Central. The building was capped by a small dome done in Spanish style. This bank, which was essentially a branch of Commerce Trust, had both Nichols and J. C. Taylor as directors.[36]

The Plaza continued to expand throughout the Depression, but other elements of the Nichols operation went through retrenchment or changed emphasis. Significant layoffs were necessary in 1932 and 1933. A rental department was opened early in 1931 to handle rentals of properties that had not been sold or had returned to company ownership and to assist the high-rise apartment buildings in getting new residents. These high-rise structures were constructed south of the Plaza along Brush Creek. Nichols's view was that the more people he could get to live near the Plaza, whether in his properties or someone else's, the more potential business would

35. Scrapbook 9:293.
36. Scrapbook 10:28, 92, 138.

be generated for the stores. It turned out to be a wise policy; according to a statement by the treasurer of the company, the only way the firm survived the Depression was with the rental income generated through the shopping centers and the Plaza in particular.[37]

By late 1925, only six years after Nichols had attempted unsuccessfully to interest his fellow subdividers in the possibilities of business-center profits and percentage leases, the editors of a national magazine on land economics thought him sufficiently qualified to write an article outlining his success with such ventures. At that time the Kansas City developer was three years into the development of the Plaza and had five years' experience with the Brookside Center. Much of the article appears to have been based on his study of ways to bring retail business to his suburban residential areas.[38]

In characteristic fashion, Nichols included what he considered important aspects of this type of development work. He cited the following as causes for the increase in outlying business activity during the 1920s: automobile congestion in downtown areas; steel-framed or reinforced skyscrapers, which compacted work areas and increased traffic snarls nearby; the kitchenette and the modern apartment house, which were bringing population concentrations to the outlying areas; the outlying motion-picture theaters, which were stifling downtown movie houses and legitimate theaters; and the development of chain stores. The Kansas City developer observed to his readers that little of the outlying business development that was springing up to meet the demands created by the factors he mentioned was well planned or capable of providing better service than might be had downtown. In fact, he noted that they "frequently are becoming the ugliest, most unsightly and disorderly spots of the entire city." To Nichols, as a realtor, the greatest potential danger was to property values. He cited his old example of changing residential neighborhoods and added to it his new concern about "neglected and blighted former business sections." Indeed, "the very home-life of the city is endangered and should be

37. Ibid., 290–93.
38. Nichols, "The Planning and Control of Outlying Shopping Centers."

protected" from unplanned and uncontrolled growth, which reduced some values as rapidly as it elevated others.[39]

As a solution to these problems, Nichols suggested general standards be applied to further development of outlying business centers. He argued that streets in these shopping areas should be one
hundred feet wide, with paving of sixty to seventy-two feet wide to
allow for diagonal parking. He had followed this along Forty-
seventh Street in the Plaza. All unloading needed to be done at the
rear of the stores to avoid traffic problems, litter, and general disruption of shopping in the fronts. This was expensive since valuable
land had to be given over to what some might consider an unpro-
ductive use. If unloading could not be done at interior unloading
courts, then alleys should be at least twenty-four feet wide to allow
for maximum unloading of two vehicles with room for a third to
pass. If necessary, buildings should be shortened to allow for
unloading room at the rear.

Control of building heights was essential from the start of the
development. Buildings in these types of centers should have one
story, or at most two stories, since rentals were not profitable for
more than two stories in the suburbs. Nichols also argued that
zoning boards should strictly limit the amount of shopping space
allowed in suburban centers in order to prevent overbuilding,
which would cheapen all property values in the area. He urged the
use of smaller blocks and more total street area in the planned
suburban shopping center to diminish traffic and parking problems. Nichols also thought that smaller blocks would increase the
pulling power of particular shops more than would be the case in
larger blocks. In 1925 the Plaza developer was advocating the by-
passing of through traffic *around* outlying shopping centers in order
to reduce traffic problems, but by 1929 he instead favored routing
as much traffic directly *through* the centers as possible in order to
create maximum drawing power.[40]

Nichols argued for the massing of business blocks radiating out
from a center point if possible, rather than being strung along one

39. Ibid., 17–18. The following paragraphs were all drawn from this same article
unless otherwise noted.
40. Nichols, "The Development of Outlying Shopping Centers."

street. He accomplished this well with the Plaza, but many of his smaller centers were more like string developments during the 1920s, although their small size limited what he saw as the drawbacks of developments that extended for several blocks. Again, his major concern with massing as opposed to string development was that the latter exposed far more residential property to potentially injurious neighboring land use.

A strong case was made by Nichols for grouping similar shops and segregating potentially injurious shops such as garages, plumbers' supply shops, or hardware stores. As has been noted, this goal was not always accomplished in the early years of Plaza development, but the company later followed the concept much more rigidly there. Nichols noted that in certain instances, as with furniture stores or music stores that did not have great drawing power, grouping these shops might be detrimental, while the interjection of a Piggly Wiggly type of grocery might stimulate traffic for the furniture store.

To Nichols, the most important thing in planning a shopping center away from the downtown area was parking. As was previously mentioned, the Nichols Company built garages and parking stations in advance of shop buildings in parts of the Plaza; the two fence-enclosed stations constructed in 1929 had space for a total of 500 cars. Nichols spent $26,000 on the fence, decorative features, and landscaping alone. The lots featured built-in sub-drained pavement throughout and lighting served by underground conduits. One of the major uses of the parking stations was reflected in Nichols's requirement that tenant employees had to use the parking stations rather than curb parking. The Nichols Company put a clause in each shop's lease that allowed cancellation of the lease if the owners or employees repeatedly parked in the wrong place. In addition, Nichols felt that the parking stations created an open, parklike space that broke up what would otherwise become oppressive continuous shops.

Nichols believed that overhanging signs should not be allowed. He also argued against billboards, "screaming advertising placards, hideous combinations of color, great scrawling, flaming advertising lettering across an otherwise pleasing storefront or plate glass window." He also argued against any obstruction of the sidewalks without some payment by the offending party. This included sidewalk vendors, newsstands, and signboards. In 1930, however, he allowed root beer stands (for a fee) on Plaza sidewalks.[41]

While Nichols believed that all stores in such a center should conform to a single overall architectural style, he also presented a case for variety in the storefront designs. Nichols argued that the developer should include restrictions to prevent changing color schemes or building designs later, that storefront and street lighting needed to be considered carefully, and that controls should be maintained over the appearance of sides and rears of buildings just as much as over the fronts. He likewise advocated the use of small open spaces, fountains, decorative ornaments, and extensive landscaping to create shopper interest.

Nichols believed that there should be neighborhood shops like Crestwood and Brookside as well as larger centers like the Plaza. The neighborhood centers needed to be approximately one-half-mile apart in densely populated areas, while the larger centers should be two miles or more apart. He advocated a series of graduated steps from a major shopping area like the Plaza to strictly residential areas. The high-rise apartments and the hillside on the south bank of Brush Creek accomplished this to the south, while duplexes helped the transition to the west up the Brush Creek watershed.

Finally, Nichols believed that it was essential for the center to be located where arterial traffic approaches would automatically bring shoppers to or by the center. He accomplished this by placing the Plaza along a boulevard connecting his Country Club District to the downtown area. When the federal highway system was established in the late 1920s, he worked to get the U.S. Highway 50 designation for Johnson Drive coming through the north part of Mission Hills and connecting with Ward Parkway as it crossed the Missouri state line. This meant that motorists coming from Olathe, Lawrence, and other Kansas points to the south and west would approach Kansas City through the Country Club Plaza.[42]

Another way Nichols attempted to help his merchants make money for themselves and for his company was to organize them

41. Ibid., 29; Scrapbook 10:236.
42. Nichols, "The Development of Outlying Shopping Centers," 22–31; Nichols, "Planning and Control of Outlying Shopping Centers," 18–22.

into merchants' associations. The Country Club District Merchants' Association formed in December 1920 to help organize activities for the Colonial shops and the Brookside shops. Crestwood merchants were included in this group when that center opened in 1922. Less than nine months after the first building opened on the Plaza, the Plaza Merchants Association was formed in December 1923. This group started the Christmas lights tradition in 1925. In the late 1920s and early 1930s, the association sponsored bridge lessons and book reviews at the Plaza Theatre, complete with style-show intermissions. At other times, merchants sponsored dog shows in the Knabe Building auditorium, began the continuing tradition of the Plaza Art Fair, adapted the Crestwood Easter bunnies (later augmented by huge plaster-of-Paris eggs) for use on the Plaza, and lighted six-foot Halloween pumpkins. They also hired a Plaza hostess who performed Welcome Wagon–type services for new residents in the district and the apartment buildings surrounding the Plaza. Direct-mail activities included a cooperatively supported newsletter, which was mailed out regularly to a list of "preferred customers" in the towns within a hundred-mile radius of Kansas City.[43]

Ironically, but also understandably, the least attractive business section on land originally developed by Nichols is in Bismark Place. This string development along Main Street south of Forty-ninth Street was built up by others on land Nichols had intended to be residential. When the ten-year restrictions lapsed before World War I, many landowners sold to commercial developers other than Nichols. It has become an uncoordinated and poorly filled business section that contrasts sharply with the highly successful Nichols business developments nearby. Another instance of encroachment by uncontrolled shop space occurred next to Nichols's Sixty-third and Brookside shopping area, where he gained control only of the land immediately adjacent to the streetcar line and on the north side of Sixty-third. Competing developers who already controlled the land directly south put up uncoordinated shops that detract from the overall effect of the area. Nichols almost certainly placed his

43. *CCD Bulletin,* December 15, 1920, 3; "Planning and Management of Nichols Shopping Centers," 50–51.

shops at this location, which is across the street from the Border Star
School, in an effort to protect his neighborhoods to the west and
north from possibly even more detracting residential sections that
might have sprung up. The result is an English-styled Tudor shopping section cheek-by-jowl with a jumble of architecturally uncoordinated shops, but which effectively insulates his residential neighborhoods.[44]

The first Nichols post–World War II commercial development
(and the last completed before his death in 1950) emerged directly
west of Mission Hills at the entrance to his moderately priced subdivision of Prairie Village. It is this commercial development, so
well coordinated with the surrounding residential sections, that sets
Prairie Village apart from Levittown and other postwar suburban
developments in a most distinct way. The Prairie Village Center
forms a transition zone between Mission Hills and Prairie Village
that is at once both subtle and important. The large homes that
dominate the western sections of Mission Hills might well over-
power architecturally the more closely set and less pretentious
houses of the newer section, but the shopping center allows the two
sections to flow into one another without an abrupt change that
might create problems either visually or socially.

Architecturally, the Prairie Village Center has the distinctive
Nichols consistency of design that brings various buildings, each
housing from one to a dozen tenants, together into a comprehensi-
ble whole. At the same time, it does not attempt to reproduce a
period style in the same way as many of Nichols's smaller centers.
Rather, the use of red brick and occasional ornamentation provides
an attractive and serviceable grouping of buildings without calling
attention to the much less distinctive residential architecture of the
surrounding Prairie Village homes.[45]

By contrast, the Levitts simply sold parcels of land to commercial
developers and individual shop and store owners along major thoroughfares without any apparent control or direction to the buyers.
The result, particularly along the Hempstead Pike running east from
the Wantaugh Parkway, is a garish mixture of strip centers, unkempt

44. Based on personal observations by the author, August 24, 1988.
45. Ibid.

vacant lots, and totally uncoordinated shopping emporiums. While the residential sections of Levittown, New York, have been remarkably well maintained and rival in appearance those in Prairie Village in certain ways, these unplanned and jumbled commercial sections give an impression of declining values that easily could invade the no-longer-suburban sections of Levittown homes.[46]

This same result is highly unlikely in the original areas of Prairie Village where Nichols managed to control land use. There the careful transitions from residential to commercial uses, the strategic plantings of trees and shrubs, and the incorporation of a passing creek into a protective boundary combine to present residents and visitors a picture of residential calm in close, but separated, proximity to the second-largest shopping center built by the Nichols Company prior to 1950.

Whereas J. C. Nichols was primarily a synthesizer of ideas in his residential developments, he was without question an innovator in the development of attractive, profitable, and long-lasting shopping centers. His use of newly constructed nearby apartments to build a local population while at the same time appealing to the newly mobile auto-borne shoppers was a successful planning technique that has been overlooked by many who have evaluated his impact on the development of shopping centers. The Country Club Plaza was both the first regional shopping center in the United States and a neighborhood center as well. Like the downtown retailers before him, Nichols learned that the best location was at traffic intersections. Unlike the downtown department-store managers who placed their confidence in traffic generated by streetcars and interurbans, Nichols tried to attract automobile traffic through the city's boulevard system and the nationally funded highway system. When after World War II this meant constructing multilevel parking garages to handle the volume of customers and workers generated by the coming of a Sears store to the Plaza, the company did not hesitate to do so.

Ultimately, the most striking thing about Nichols shopping areas was their staying power, just as it was with his residential neighborhoods. In the late 1980s, more commercial and office construc-

46. Based on personal observations of the author, July 2, 1988.

Adequate parking was always a major concern for Nichols in his shopping areas. After World War II, he had this triple-deck parking garage built along 47th Street to accommodate both shoppers and office workers in the first office building on the Plaza—the Skelley Building. By 1990, the offices have proliferated both in areas controlled by the Nichols Company and in adjacent areas over which they have no control. Other parking garages of similar style have been built, and most of the office structures have their own parking in basement garages. Note the decorative ornaments designed to divert the shopper from the utilitarian use to which the structure is put. KC54n61.

tion was going on in the Country Club Plaza area than anywhere else inside the city limits of Kansas City, Missouri. The Plaza had become, for all intents and purposes, the new downtown of Kansas City. Sharing in this rise in interest, the nearby Nichols neighborhoods were holding their property values just as securely as the shopping centers. Without question, Nichols's shopping centers were the heart of the success of his planned residential communities.

9

ADVERTISING OR SPIRIT BUILDING?

Community Features in a Planned Subdivision

> There has been a vast deal of speculation by preachers and teachers of
> late on that familiar theme, "The Matter With America." None of
> them seems to have a cure-all for all the things that ail the rest of us,
> but there is one general conclusion on which all modern moralists
> agree. It is that Americans need to build their lives on a more solid
> foundation of homely, wholesome home life with relevant neigh-
> borliness and closely interwoven community interest. The carrying
> out of that idea is the very breath of life of the Country Club Dis-
> trict.
>
> —J. C. Nichols, 1920

One of the aspects of real estate subdivision development that
J. C. Nichols enjoyed most and accomplished best was the creation of a community spirit among his residents. This type of activity was designed to accomplish at least two goals: to build a high
degree of satisfaction among those who were already lot owners
or residents, and to create a picture of an active and enjoyable life-
style for those who had not yet purchased in the Country Club
District.

Strictly speaking, "community work," as Nichols liked to call it,
was expected to help sell lots and build houses in the district. That
this activity also resulted in a heightened sense of identification with
the neighborhood is another instance in which Nichols's promotion
of his own interests turned out to have a positive outcome for many
of his residents.

An element of direction by an all-knowing hand may seem present in all this. Nichols was attempting to increase interest in his
residential neighborhoods by creating value through what were
essentially public relations ventures. In many instances he described
these as "services" both to residents and to the public at large, but

they remained conscious efforts to bring more people to the doors of his real estate offices.

In many ways the methods Nichols used to advertise his subdivisions would be classified as public relations in the post–World War II era. The term did not exist in pre–World War I America, so he and other subdividers called these types of promotions "community features." This category of promotional activities covered a multitude of efforts by the company and district residents to develop institutions and events that would involve residents and gain publicity for the subdivisions. Everything from the development of private schools to the creation of interest in bird life to the sponsorship of Christmas celebrations, school athletic competitions, and flower shows was part of the Nichols repertoire. Sometimes he borrowed ideas for community features from other subdividers; in other cases, he conceived his own projects.[1]

When Nichols was with his fellow subdividers in their annual meetings during the World War I era, he felt relaxed enough to share with them the ways in which he justified many of the actions he took. The aspect of "community features" was a part of his development work that he thoroughly enjoyed and that he believed paid rich dividends. In 1917, Nichols was completing the first phase of his community development work, in which he and his company were attempting to create a positive impression toward his subdivisions in the minds of Kansas City residents at large. At that point, he perceived the value of community features primarily in the satisfaction felt by residents who had chosen to buy from him and move to the area. His methods centered on keeping up with the activities of residents, sending letters of congratulation or condolence when appropriate, and keeping in personal contact with as many as possible through the clubs and organizations to which Nichols belonged. In 1917, that meant he was on the rolls of twenty-eight clubs or organizations. He attended the club meetings as often as possible and used their membership lists to develop contact lists for his salesmen.[2]

1. Nichols, "Suburban Subdivisions with Community Features"; Kissell, "Community Features," 124–37.
2. 1917 *Proceedings*, 214–23.

His goal was to attract as many people as possible to his subdivisions and to keep them there. The first part of the goal was common to all subdividers; the second was what set Nichols apart from the average subdivider. He was so committed to having people stay in his houses and in Kansas City that he would call men who had announced publicly they were moving and try to convince them to stay. He told a group of real estate men in 1916 that it was "a deplorable thing, especially in our western towns and counties, that any man will offer his home for sale." Too often, Nichols believed, the man's view was that he would willingly sell his home if there was profit in it. Nichols cited an instance in which someone had asked a man whether he would sell his home. "You bet your life," came the response. "I will sell anything I have except my wife and children."[3]

To Nichols this was a shameful attitude because of the effect it had on children. "It is an awful thing to raise children and have them think, 'Daddy doesn't own anything, he is here today and there tomorrow.' They have no playmates with any lasting feeling in life, they have no chums of their youth." To counteract this, Nichols had his company send out postcards to both prospects and current residents "with a picture of a quiet residential street where children could take their naps in the afternoon." Nichols summed up his philosophy for a national real estate magazine in 1920:

> It is the belief of the founders [of the Country Club District] that there is no safer way of bringing about a constant increase in value in its remaining holdings than the creation of an enthusiastic belief and assurance among the residents of the district that they and their children may continue to live safely and comfortably in their same house and same location in this rapidly growing city for a long term of years.[4]

The Kansas City developer capitalized upon the mobility of his fellow citizens in luring them from old neighborhoods into his subdivisions, yet he argued for breaking that cycle of mobility in the future. With the attitude he expressed in 1920, Nichols forced himself constantly to open new subdivisions as soon as his older

3. Nichols, "Financial Effect of Good Planning," 102.
4. "Kansas City Country Club District."

areas were built up. To a remarkable degree, given the stability of his neighborhoods throughout the twentieth century, he achieved his goal. Nichols appears to have been convinced that he would make more money if the people who moved into his houses or bought his land were satisfied with their choice and then told friends and former neighbors how they felt. If the residents felt that way about his neighborhoods, they would probably recruit their friends directly or indirectly to join them.

The result of these policies by 1924 was that Nichols believed that "very few people in our subdivision would sell to an undesirable purchaser." Although just who this "undesirable purchaser" might be was never clearly identified, Nichols probably meant anyone who did not fit in socially or economically with the others to whom he had sold land. Thus the overt purpose of community-centered programs was to build a sense of belonging on the part of his residents, but the underlying reason was to bolster land values by reducing the turnover of residents in the already developed parts of the Country Club District. Nichols was primarily in the business of selling land for new houses, and secondarily of building new houses on those lots. His real estate firm did handle resales of houses in the Country Club District and in other parts of the city, but this was the least important aspect of his business. Nichols saw this brokerage business as a service to new buyers more than as a source of income.[5]

In a candid moment with his fellow developers in 1918, Nichols admitted that he had not achieved his goal of community involvement by everyone in his subdivisions. Many of his residents were, like himself, already heavily involved in organizations, and affiliation with yet another club or activity was the last thing this type of resident wanted. They wished to come home to relax. Also, there was the class factor. Nichols had to recognize that for some, "getting close to the people in their neighborhoods does not mean much to them; they belong to another grade or social set."[6]

From his earliest advertising, Nichols often associated his development with an adjacent organization to which he did not initially belong. The proximity of the Kansas City Country Club (KCCC)

5. Nichols, "Suburban Subdivisions with Community Features," 17.
6. 1918 *Proceedings*, 290–91.

provided Nichols with the trademark he needed. As early as the fall of 1908, he referred to his subdivisions as "The Country Club District." He got the streetcar company to rename its Westport line as the Country Club line, and his name for the district gradually was accepted. In 1988 the bus route that followed the old car line still carried the Country Club designation, even though the KCCC had moved to Kansas years ago.[7]

The KCCC traces its origins back to an informal organization called the Hyde Park Country Club, founded by some Scots golfers in the early 1890s. The Hyde Park neighborhood attracted defectors from Quality Hill in the late 1880s and early 1890s, while other new residents to the city moved into speculation homes built by Jarvis, Conklin, and other developers. Among these were some Scots accountants who had brought golf with them from Scotland. These Scotsmen recruited some of their neighbors to play golf on a nine-hole course laid out on a flat pasture east of Hyde Park in Kenwood Addition. By the spring of 1896, these golfers thought they needed a full eighteen-hole course, but the Hyde Park neighborhood did not have the space they required.[8]

One neighbor and fellow golfer owned land south of Brush Creek on a high, flat plain that had previously been best known as the site of the Civil War battle of Westport. Hugh Ward donated part of his family's cow pasture south of Brush Creek to the small golf group in 1896 on condition that the newly organized KCCC would simply pay the taxes. Thus, the setting for J. C. Nichols was erected some nine years before he sold his first lot. Initially, membership in the KCCC was limited to one hundred. The first officers were all northern men who had moved to Kansas City since the Civil War, except for the president, Hugh Ward. All lived on Quality Hill or in Hyde Park in 1896.[9]

The KCCC served as the community force for the first eight years of Nichols's development. By 1913, however, it was proving impossible to get "some of the very best men in our section" into the KCCC because of the selectivity of the current membership. Nich-

7. Nichols Co. advertisement, *Kansas City Star,* October 11, 1908, 18C.
8. Scrapbook 1:132A.
9. Ibid., 132A–32B.

ols asked E. H. Bouton of Roland Park how to control membership so that "in after years any good desirable man in the Country Club District can become a member of this club." Bouton explained that his method with the founding of the Baltimore Country Club (also in 1896) was to get himself on the board of governors of the club. He had donated the land for the clubhouse and golf course. Bouton explained to Nichols that he simply told the other governors "at the outset that I should expect that practically any person that I would possibly sell property to in Roland Park would make a good member in the Country Club."[10]

Bouton correctly recognized that the membership selection process of any country club would be one of "friends picking friends." Because friendships were largely a function of economic and social similarity, Bouton believed that the type of person buying land in Nichols's district would definitely be acceptable to others of similar background. He concluded, "I feel quite sure that this would take care of itself once you got it started the right way." Nichols followed Bouton's advice, for when his new country club—the Mission Hills Club—was opened in 1915, Nichols was on the board of directors. He controlled membership through influence rather than by dictate.[11]

Nichols did not fail to recognize the one geographical necessity in determining the location of the Mission Hills Club. The golf course could be in Kansas, where Nichols owned land and had access to more; that was no problem. The difficulty arose because the state of Kansas had enacted statewide prohibition in 1880. Nichols needed a clubhouse physically located in Missouri so that alcoholic drinks could be served. The solution lay in having the clubhouse located on a small parcel of land purchased from the Hugh Ward estate on the east side of State Line Road, approximately at Fiftieth Street. The Mission Hills Country Club was a two-state club from the start.[12]

Between the KCCC and the Mission Hills Club, the demand for status-bearing membership in country clubs was satisfied until the

10. Letter from J. C. Nichols to E. H. Bouton, November 21, 1913, Roland Park Papers. See also reply from Bouton to Nichols, November 25, 1913.

11. Scrapbook 3:75.

12. The necessity for this arrangement was mentioned by Nichols in a letter to Bouton, November 21, 1913, Roland Park Papers.

mid-1920s, but the demand for golf courses exceeded the supply somewhat earlier. In 1918 Nichols organized a Community Golf Club on land he had arranged for purchase by the KCCC. Adjacent to the Mission Hills Club course, the new KCCC site was made necessary by the fact that Mrs. Ward, by that time remarried to the president of the University of Missouri, Dr. A. Ross Hill, had notified the KCCC that she wanted its land back.[13]

Nichols had a golf expert from Chicago lay out the course. Membership in the Community Golf Club was open to any resident of the district for an annual fee of thirty dollars, with five dollars charged for each additional family member who wanted to play. By 1923, so many members wanted to join the Community Golf Club that Nichols had to lay out another course for a fourth organization, the Armour Fields Golf Club. In little over a month, more than one hundred families had joined the new club.[14]

When the KCCC moved to its Kansas-side location after the enactment of national prohibition in 1920, Nichols arranged for a new site for the now-displaced Community Golf Club. The members, with the help of Nichols, organized themselves into the Indian Hills Country Club. Exclusive membership was thus assured for this group as well. The effect of this arrangement was measured in 1952–1953 when a research group from Boston measured social status and its sources in Kansas City. They found that these three country clubs "had themselves become the rungs of a finely graded social ladder." The authors of the study substituted fictional names for the actual club names. In the following excerpt, "First Jackson" represents the KCCC, "Missoukana" stands for Mission Hills, and "Silver Hills" is the equivalent for the Indian Hills Country Club.

A society reporter quipped, "Golfdom's fairways are Kansas City's social stairways"; and all higher status citizens recognized that "anyone in the First Jackson Country Club is automatically top rung and higher up the social ladder than anyone in Missoukana." In turn, Missoukana, the country club ranked second, was widely perceived as enough better than Silver Hills so that "anybody in Silver Hills would quit it in a

13. Scrapbook 5:18, 49; Scrapbook 7:48.
14. Scrapbook 5:18, 49.

minute if he were asked to join Missoukana." Silver Hills members were described as "well-to-do," "socially very active," and "almost big wheels but not quite."

This section of the report concluded that all other country clubs in the Kansas City area ranked lower in social status than the ones mentioned.[15]

By the mid-1920s it had become fairly common for subdivisions to include or be built around golf courses. In some cases, such as in the Broadmoor subdivision in Seattle, Washington, and the Country Club District developed by the Perkinswood Realty Company in Warren, Ohio, course membership was part of the homesite purchase. The purchasers each received a share of stock in the club. A $100 initiation fee was part of closing costs at Broadmoor in order to create a permanent fund for the organization. As is evident by the name chosen by the Perkinswood group, Nichols's name—Country Club District—was sometimes used along with the idea itself.[16]

The creation of *the* country club for the city was central to several developments by Nichols's contemporaries in other states. Bouton had the Baltimore Club in Roland Park, Prather had the Dallas Club in Highland Park, Kissell had the Springfield Club near his Ohio developments, and the Palos Verdes subdivision near Los Angeles had golf courses with country clubs as a central element. Lake Forest had its Onwentsia Club, one of the most exclusive golf clubs in the country. No developer in the United States but Nichols, however, could boast of four golf courses within the boundaries of his property in 1930.[17]

Very likely the second-most-important factor in distinguishing Nichols's developments from others in Kansas City was the presence of the best private *and* public schools in the city. One of the things that made the last week of April 1908 special for Nichols was the

15. Scrapbook 7:42–43, 48; Coleman and Neugarten, *Social Status in the City,* 41. The equivalents of the fictional names with their real counterparts have been communicated to the writer in several interviews with Coleman.

16. "Golf Courses in Subdivisions."

17. A fairly complete summary of the founding of country clubs with their reliance on golf as a common denominator is in Jackson, *Crabgrass Frontier,* 97–99.

land deal between his clients the Yeomans and St. Theresa's Academy. This land purchase made the agency arrangement between Nichols and the Yeomans possible. Possibly even more important was the amount of publicity occasioned by the move of the girls' school from Quality Hill to the County Club District. St. Theresa's was the most prestigious Catholic girls' school in the city, and many prominent Protestant families as well as the leading Catholic families sent daughters there. Miss Barstow's School was probably even more elite than St. Theresa's, but not by much.

Far more important in the long run, however, both Country Day (later Pembroke Country Day) for boys and Sunset Hill School for girls (now combined as Pembroke–Sunset Hill School) originated in the midst of the Country Club District. The widow of the KCCC land donor, Vassie James Ward, was instrumental in the founding of these private schools in 1910 and 1913, respectively. Nichols donated sites and arranged favorable land purchases for these schools, which provided college preparatory training for the children of Kansas City's elite for generations. Though the idea was incorporated into the name of only one of the two schools, both were inspired by the country day school movement of the turn of the century. This type of school allowed students to live at home while receiving the type of education previously available only from residential preparatory schools in the East. It is significant that the Gilman School, founded in 1896 in Roland Park, was the very first of this movement. While Nichols always had some ambivalence about private schools, he nevertheless recognized a drawing card when it was placed before him. The first home of Pembroke Country Day was in the historic Wornall homestead, which Nichols had bought from the Wornall family along with several acres of surrounding land for homesites. Later he and Mrs. Ward collaborated in expanding the prospects of the schools by giving them excellent locations and mentioning them in advertising.[18]

One other private school claimed the loyalties of residents. Visitation Catholic Church sponsored a parochial school for its parish at Fifty-first and Main in the old Bismark Place subdivision. Visitation

18. Scrapbook 2:159, 167; Henry M. Hyde, "Roland Park–Guilford: An Appreciation," 9, 20; and see 1919 *Proceedings,* 686–87.

School opened in the fall of 1916. Within two years, enrollment pressures forced the construction of an addition, completed in March 1919. Nichols's Catholic population, while always in the minority, was well served by St. Theresa's and Visitation School. Some developers across the country totally banned Catholics from their subdivisions; Bouton at Roland Park did not favor them, although he had no written restrictions against them. Nichols, on the other hand, had a Catholic presence in his neighborhoods from the beginning and stated that he had no problems with them at all.[19]

While several of the developers who met for the first conferences near the time of World War I primarily encouraged private schools in their developments, Nichols gave at least equal time to public schools. At the same time that Mrs. Ward was getting the Country Day School started at the Wornall mansion in 1910, the Kansas City school board was moving ahead of the city annexation proceedings by placing E. C. White School at Fifty-first and Oak streets on the extreme east edge of the Country Club District. In 1913 the school board moved the school to a site provided at a subsidized price by Nichols at Forty-ninth and Main streets, where the Plaza Library is now located. The school board acquired the site for William Cullen Bryant School at Fifty-seventh and Wornall Road in 1915. This school still operated in 1990 at the same location and served as an anchor for the public schools in the most exclusive section of Kansas City.[20]

In 1922 the school board, with Nichols as a member, purchased fifteen acres from the Nichols Company as a site for what was initially referred to as Wornall High School. Construction began in February 1925. The first classes were held in the almost completed first unit the following September, with 956 students attending during the first year. Southwest High School, as the school district finally named it, went on to become the school showpiece of the district during the later 1920s and 1930s. It had outstanding sports

19. 1917 *Proceedings*, B73.
20. Scrapbook 2:149. Nichols's policy with regard to schools was to sell land to the school board at a somewhat reduced rate. See 1917 *Proceedings*, B72; Scrapbook 3:160.

teams and was in 1930 considered to be "among the most admired college-preparatory institutions in the United States."[21]

In the same year that the ground was purchased on the Missouri side for Southwest High School, Johnson County, Kansas, organized what was first called Shawnee Mission Rural High School. Located just west of Mission Hills, it was available to students from the Country Club District living on the Kansas side. Most Mission Hills children, however, attended Bryant and Southwest High public schools, or Country Day and Sunset Hill private schools, on the Missouri side throughout the 1920s. The reputation of Southwest High was too good to ignore. Also, the Kansas City School District did not charge extra tuition to out-of-district students during that period. After World War II, the pendulum swung toward the Kansas-side schools. The Shawnee Mission School District and its East High School in particular took over the top ranking among public schools in the Kansas City area. That district draws a large portion of its students from Nichols's neighborhoods. The attraction was strong enough in the late 1970s for one commentator to state that the difference in school quality was responsible for most of a 10 to 20 percent differential in property values between lower-valued Missouri-side and higher-valued Kansas-side Nichols neighborhoods.[22]

Following his concern for the golf and country clubs he organized and the schools he subsidized, J. C. Nichols was most interested in getting churches to move to or be established in his subdivisions. Actually, he subsidized the churches as well as the schools, but in a different way. With the schools he sold the land at a discount; in the case of churches, Nichols chose to sell the land at full price and then to make a substantial contribution to their building fund.[23]

It took seven years after offering his first house for sale before any church would make a decision in his favor. When it happened, however, it was the best possible church to achieve the effect Nichols wanted. Three churches had dominated Quality Hill life. The Roman Catholic Cathedral and Grace and Holy Trinity Cathedral

21. Scrapbook 7:262; Scrapbook 8:61; Jackson, *Crabgrass Frontier,* 178.
22. Scrapbook 6:187; see Mayer, *The Builders,* 59–60.
23. 1917 *Proceedings,* B72.

(Episcopal) were there because cathedral churches were always downtown in large American cities. There was not then, and has not been since, any plan to move them elsewhere. These were not residential churches; they were the seat of the bishop. The third church, Second Presbyterian, was of a different polity. Affiliated with the northern branch of the Presbyterian denomination, Second was very much a church that drew from its surrounding neighborhood. Most residents of Quality Hill had been born north of the Mason-Dixon line, and many were Presbyterian.

In 1900 the fire there destroyed Convention Hall just months before the National Democratic Convention was to meet there also destroyed the Second Presbyterian building at Fifteenth and Broadway. There had been some movement out of Quality Hill by this time, so the church leadership took a census of the membership to determine the best location. The elders of the congregation found in 1900 that 129 families listed as church members lived within walking distance of the site at Fifteenth and Broadway. This was enough of a core of membership for the Session of the Church to decide to rebuild at that location.[24]

Just ten years later, in 1910, the church's governing body discovered that only five member families still lived within walking distance. They considered consolidating with a sister congregation in Westport, which would have put them closer to the members who had moved to the Hyde Park neighborhood a few blocks away. In 1912 the leadership decided they could delay no longer. As one put it, while their members had moved south, "Quality Hill has become a district of boarding houses." Another elder stated that it was "better that we should follow our own membership and keep them together."[25]

Following their congregation meant a move to Nichols's Country Club District and a site at Fifty-fifth and Oak streets. They started a building campaign and opened their first unit in November 1915. Being first had its advantages; by 1922 they had eight hundred members, more than three hundred larger than any other congregation in the district. The congregation has not moved from the Fifty-

24. *Kansas City Star,* September 22, 1912, 14A.
25. Ibid.; also November 10, 1912, 11C.

Country Club Christian Church serves as something of a cathedral for the district. Located on Ward Parkway, its Gothic windows and high-reaching spires certainly invoke a feeling of awe. The Christian Church, of course, has no bishops or even district superintendents who might sit ex cathedra in the pulpit of this imposing structure. As a result, it has tended to be more famous for its membership and architecture than for its clerical leadership. KC54n38.

fifth and Oak location to the present time, which means that they have worshiped in Nichols's area much longer than they previously occupied their Quality Hill locations.[26]

Once Second Presbyterian had taken the lead, other churches began to follow suit. Visitation Catholic opened its church building and parochial school in 1916 as a new parish. That same year, an Episcopal parish from the northeast section bought land at Wornall and Meyer Boulevard. St. Andrew's Episcopal, as the parish renamed itself, had become the most elite church in the district by 1952, followed by Second Presbyterian. The next congregation to organize and the next to achieve a relatively high status as a social church began with a meeting in the Brookside Community Hall above the shopping center in the fall of 1920. This was Nichols's own church—Country Club Christian Church. Nichols had been

26. Scrapbook 3:175; Scrapbook 6:103.

raised a Presbyterian, but from 1920 forward he seems to have been more at home in the Christian Church (Disciples of Christ). In the 1952 study of social status in Kansas City, the researchers interviewed prominent Kansas Citians about this and other congregations. One interviewee described the position of Country Club Christian Church (called the Ward Parkway Christian Church in the study) in Kansas City society:

> The Ward Parkway Christian Church was founded by twelve millionaires, and they have more millionaires in that congregation than in any other in Kansas City. It's right in the heart of the wealthy neighborhood, and when anybody moves into town who is high up in the executive ladder he joins that church—that is, if he isn't strongly committed to some other denomination. That's the church to be with for business advantage.

J. C. Nichols was one of the twelve millionaires. The Wornall Road Baptist Church was also organized in 1920, with Country Club Methodist and Country Club Congregational coming shortly thereafter. The Sixth Church of Christ Scientist was organized about the same time and moved into their building at Sixty-sixth Street Terrace and Wornall Road in October 1925.[27]

Nichols was as interested in developing community events as in attracting other institutions that might accomplish similar goals. Just as he had done with some of the golf and country clubs, the developer used any opportunity to attract attention to his subdivisions. One of the earliest "community features" organized by Nichols was his bird campaign of 1912–1914. It was essentially a public relations campaign designed to get residents and potential buyers to think about the beauties of nature available in the Country Club District. The expressed goal was to build birdhouses, provide nesting grounds, create interest in birdwatching, and generate wide

27. Scrapbook 3:242; Coleman and Neugarten, *Social Status,* 50; Scrapbook 4:167; Scrapbook 5:253; Scrapbook 8:62. On the rankings of churches in a social sense, see Coleman and Neugarten, *Social Status in the City,* 49–50, and Scrapbook 5:119.

awareness of the presence and activities of the bird population in the district.

Nichols started by experimenting with cigar-box birdhouses in his own backyard. He found a source for ready-made birdhouses that were well adapted to the types of birds commonly found in the area, and he had these shipped in to be sold at cost to residents. Similarly, he had his nurserymen obtain trees, rose bushes, shrubs, ornamental grasses, vines, and bulbs that could be provided at cost to residents both for beautification and for nesting sites for the birds. Next he found a government pamphlet describing birds and their habits. He distributed thousands of these pamphlets to residents and potential buyers and to doctors' offices, teachers, ministers, and others. He had his salesmen put pamphlets in waiting rooms about the city. Each was stamped with the inscription "Compliments of the J. C. Nichols Company, Developers of the Country Club District." Postcards extolling the wonderful contributions of birds to humanity were sent to a mailing list of 15,000 people in and about Kansas City. A few weeks later, the company sent a postcard to the same list that served as a coupon to be returned for a booklet on homes in the Country Club District. Nichols received 5,700 replies. He had his salesmen check the replies for the respondents' financial condition by using the city directory, which showed residence location and employment status. The booklets cost the company fifty cents each and were mailed to all respondents who appeared able to buy.[28]

To complement the campaign, Nichols sponsored a lecture by a visiting naturalist. A bird census conducted in 1914 revealed the presence of over one thousand birdhouses in the district and fifty different species of birds. Nichols offered prizes to schoolchildren for the best birdhouse designs and for viewing the first arrival of different varieties of birds in the spring. The bird campaign was one of the most copied activities Nichols ever began. His fellow subdividers at Forest Hills, Roland Park, St. Francis Woods, and the Kissell Developments of Springfield, Ohio, all used the concept in one way or another to call attention to their developments.[29]

28. *Kansas City Star,* December 7, 1913, 14A; 1917 *Proceedings,* 185–90.
29. *Kansas City Star,* December 7, 1913, 14A, and August 2, 1914, 11C; *CCD*

The bird campaign did not end in 1914, however; Nichols promoted the idea in different ways until the 1920s. In one of the earliest issues of the *Country Club District Bulletin,* he expounded on the benefits of birds in reducing the insect population. He reminded his residents, "You cannot be a friend to both the bird and its enemy, the cat. It is hard to conceive that any tenderhearted person would harbor a house cat when it will deliberately destroy the little birds." At the same time, he ordered the delay of the spring mowing of vacant lots in order to give the meadowlarks sufficient nesting time. He did not tolerate boys shooting at birds and asked for residents to report to him any instances of this activity.[30]

Just as he was getting the bird campaign underway, Nichols developed a way to stimulate interest in lawns and gardens. During the summer of 1912 he sponsored the first lawn beautification contest for the district, offering cash prizes to winners in each of three categories based on property frontage. The following year Nichols drafted more well-defined rules. Consideration of the arrangement of plants constituted 35 percent of the score, while judges allotted up to 15 percent for flowers arranged to bloom consecutively and another 15 percent for the condition of the newly mowed grass. The artistic use of flower pots and boxes accounted for up to 10 percent of the rating, while the assessment of the condition of the rear yard and the front parking comprised the last 25 percent. Using these rules or variations upon them, judges rated Country Club District lawns from 1912 until the 1930s.[31]

Other developers with whom Nichols had regular contact, including Bouton of Roland Park and Jemison of Birmingham, Alabama, copied the lawn contest idea. Bouton did not adopt the practice immediately, however. He indicated to Nichols at one point in 1918 that he had resisted the idea up to then because he wondered how the contests went over with "the important people of your subdivision." Nichols responded with an example of one owner of a $35,000 house on a large lot who dearly loved the idea of having people drive by to point out his prize-winning lawn and

Bulletin, March 1922, 3; Kissell, "Community Features," 128–29.

30. *CCD Bulletin,* May 15, 1919, 2.

31. Scrapbook 2:128–29.

flower garden. Bouton was amazed: "I was associating that kind of thing more with industrial communities, wage-earning communities, than with homes of the better sort. I have supposed that our people [in Roland Park and Guilford] would not take any interest in the matter largely on that account." Later, he discovered that it worked for him, even in elite Guilford.[32]

Robert Jemison's exclusive developments in and around Birmingham were only part of that company's enterprises, for it also built wage-earner homes for black and white workers in the steel mills. His company offered prizes for the best vegetable gardens in all of their neighborhoods. The response was enthusiastic: "The people did not resent [the offering of prizes in the different neighborhoods] at all. The people in the best sections took the same degree of interest in that district as the negro did in his."[33]

Nichols planned competitive flower shows as early as 1918. An annual flower show was instituted in April 1921. Nichols held the show and judging in the Brookside Community Hall during the early years. Women and men arranged their best spring blooms in their favorite vases, which were then set apart in categories on tables in the hall for the judges and their neighbors to see. It turned out to be an excellent way to promote flower gardening in the district. This was helpful to Nichols because the flower gardens made existing homes seem more beautiful to prospects. The small cost of prizes and a traveling trophy were more than repaid in improved appearance and heightened morale among many of the female residents, for whom this contest became a highlight of the year. Nichols even sponsored a dandelion contest for children in the schools of the district. They were to pull all the dandelions they could, put them in a bag, and bring them to school in the spring of 1921. The winners were photographed standing behind the mounds of dandelions. Nichols occasionally sponsored essay contests in the schools as well. In 1919, he offered prizes for the best themes written on the subject "Why Father and Mother Should Own Their Own Home." Prizes

32. 1918 *Proceedings*, 296.
33. Ibid., 297–98.

included having the picture of the winner printed in the *Kansas City Star*.[34]

Possibly the most successful activity of this sort was the series of games sponsored by Nichols each spring for the students in the schools of the district. Sometimes he included neighboring schools such as those from Westport so that the parents could see what fun children in the Country Club District schools could have. These events were called "Community Field Days." Nichols Company personnel planned the field days in conjunction with an executive committee composed of a representative from each participating school. Every school selected one particular event or display that would show off its abilities, and it also had the right to enter representatives in the general events.[35]

Nichols attended each field day personally to award prizes and to congratulate the winners and runners-up. The first field day was on May 12, 1921, with six schools and one kindergarten participating. The youngsters engaged in races and relays that included three-legged races, sack races, potato races, handicap races, dashes, pole vaulting, kiddie car races for the pre-schoolers, broad jumps, and tug-of-wars. There was a ceremonial winding of the Maypole, an idea borrowed from St. Francis Woods in California. In only three years the event grew from its small beginnings to an involvement of over three thousand youngsters from eleven public and private schools. It continued to be a popular and relatively low-cost affair for the company. Nichols continued it well into the 1930s, after he had dropped some other community features because of the Depression.[36]

Another contest was the annual model boat regattas normally held at the lily pond in the middle of Ward Parkway just north of Meyer Circle. These were elimination races by youngsters with model sailboats they had built. Begun in the early 1920s, the regatta was switched to a new location, Lake Hiwassee, in 1927. Because the boats were small and intricate, the building and sailing often

34. Scrapbook 5:241, 232–33; *CCD Bulletin*, April 15, 1919, 4.

35. Nichols, "Suburban Subdivisions with Community Features," 11.

36. Scrapbook 5:223–27; 1917 *Proceedings*, 153–56; Nichols, "Suburban Subdivisions with Community Features," 11.

Community Field Days were major events for the district throughout the 1920s and into the Depression years. They were not really track meets since the events were designed to include boys and girls from kindergarten through high school, who could participate in regular school dress. Note the boys, many in ties and knickers, preparing to wheel the girls, who wear full dresses. The abbreviated costumes of later school-coordinated athletic events would probably have shocked Nichols and prevented his sponsorship, given his questioning in 1919 of the morality of boys and girls swimming in the same pool. The events were usually conducted on the grounds of the private Country Day (now Pembroke Hill) School. KC54n39.

turned out to be a father-son affair, which was even better as far as Nichols was concerned. The developer seemed to have little trouble devising activities that would appeal to the female residents, but male-oriented activities were seemingly more difficult to formulate.[37]

The games and contests were all designed to do at least two things: to increase the interest of current residents in their homes, neighborhoods, and schools, and to draw attention to the active community life available in the Country Club District. Nichols was a man who tried to find the monetary value in almost everything he did. To him, the games and contests were valuable tools for keeping people who bought his lots and houses. Otherwise, if they became dissatisfied and sold their houses, they would place their older homes directly in competition with the new houses and lots Nichols was constantly developing. The Community Field Days cost

37. Scrapbook 9:78.

between $200 and $250 per year, which made them some of the cheapest advertising he did. If these activities also brought inquiries from potential buyers, so much the better.

At Christmastime in 1919, Nichols organized what became a tradition through the 1920s—a hayrack Christmas caroling party. Using an approach he borrowed from Forest Hills, Nichols had the carolers cover themselves with white sheets so that the actual caroling was done anonymously. Looking very much like members of the Ku Klux Klan, Nichols, some of his salesmen, and their families went through many parts of the district on their mule-drawn wagons that Christmas Eve of 1919. By 1921 the tradition had grown to include a Christmas pageant held about a large decorated tree at Fifty-fourth and Brookside. The carolers then embarked on nine wagons provided by the company, leaving a candle at each home they caroled. Afterward the wagons brought them to the Country Club Coffee Shop in the Colonial shops for coffee and donuts. The entire event in 1921 was coordinated by the sales department, which gave an indication of the importance attached to such activities.[38]

Nichols discovered that sometimes the most effective way to stimulate activities was to create an organization that would do most of the work. Immediately after he returned from the Developers' meeting in 1919, where he had expressed doubts about his future as a developer in Kansas City, he formed the Women's Community Council as an auxiliary to the evolving Country Club District Improvement Association. To support the work of the Women's Council, he began publication of the *Country Club District Bulletin* in April. By September he had hired a young woman to serve as community secretary. Her job would be to carry out many of the ideas formulated by the Women's Council, as well as to develop activities on her own. The success of the Women's Council in stimulating activities between 1919 and 1921 was largely due to the efforts of the community secretary and Mrs. A. I. Beach, the wife of the future mayor of Kansas City, who served as chairwoman of the council during this period.[39]

38. *CCD Bulletin*, December 15, 1919, 1; ibid., January 15, 1920, 1; reference on Forest Hills is taken from 1918 *Proceedings,* 663, 679; Scrapbook 6:48–49.

39. *CCD Bulletin*, April 15, 1919, 2, and September 1, 1919, 1.

284 J. C. NICHOLS AND THE SHAPING OF KANSAS CITY

Initially, the Women's Community Council publicized ideas and concerns of many of the female residents. In 1919 this included concern about speeding automobiles and the use of muffler cut-outs on cars and motorcycles. At Christmastime that year the council advocated using electric lights on Christmas trees and noted that "lighted candles on the Christmas tree are no longer in favor because of the fire danger." As time went on, the tactic changed from making statements to taking action that would hopefully alleviate the problems or get the proposed idea accomplished. Many of these women were concerned about "the servant problem," which involved a lack of women who were willing to work as domestic servants after World War I. The solution of the Women's Council was to establish an employment exchange, where women who did want to work in this line could be paired with women who wanted to hire domestic help.[40]

During the winter of 1920, as a consequence of the adoption of woman suffrage, the women began citizenship classes for themselves. They also planned a spring pageant for their children in order to keep them occupied during nonschool hours and set up a vigilance committee to watch for and report speeders. The women also established a Common Courtesy Committee to deal with neighborhood disputes and to preserve harmony. Later in the spring they hired a summer athletic director to set up boys' baseball leagues; organized rifle, bicycle, riding, nature, and bird-watching clubs; set up a weekly story hour for younger children; and organized a committee to work for the preservation of historic landmarks throughout the district. In most cases the money to fund these activities came from the Nichols Company through the community secretary.[41]

The children's pageant took place out-of-doors in June 1920, with more than one thousand children dressed in appropriate costume and dancing to the accompaniment of a full orchestra. The site was near one of the oldest trees in the district, located at Fifty-sixth Street and State Line Road. During that summer of 1920 the Women's Council helped develop baseball fields for their boys'

40. Ibid., September 1, 1919, 4, and December 15, 1919, 1.
41. Ibid., February 1, 1920, 2; April 1, 1920, 2; and May 10, 1920, 1.

leagues on land provided by Nichols at Fifty-fifth and Wornall. Additionally, they staffed two summer playground programs at Fifty-second and Fifty-eighth streets at Brookside.[42]

In December 1920, Mrs. Beach organized a somewhat different forum for dealing with what she perceived to be a major problem. She set up a Children's League in which the members were mothers, not children. The requirement for membership was the signing of a pledge to keep holiday parties to a maximum of two each week. The concern was that children were getting too many experiences too fast. In line with this concern, the league also recommended keeping children's clothes simple rather than following the latest fashions. Girls' behavior was to be strictly regulated until they reached the age for their official debut into society. The boys' behavior should also be regulated closely until they were "pretty well along in high school or go away to school, or meet some other crisis."[43]

After 1921, some of the activities were continued through the homes associations that began to be organized on the Missouri side. Other activities were dropped for three reasons: Mrs. Beach became more interested in politics with her husband, the community secretary left the company, and Nichols was selling all the houses and lots he could without any further stimulation by such public relations activities as the Women's Community Council. As the 1920s drew to a close, the building of single-family homes fell more rapidly than the overall economy. By 1930, when the country knew it was in a real depression, Nichols was cutting back where he could while keeping some activities that were less costly. The *Country Club District Bulletin* ceased publication after its October 1930 number. The only way Nichols could have continued it was to take outside advertising, which he refused to do. He used it to advertise his own company's activities, but not those of unrelated companies. Lawn contests ended in 1930. These were not costly activities, but they called for the expenditure of more on the part of residents than many would have been able to afford, so they were discontinued. Other events such as the field days and the annual flower shows were

42. Ibid., June 1, 1920, 1, and July 1, 1920, 1.
43. *Kansas City Star,* December 20, 1920, 2A.

kept alive to sustain some feeling of community activity during the worsening situation.[44]

Overall, the period of innovation by J. C. Nichols in developing a spirit of identity between his purchasers and their neighborhoods was over. Some things were continued, but few new ideas were added after 1930, for it was all the company could do to remain in business. Nichols and his staff gave most attention to the shopping centers, which continued to provide needed income. Later in the decade, Federal Housing Administration money served to stimulate some new homebuilding, but this was done in a more utilitarian manner, with little of the flair of the 1920s. The onset of the Depression thus signaled the end of an era. For Kansas City at least, this era brought together the best in residential landscape and housing design, the most complete deed restrictions, the most comprehensive homes associations, the newest ideas in shopping center design, and the most innovative array of community development activities.

J. C. Nichols went on to become involved in the founding of the Federal Housing Administration, in the mobilization effort for World War II, in the founding of the Urban Land Institute on a national scale, and in the founding of the Midwest Research Institute locally in Kansas City. Never again, however, would he put his considerable talents into the fusion of such an array of ideas as those with which he developed the Country Club District and the Country Club Plaza.[45]

44. Scrapbook 5:45–46. The job of community secretary evolved into the position of assistant secretary of homes associations. Scrapbook 4:101.

45. The presence of the shopping block in 1903 is attested to in Fawcett, "Roland Park," 190. *Baltimore American* article on May 16, 1912, 12.

10

J. C. NICHOLS

The Man and the Myth

Planned residential communities have been called "a glory of American life." They constitute "one of the most significant contributions to American urbanism as [they serve] to make real our most extravagant and lyrical fantasies." J. C. Nichols was not the first developer to use this controlled form of urban growth, but he was one of the most effective. Nichols was a great synthesizer of other people's ideas and experiences. If an idea worked somewhere else, he tried it in his own setting. Many of the design characteristics that distinguish his neighborhood planning were borrowed from his Kansas City mentor, William Rockhill Nelson, or suggested by landscape architect and urban planner George Kessler. After 1912, Nichols frequently traveled to Roland Park for ideas.[1]

Deed restrictions had a long history before the Kansas City developer began to put them into practice. Mandatory homeowner associations were not entirely new when he began the Mission Hills Homes Company in 1913. However, the degree to which he used both mechanisms to maintain direct and indirect control over the quality of development in his areas *was* unprecedented. His goal was to protect property values—both his own future values and the current values enjoyed by his residents. In building homes for sale to residents, the J. C. Nichols Company preferred conservative styles that blended harmoniously with each other. Most of the construction done by the company served to stimulate development during periods of economic slump. Nichols's major accomplishments included the extensive use of model homes in the early 1920s, often partially subsidized by materials suppliers or utility companies. The Nichols Company's most innovative work was concentrated in the area of shopping center development. Few people in the United States were thinking about retail centers that might capitalize on the

1. Stern, *Pride of Place,* 158.

automobile trade as early as World War I. The Country Club Plaza rightfully claimed the title of first regional shopping center in the country, even though it was sustained to a great degree by the apartment dwellers housed in surrounding units. Nichols's mix of neighborhood and regional shops has remained an enviable plan through the rest of the twentieth century.

From 1910 through 1930, Nichols concentrated a great deal of personal effort in developing a sense of community spirit among his buyers. The company emphasized the creation and maintenance of high-amenity features, including golf and country clubs, lawn and flower contests, and school and recreational events, as well as effective communication between the company and the residents. Nichols's Country Club District became a model for similar developments around the country in the same way Nichols had borrowed from previous planned subdivisions early in his own career. His planning and construction of residential areas had considerable impact on local Kansas City developments as well as on national patterns. The Country Club District served as a model for other developers in the immediately adjacent sections of the metropolitan area.

It should not be too surprising that a person of the stature and accomplishments of Nichols should have something of a myth evolve about his origins and work. On occasion, Nichols contributed to the formation of this myth through statements in speeches and interviews. Perhaps the most complete statement of the J. C. Nichols myth appeared in an article in the February 1939 issue of the *National Real Estate Journal,* which was devoted entirely to the Nichols Company. The fact that the magazine chose to honor the firm in this unprecedented manner illustrated the high esteem accorded Nichols nationally.[2]

The basic elements of the myth served to heighten the popular image of Nichols as a self-made man. According to the tenets of the myth, the real estate executive began with a ten-acre subdivision in 1907, a year of financial distress, with little financial backing. The initial subdivision was lacking in natural advantages, and the main thrust of the city's growth was in another direction. Downtown lay a full day's drive by horse-and-buggy with no streetcar service

2. "Portrait of a Salesman," 76.

Nichols wanted to encourage families in his neighborhoods to use as-yet-undeveloped areas near Mission Hills for recreational purposes. In this picture, a knickered patriarch surveys his children and three employees preparing to roast hot dogs at an outdoor oven erected by his company. Miller Nichols is shown reaching into the picnic basket sitting before his older sister Eleanor. Clyde, Jr., is the youngster perched atop the oven chimney with the family dog. An unidentified family group looks on. This is a most unusual pose for Nichols in that he normally spent full weekends working with his salesmen as well as every weekday. The fact that this was a posed shot for company publicity purposes probably helped assuage his guilt for not working with buyers at that moment. KC54n43.

nearby. No paved roads extended from the downtown section for many years until Nichols paved one himself. In spite of all the problems, the mythical Nichols quickly sold his original subdivision to buyers who immediately built homes. Neighborhood shops were added regularly for the convenience of the residents.[3]

As has been shown, the actual Nichols began his homebuilding enterprises in 1903 with the quite modest workmen's houses in

3. The main elements of the myth are distilled from ibid., 19–20. Hoyt, *Structure and Growth*, 119; *The J. C. Nichols Company: Seventy-Five Years*, n.p.

Kansas City, Kansas. From the beginning, he worked with financial backing. From 1903 through 1905, when he moved to Bismark Place on the Missouri side, his primary financial support came from farmers in the Olathe, Kansas, area who were friends of his father. Late in 1905 he aligned himself with grain merchants Crowell, Hall, Simonds, and Shields.

In 1905 W. R. Nelson's Rockhill District extended to Brush Creek, and large residences lay only one-half mile directly north of Nichols's first subdivision. The Kansas City Country Club had been located five blocks due west of Bismark Place since 1896. Some middle- and lower-middle-income housing had been started further south and east of Nichols's subdivision, but he placed his developments squarely in the path of movement of upper-income residences. Nelson had paved Warwick Boulevard from the downtown area into his Rockhill District and had persuaded the streetcar company to extend tracks through his land to Forty-eighth Street by 1904. The newspaperman commuted by horse-and-buggy between his home in Rockhill and his newspaper office downtown in a few minutes each day. Nelson's home was five blocks straight north across Brush Creek from Nichols's first house. When Nichols began advertising Bismark Place in the spring of 1905, customers could ride a streetcar from downtown to within a quarter mile of his first houses. It was only a quick walk across one of Nelson's picturesque stone bridges over Brush Creek and up the hill on the south side to the Nichols neighborhood. The first Nichols "shopping center" opened as a grocery store and drug store next to the streetcar tracks in 1907. The next center constructed was the one at Sixty-third and Brookside in 1919–1920, at which time the original two stores were being remodeled and enlarged. Planning and land acquisition for the Country Club Plaza commenced at the close of World War I, but it was not officially announced until 1922. The pattern of placing neighborhood shops in newly developed subdivisions did not become commonplace until the 1920s.

The Nichols myth is not an untruth in most instances. Rather, it is more of a distortion of the truth—a smoothing over here, a convenient lapse of memory there—which resulted in the creation of a portrait of the developer that heightened his personal reputation as a self-sufficient entrepreneur whenever possible. This is not a great sin. Nichols did much to build his own reputation without any enhancement being necessary. Possibly the most important thing is that he was always a better student than he was an innovator. He studied what others had done, borrowed ideas from here and there, and put them together in ways no one else had done.

The Country Club District is not so much an innovation as it is a synergistic enterprise: a bringing together of the best thinking available at the time toward the creation of a living environment second to none in the United States—for those who could afford it. By 1984 the J. C. Nichols Company had developed 8,000 acres (double the amount developed by the onset of the Great Depression) with 18,000 homes. The company had another 6,000 acres available for future residential, shopping, or office development. It was the single largest private landowner in Johnson County, Kansas, and a major landowner in undeveloped portions of eastern Jackson County, Missouri. Indeed, in something of a perpetuation of the myth, a newspaper writer said on Thanksgiving Day, 1984, "It would be hard to imagine what Kansas City would be today without the influence of the J. C. Nichols Company."[4]

Actually, without Nichols, Kansas City would be very much like it is today. The wealthy would probably still live along its extreme western edge and south of Brush Creek—there was really no other place for them to go. The subdivisions that ranged along the bluffs overlooking the Missouri valley east of downtown were the only other historic possibility, and those limited areas were almost completely filled before Nichols established himself. The southwesterly angle of the Blue River valley hemmed in high-value development on its western edge to the south of Brush Creek. However, the wealthy probably would have moved further south and west into Johnson County than is currently the case. Nichols's deed restrictions and homes associations served to stabilize property values to a remarkable degree. The social center of upper-income residences would very likely have shifted much further south and west as well. Above all, while there might have been shops built in the swampy Brush Creek valley, there would definitely not have been anything like the Plaza forming a second in-town downtown as it

4. Wenske, "Fulfilling a Vision," C-1, C-2.

does today. No one else attempted to build such a large, regional shopping complex in the Kansas City area until the inauguration of sizable strip shopping areas along Ninety-fifth Street in Johnson County during the late 1950s and early 1960s.

An additional role played by the Nichols Company was that of model for other subdividers who used several of Nichols's planning features on a smaller scale. If one looks at the 1980 census maps for the Kansas City Metropolitan Statistical Area, there is a rather clear dividing line with regard to subdivision layouts. In the areas north and east of Nelson's small Rockhill development and Nichols's much larger Country Club District, there are almost no examples of curvilinear streets that conform to the shape of natural landforms in private subdivisions. To the south and west of Nichols's developments in Jackson County, Missouri, and Johnson County, Kansas, most subdivisions are laid out using the curvilinear technique.[5]

An examination of the plat books for later subdivision development reveals that no developer on the Missouri side or in Kansas came close to subdividing the more than four thousand acres that had been developed by the Nichols Company by 1930. What appears superficially is that Nichols's competitors did attempt to copy many of his design characteristics, but on a much smaller scale. Some of the higher-income developers, working in areas immediately adjacent to Nichols, copied other details, such as the use of outdoor ornamentation at street intersections, similar building restrictions, homes association in some cases, and small neighborhood shopping centers. The trite phrase "Often imitated, never duplicated," fortunately was not used by the Nichols Company, but it is a fairly accurate description in southwest Kansas City, Missouri, and northeast Johnson County, Kansas.

A more important issue is whether Nichols's development had the effect alleged by such critics as Sam Bass Warner, Jr. Warner claimed that Nichols's projects skewed the development of the city in such a way as to make later race conflicts and class differentiation inevitable, creating "a social disaster" for the city. The pattern of de facto racial separation predated Nichols's arrival on the scene by some forty years. If any single subdivider was responsible, it would

5. U.S. Bureau of the Census, *1980 Census,* Document PHC80–1–200.

have to be the abolitionist Kersey Coates, who developed his Coates Addition and surrounding subdivisions exclusively for the wealthy (whites, by definition). He also created the Peery Place subdivision for people of much lower income to the east of downtown and gave land for a black school and black churches within its confines. Later subdividers simply followed Coates's lead, with the single exception that pressure from whites forced blacks to move further east across Troost prior to the 1880s. What has been called the "Troost Wall" of racial separation has continued to the present. Troost Avenue is no longer an absolute barrier, but it is still a potent dividing line. In 1980 not one of the census tracts west of Troost had more than 50 percent of its population made up of black citizens. Most tracts west of Troost as far south as Gregory (the southern edge of Nichols's original contiguous development in Missouri) had less than 25 percent black population. The majority of tracts south of Forty-seventh and west of Troost had less than 2 percent black population in 1980. Meanwhile, east of Troost, very few census tracts between that street and the Blue River had less than 50 percent black population. Most tracts in the area between Independence Avenue on the north and Gregory on the south had between 75 percent and 100 percent black population. It is undeniable that racial separation existed in Kansas City in the 1870s and in the 1980s.[6]

Possibly the most useful analysis of racial concentration was an unofficial census taken in 1912–1913 by the Research Bureau of the Board of Public Welfare of Kansas City, Missouri. That study revealed that in 1910 blacks comprised just under 10 percent of the total Kansas City, Missouri, population. Of the 23,566 black residents in the city at the time, a little over 20 percent lived west of Troost. A large number of these black families were actually living quite near Troost in extensions of the Belvedere Hollow section and the main black neighborhood centered around Eighteenth and Vine.[7]

The pattern was clear in 1913, just as it was clear in 1980. Whites

6. Warner, *The Urban Wilderness*, illustration captions after 222; Melissa Berg and Mary Lou Nolan, "Many Blacks Join Migration from Central City," *Kansas City Star*, April 12, 1981, 31A.

7. *Social Prospectus of Kansas City*, 9–11.

predominated west of Troost, and blacks were more numerous east of that street. The biggest change has not been movement by blacks across Troost, but south along the east side of that thoroughfare. In 1913, far fewer blacks lived south of Twenty-seventh Street and *east* of Troost than lived *west* of Troost. The Troost barrier held to a significant degree into the 1980s, but the Twenty-seventh Street barrier, which was stronger in 1910, has given way. In 1980, there are neighborhoods of 75 percent to 100 percent black population as far south as Seventy-fifth Street.[8]

More to the point in regard to Nichols neighborhoods, blacks account for less than 2 percent of the population in the census tracts that are largely or entirely covered by Nichols's restrictions and homes associations. In no case does the black population comprise more than 5 percent of the population in a given census tract. De facto segregation certainly does exist in Nichols's subdivisions. The areas immediately to the south of Nichols's territory show a slight change, but not much. From Gregory to Bannister Road between Troost and the state line, two of the census tracts had between 5 percent and 10 percent black population in 1980. The other four tracts had less than 2 percent black population, just like the Nichols areas. Furthermore, the average black population of the six tracts directly south of Nichols was less than 5 percent.[9]

One simple explanation for this pattern, besides pure racial preju- dice, is mean income. For the Jackson County portion of Kansas City, Missouri, as a whole, the mean family income in 1980 was $21,905. In the Country Club District census tracts, mean income ranged from just under $28,000 in the three tracts on the east side (one of which adjoins Troost and includes some non-Nichols areas) to a high of $62,586 in the lower Sunset Hill area (census tract 84) from Fifty-fifth to Sixty-third, State Line to Wornall. This tract had the highest mean income of any tract in the Jackson County portion of Kansas City. (See the map on p. 87 for locations of the census tracts.) With regard to median estimated housing values of owner- occupied housing in 1980, the Kansas City median was $30,700. The Nichols neighborhood with the lowest median housing value

8. Ibid., 10; Berg and Nolan, "Many Blacks," 31A.
9. U.S. Bureau of the Census, *1980 Census,* Document P-101-102.

was the Plaza area with $41,900, which had only 21 owner-occupied units out of 3,695 total units. Three east-side Nichols tracts were in the $55,000 range in estimated value. Tract 84 had a median value of $103,000, which more than tripled the city-wide median.[10]

One final, telling point is a comparison of mean income for whites and blacks. For black Kansas City families in 1980, the mean income was $17,068. For white Kansas City families in 1980, the same category showed $24,311. The lowest mean income of residents in the Country Club District was almost $28,000, or more than $10,000 per year higher than the mean income for black families. Just over 27,000 white households earned more than $25,000 in Kansas City; slightly more than 13,200 of those households were in the Country Club District.[11]

All of this statistical data would seem to confirm the Warner hypothesis concerning race and class separation. The residents of the Nichols neighborhoods, even in 1980, were among the wealthiest and best-housed groups in Kansas City. Despite open housing laws, the removal of racial restrictions, and the outlawing of "redlining" by lending institutions, race and class distinctions continue to exist.

Nichols's policies of racial exclusion obviously contributed to this situation, even though he was only following common white realtor and developer practice of the time in Kansas City. What has made the difference in Nichols's territory has been the stability of housing values. The difference in income between blacks and whites has allowed blacks to buy into white neighborhoods only when the resale value of housing stock has declined considerably.

Nichols had observed this phenomena on Quality Hill and in the old, exclusive sections of the Northeast and Hyde Park. What he had seen was not blacks buying white houses, but rooming-house landlords and businesses buying devalued residential property and putting it to other uses. The more people moved out, the more the prices of the remaining property fell. He wanted to avoid that cycle, so he instituted deed restrictions calling for certain types of houses to be built, and he went out into the neighborhoods to make sure

10. Ibid., P-235, P-269-270, H-3, H-37-38.
11. Ibid., P-293, P-312.

that the properties were being maintained over the years. The officers of the current homes associations assume this responsibility to prevent practices that would devalue their houses and those of their neighbors. Previously, the mere presence of a black family would accomplish this devaluation. It is just as important to note that there *are* a few black families in Nichols neighborhoods as it is to note that there are only a *few* black families in Nichols neighborhoods. This means that the ultimate restriction is the resale value of the property rather than racial clauses. If and when more black families achieve a financial level that allows them to do so, it may well be possible to see more black families in the Country Club District.

Sam Bass Warner proposed in *The Urban Wilderness* that the antidote to this type of class and race segregation would have been "public financing and control of land and housing development." This is another way of saying that the maintenance of high property values in the Country Club District operates to limit the number of black families who can afford to live there. Warner is correct in his assertion that public control might have accomplished such a goal, but it would have required a course of events totally at odds with what actually took place in Kansas City and in American history. For Warner's proposed solution to have worked, not only would J. C. Nichols have had to have been quite a different person, but Thomas J. Pendergast would have had to have been a reform-minded city planner as well.

It is difficult to think of Kansas City in the 1920s and 1930s without thinking of the Pendergast Machine. Tom Pendergast inherited a political arrangement from his older brother Jim in 1910, when J. C. Nichols was just beginning to sell houses and lots on the south side. Over the next twenty-five years, Tom Pendergast built that arrangement into a machine that dominated city and state politics and even spawned a president in Harry S. Truman. This was the government that would have had to direct homebuilding and subdividing to prevent racial and class distinction according to Warner's thinking.

By 1921 Tom Pendergast had a home in the Country Club District. Within ten years, he had moved his family to a $175,000 mansion on Ward Parkway. Pendergast exercised his control of city policies through City Manager H. F. McElroy, who resided in a much more modest home in the eastern portion of Nichols's sub-divisions. The mayor of Kansas City, and an implacable foe of Pendergast during part of the 1920s, was none other than A. I. Beach, husband of the indefatigable chairwoman of the Woman's Community Council of the Country Club District. These were hardly the people to accomplish the type of supervision that Warner argues would have prevented "the social disaster" caused by Nichols's development in the social fabric of Kansas City.[12]

Another issue raised by the Pendergast presence is whether Nichols worked with or against the political boss. The answer is that he worked with the machine when necessary and worked against it when he disliked the proposals of its spokesman, McElroy, or the effects of its policies. The only time Nichols stood for public office was when he was elected in 1918 to the Kansas City School Board as a Democrat. The *Star* endorsed him even though it considered him "a machine Democrat." Nichols served on the school board for eight and one-half years.[13]

One key to T. J. Pendergast's success in the domination of local Kansas City politics was money paid to his concrete company for construction contracts. This type of work lent itself to rake-offs and kickbacks. Nichols went along with this as far as the city was concerned in the early 1930s. When it came to similar "improvements" in his Country Club District, however, Nichols drew the line. He particularly did not like the concrete creek bed for Brush Creek as it passed the Plaza. City Manager McElroy got his project inserted back into a bond-issue proposal in 1933 after the measure had been dropped by the executive committee of which Nichols was a member.[14]

The breaking point between the developer who wanted Kansas City to grow even if it took cooperation with Pendergast and the machine he had formerly supported for the most part began in 1937. During that summer, trade unions were beginning to exercise their new muscle as a result of Second New Deal legislation allowing for closed shops and the like. Nichols had always run an open shop

12. Reddig, *Tom's Town*, 342, 358.
13. Scrapbook 5:31–32.
14. Reddig, *Tom's Town*, 342, 358.

with regard to his construction activities. He apparently took any effort at organization by his employees as a personal affront. At any rate, his construction crews became the target of "flying squadrons" of union members, who visited Nichols construction sites to either enlist or disperse nonunion workers.[15]

Nichols called for police protection against such tactics, but the Pendergast machine had aligned itself with the largely American Federation of Labor–affiliated unions, which were also staunchly Democratic. The machine was coming under increasing pressure from federal and Missouri investigations and needed all the allies it could get. When Nichols could not get the protection he sought, he organized a "Law and Order" campaign, which resulted in a rally of more than three thousand people in the Municipal Auditorium (built with massive amounts of Pendergast concrete) to protest the lack of police protection for law-abiding (and antiunion) citizens. Nichols made his point; gradually the workmen who had been scared off by the union organizers returned to work, and the episodes were not repeated.[16]

According to Nichols's correspondence, this was just the beginning of what he considered to be harassment by the administration of City Manager H. F. McElroy, a man with whom he had worked closely on many projects for more than twenty years. Taxes were raised on vacant land within the district. The Kansas City, Missouri, Fire Department suddenly discovered that it did not have the manpower to provide fire protection in Mission Hills, Kansas, which it had done since 1913. McElroy reversed a long-standing policy of charging the Nichols Company a single-meter rate for water delivered to the state line connections to Mission Hills. From that time, the city charged according to usage at each meter location. McElroy even threatened to raise sewer rates and to build a viaduct over the Plaza to connect the Broadway extension with Wornall Road, which would have meant that all through traffic would have to bypass the shopping area. The latter two threats gained a degree of

15. Letter from J. C. Nichols to Mrs. Raymond Lee, January 16, 1939, in company general correspondence file for 1939, J. C. Nichols Collection. See also Reddig, *Tom's Town*, 302, for confirmation of the incident.

16. Letter from J. C. Nichols to Mrs. Raymond Lee, January 16, 1939.

publicity but were never carried out. In the wake of indictments of Pendergast and former insurance commissioner O'Malley for income tax fraud in 1939, McElroy resigned his position as city manager. Five months later he died from heart disease while under indictment for some of his actions as city manager.[17]

In sum, Nichols often supported machine initiatives during the early years of its activities. He began to have doubts when the concrete bed for Brush Creek was restored to the city bond issue after he thought he had quashed it in 1933. The labor unrest and the failure of the city officials to follow his requests brought him into much more open opposition. In all of this, he presented the position taken by many business leaders during the period: when the goals of the machine coincided with his goals, he was cooperative; when the goals diverged, he was willing to go the other way.

Throughout the 1920s Nichols served as an appointed member and sometimes as chairman of the Kansas City Planning Commission. At one point during his tenure, a proposal was put forth to expand the membership of the commission to include more elected officials. Nichols argued publicly that the commission needed to be small enough to work effectively and that members like himself should serve without pay. He won the point, which resulted in the continuation of a small, rather elite Planning Commission over which he could exercise considerable influence.[18]

The Kansas City developer's civic leadership was one aspect of his life not warped through the interpretation of the Nichols myth. He served as an elected official only on the Kansas City School Board; in other areas of civic involvement, J. C. Nichols was "a joiner." At one point he belonged to twenty-eight clubs and organizations. Part of his rationale for so many memberships was to obtain the membership lists for his salesmen. The civic booster served as vice-chairman of numerous Liberty Loan Drives and Red Cross campaigns during World War I. After the war he was named vice-chairman for several of the Allied Charities (a forerunner of the United Way) annual drives. The main duty of a vice-chairman in all these drives was to raise money. Nichols appears to have done that very

17. Reddig, *Tom's Town*, 336–37.
18. *Kansas City Times*, August 27, 1919, 2.

well, partly due, no doubt, to his extensive contacts through his various club memberships. When Kansas City leaders decided to construct a memorial to the city's World War I dead, the south-side developer was called on to serve as vice-chairman (once again) of the Executive Committee and as chairman of the Location Committee, which was involved in acquiring the land for the site. Ultimately, the memorial was formed in the shape of a large obelisk with two accompanying buildings to house a small museum and meeting room. The designers surrounded these structures with extensive landscaped grounds overlooking the city's Union Station.[19]

Nichols also served as director or officer for several business groups and philanthropic organizations. In 1921 he was a director of Commerce Trust (since 1908), Kansas City Title and Trust, Businessmen's Assurance Company, and the Kansas City Real Estate Board. As a community service, he served as director and treasurer of the Kansas City Conservatory of Music, president of and a major fund-raiser for the Kansas City Art Institute, a member of the public school board, acting chairman of the Sunset Hill private school board, a director of the Provident Association, and vice-president of the Kansas City Symphony. In 1926 he was selected along with two others to serve as a trustee for the William Rockhill Nelson estate. This was a time-consuming job, and he resigned his position on the public school board to free some time. During the late 1920s this responsibility caused his greater involvement in the formation of the Nelson Art Gallery and the acquisition of many of its art works.[20]

Above all else, J. C. Nichols was a booster of Kansas City. This was not totally without self-interest, of course. If Kansas City grew in population, more people would need houses. Some of them would even need his kind of houses on his beautifully landscaped plots in his neighborhoods. The pages of the *Country Club District Bulletin,* which was distributed to all residents, landowners, and city officials, often served as a vehicle for his boosterism, as this 1923 example demonstrates:

19. *Kansas City Star,* November 20, 1921, 5A; November 2, 1919, 1A; November 23, 1919, 13A.
    20. Scrapbook 5:256; Scrapbook 8:131–32.

We believe Kansas City has a great future as a residential Mecca for many splendid families. We believe our city's cultural, educational and recreational facilities, as well as our intimate commercial relation with our trade territory, is appealing with increasing force to prominent and well-to-do families throughout our trade territory.

We believe that Kansas City's splendid growth in recent years in her school facilities, Art Institute, Conservatory of Music, Horner Institute, Symphony Orchestra, Grand Opera Company, Kansas City Theatre, Golf Clubs, Parkview Riding Academy, Speedway, splendid new ballpark, our Fall Festival, our various exhibitions and annual entertainment events are offering more and more for the real enjoyment of life.

We believe that as our city offers proper facilities and attractions as a residential center, in the same ratio desirable families will be attracted to our city.

We believe that the Country Club District is today one of the strongest proofs that life in Kansas City is worth while.

And in evidence of our belief in Kansas City, and our faith in her future growth, we pledge ourselves to continue our efforts to endeavor to make every subdivision we develop a credit to the Country Club District and to Kansas City.

J. C. Nichols seems to have enjoyed his role as city booster more than any other. Such statements as the above quotation seem to have come naturally to this Kansas farm boy who was a Phi Beta Kappa in college and held degrees from the University of Kansas and from Harvard.[21]

It is impossible to separate Nichols the builder from Nichols the booster. He did not try to do so himself. To this participant in the city-building process, building on his own land and boosting economic growth for the city and the region were all of one piece. Literally, what was good for Kansas City was good for J. C. Nichols because he then attracted the top echelon of leadership, along with many in middle management, from newly attracted industries and businesses to buy his land, live in his houses, and shop in his centers. This role became so important to Nichols that he devoted almost the last ten years of his life, during and after World War II, to

21. *CCD Bulletin*, August 1923, 1.

attracting new concerns to Kansas City. He served on the War Production Board prior to our actual involvement in the conflict. In 1944 he served as the founding chairman of the board of trustees for Midwest Research Institute, an agency dedicated to providing research services to enhance regional products and to support Kansas City–area industry.

Finally, J. C. Nichols played a role as both critic and booster in the fields of land development and homebuilding. He borrowed liberally from, and contributed to, the idea exchange that grew up around the profession of land subdivision in the early twentieth century. He significantly affected the land and building industries, particularly in the years between 1912 and 1930. Nichols's favorite medium was public address. A study of the primary trade journal for realtors, the *National Real Estate Journal,* from 1912 through 1930 reveals that no other realtor, subdivider, or developer had more speeches by him or articles about him in that publication. William Harmon, who started the modern subdivision movement with time payments in the 1880s, addressed the National Association of Real Estate Boards (NAREB) conventions in 1916 and 1924, but Nichols had major addresses before the group in 1912, 1916, 1924, and on into the 1930s. In 1912 he gave identical speeches calling for higher standards in land development work to the NAREB and to the American Civic Association (ACA), a national group that advocated park expansion in particular and good city planning in general. Nichols later served as national vice-president of the ACA. In 1922 he represented the group at the English Town Planning Conference.[22]

On May 26, 1926, President Calvin Coolidge nominated Nichols to serve on the National Capital Park and Planning Commission. Senator Arthur Capper of Topeka supported the Kansas native's initial appointment with this comment: "Mr. Nichols is one of few men who is a great builder and developer and who at the same time gives full weight to the artistic side of city planning." The Kansas City developer was reappointed by Presidents Hoover and Roosevelt. Nichols was forced to submit his resignation to President

22. A selected list of his speeches and articles is included in the Chronology. Scrapbook 6:129.

Truman in 1948 when his lung cancer required him to curtail many of his outside activities.[23]

In his chosen profession of land subdivision and homebuilding, Nichols served as the founding chairman of the Annual Conference of the Developers of High Class Residential Property. He was a founding director of the Home Builders' and Subdividers' Division of NAREB, which developed out of the annual conferences. Later he was a founding director of the Urban Land Institute (1944) and the founding chairman of the Community Builders' Council within the institute. He wrote two articles for the Land Institute's series of technical papers.[24]

From all of this, it would seem probable that Nichols has been the most published, and the most honored, land subdivider in American history. His acceptance on a national level may have been even greater than in his own scene of activity in Kansas City. At any rate, his ideas found their way into hundreds and possibly thousands of subdivisions across the United States. Nichols put land development ideas together in a more complete package than anyone else of his era. Few of the ideas, beyond the creation of a court-accepted formula for self-perpetuating restrictions, were new or radically different. He achieved results that went beyond the scope of other subdividers prior to the onset of the Great Depression.

His carefully planned and protected residential sections have lasted and retained value, as he hoped they would. They form an important part of the built landscape and social framework of the city. Of even more importance nationally, the Country Club Plaza has formed a lasting tribute to the creativity of J. C. Nichols. In fact, the Plaza is his legacy to the United States—the first regional shopping plaza designed for automobile traffic. After the creation of the Spanish-style consumers' paradise, downtown Kansas City and downtowns across the nation would never be the same.

Nichols's work is easier to evaluate than Nichols the man. Because so much of his correspondence was destroyed, it is necessary to view him in the few candid glimpses that are available. To the

23. Scrapbook 8:163; *Kansas City Star,* June 13, 1926, 7A.
24. Nichols, "Mistakes We Have Made in Community Development" and "Mistakes We Have Made in Shopping Center Development."

J. C. Nichols, about 1945, with telephone in one hand and lighted cigarette in the other. Nichols continued to influence the growth and development of southwest Kansas City, Missouri, and northwest Johnson County, Kansas, until the last few months before his death in 1950. The telephone was a major tool in his land and house sales as well as his city promotional work. Early in his life when there were competing local telephone companies, he had lines on each in order not to miss a sale. The cigarette was part of his character until the diagnosis of his ultimately fatal case of lung cancer. The man seldom slackened his pace except when he left Kansas City on infrequent two- and three-month fact-finding trips to the East Coast, Europe, Spain, or South America. KC54n56.

other developers in the World War I era conferences on subdivisions, Nichols came across as the man who wanted to be the leader even though he was not yet forty years old. He attempted to sway their thinking on a host of issues. With regard to subdivision design and business management, others generally agreed with his positions. When it came to branching out into commercial development or selling residences to Jews, Nichols's ideas did not carry the day. To his credit, he went ahead anyway.

Jesse Clyde Nichols knew what he wanted to do relatively early in his business career: his goal was to build permanently stable residential neighborhoods. That had not been done elsewhere in Kansas City, and such protected and stable subdivisions were rare across the United States as the nation's cities grew with unprecedented rapidity. He added to his vision of long-lived neighborhoods the proposition of furnishing residents with high-value, permanently attractive shopping centers. To a degree unparalleled in scope elsewhere in the country, Nichols achieved his goal. This single-mindedness of purpose and unwavering devotion to achievement are among the qualities of his personality that reveal him as one of the great entrepreneurs of the first half of the twentieth century.

Not everything that Nichols did was admirable. His adherence to racially restrictive deed restrictions with regard to blacks is regrettable. One could wish that he had taken the principles of land development he espoused in his 1914 article "Housing and the Real Estate Problem" and put them into practice building neighborhoods for working-class families. In these areas, Nichols was a creature of his times. He might go well beyond other developers in encouraging Catholics to buy land from him and in dropping previous unwritten restrictions against Jews, but he could not go further because others, most importantly his potential buyers, would not go further. Kansas City was not ready for such ventures as integrated housing for blacks and whites, and J. C. Nichols did not force them.[25]

On balance, Jesse Clyde Nichols changed Kansas City as he participated in evolving patterns of real estate development that have shaped the nation. As a person, he exhibited tremendous energy and singularity of purpose. He was a joiner, a booster, a philanthropist, a businessman, but the line separating commercial goals from altruism remains unclear. Actually, Nichols probably never thought about separating his business and altruistic activities. He did the latter because they served to reinforce the former. He also appears to have enjoyed public attention immensely, which meant that his public activities also served to feed his considerable personal need for acceptance.

Perhaps the secret to Nichols's success lay in the fact that he was able to enjoy doing the things that also made him wealthy. His only hobbies seem to have been the promotion of the various Kansas City activities that have been cited throughout this book. Because he so successfully combined what he enjoyed with what he wanted to do to make a living, J. C. Nichols became a city builder without parallel in his time.

25. Nichols, "Housing and the Real Estate Problem."

BIBLIOGRAPHY

Books and Articles

"Another Realtor Built Group." *National Real Estate Journal,* April 29, 1929, 24–27.

Atlas of Jackson County, Missouri. Rpt. Kansas City: Jackson County Historical Society, 1976.

Bender, Thomas. *Toward an Urban Vision: Ideas and Institutions in Nineteenth-Century America.* Baltimore: Johns Hopkins University Press, 1975.

Berg, Melissa, and Mary Lou Nolan. "Many Blacks Join Migration from Central City." *Kansas City Star,* April 12, 1981, 31A.

Boorstin, Daniel. *The Americans: The Democratic Experience.* New York: Random House, 1973.

Bouton, E. H. "Development of Roland Park, Baltimore." In *Proceedings of the 1923 Homebuilders' and Subdividers' Division Meeting.* Chicago: National Association of Real Estate Boards, 1923.

Brown, A. Theodore. *Frontier Community.* Columbia: University of Missouri Press, 1963.

Brown, A. Theodore, and Lyle Dorsett. *K. C.: A History of Kansas City, Missouri.* Boulder, Colo.: Pruett Publishing Co., 1978.

"A Brush Creek Parkway." *Kansas City Star,* January 14, 1906, 1.

Burleigh, Brown. "Ridgewood Development at Springfield." *National Real Estate Journal,* March 1, 1920, 15–18.

Case, Mason. "Outlying Business Districts." *National Real Estate Journal,* September 15, 1930, 27–30.

Case, Theodore B. *The History of Kansas City.* Syracuse, N.Y.: D. Mason and Co., 1888.

"Chart Showing Building Activities." In *City Planning, 1920–1941* (unpaginated). Kansas City: City Planning Commission, 1941.

"City Builders and Railroad Kings." *National Real Estate Journal,* July 13, 1925, 38–40.

City Planning, 1920–1941. Kansas City: City Planning Commission, 1941.

Clugston, W. G. "Kansas City: Gateway to What?" In *Our Fair City,* edited by Robert S. Allen. New York: Vanguard Press, 1947.

Coleman, Richard P., and Bernice L. Neugarten. *Social Status in the City.* San Francisco: Jossey-Bass, 1971.

Coleman, Richard P., and Lee Rainwater. *Social Standing in America: New Dimensions of Class.* New York: Basic Books, 1978.

Connell, Evan S., Jr. *Mr. Bridge.* New York: Alfred A. Knopf, Pocket Books Edition, 1977.

Country Club District Bulletin. A series of company newsletters issued on a varying schedule between 1920 and 1931. Available in bound form in the Missouri Valley Room of the Kansas City Public Library. (Cited in notes as *CCD Bulletin.*)

Davies, Pearl Janet. *Real Estate in American History.* Washington, D.C.: Public Affairs Press, 1957.

Dopking, Al. "From a Tract Beside a Hog Lot Grew His District of 10,000 Homes." *Kansas City Star,* August 2, 1947, in J. C. Nichols Clipping File, Missouri Valley Room, Kansas City Public Library.

Dorsey, William R. "Roland Park: A Modern Suburb." *Baltimore American,* May 16, 1912, 10.

Doucet, Michael J. "Urban Land Development in Nineteenth-Century North America." *Journal of Urban History* 8:3 (May 1982): 299–342.

Doucet, Michael J., and John C. Weaver. "Material Culture and the North American House: The Era of the Common Man, 1870–1920." *Journal of American History* 72:3 (December 1985): 560–87.

Douglass, Harlan P. *The Suburban Trend.* 1925. Rpt. New York: Johnson Reprint Corp., 1970.

Dyos, H. James. *Victorian Suburb: A Study of the Growth of Camberwell.* Leicester: Leicester University Press, 1961.

Ehrlich, George. *Kansas City, Missouri: An Architectural History, 1826–1976.* Kansas City: Historic Kansas City Foundation, 1979.

Eichler, Ned. *The Merchant Builders.* Cambridge, Mass.: MIT Press, 1981.

"The Entrance to Janssen Place." *Kansas City Star,* January 30, 1897, 8.

Fawcett, Weldon. "Roland Park, Baltimore County, Maryland: A Representative American Suburb." *House and Garden* 3:4 (April 1903): 180–95.

Fein, Albert. *Frederick Law Olmsted and the American Environmental Tradition.* New York: George Braziller, 1972.

"The First Hollow Tile House." *Kansas City Star,* June 8, 1913, 6C.

Fishman, Robert. *Bourgeois Utopias: The Rise and Fall of Suburbia.* New York: Basic Books, 1987.

Foley, Mary Mix. *The American House.* New York: Harper and Row, 1980.

"For South Side Acres: $75,000." *Kansas City Star,* April 23, 1908, 1.

Ford, George B. "City Planning and Unbuilt Outlying Areas." *Third Annals of Real Estate Practice.* Chicago: National Association of Real Estate Boards, 1925, 247.

Fowler, Richard. "How J. C. Nichols Reached His Turning Point." *Kansas City Star,* December 8, 1929, 6C.

———. "J. C. Nichols." In *Leaders in Our Town.* Kansas City: Kansas City Star Publishing Co., 1951.

"From the District's Archives." *Gardens, Houses and People,* July 1931, 4–5, 20.

Glaab, Charles N. *Kansas City and the Railroads: Community Policy in the Growth of a Regional Metropolis.* Madison: State Historical Society of Wisconsin, 1962.

Glaab, Charles N., and A. Theodore Brown. *A History of Urban America.* 2d ed. New York: Macmillan Publishing Co., 1976.

"Golf Courses in Subdivisions." *National Real Estate Journal,* August 23, 1926, 52–53.

Gottlieb, Manuel. *Estimates of Residential Building, United States, 1840–1939.* Washington, D.C.: National Bureau of Economic Research, Technical Paper no. 17, 1964.

"Guilford Information for Buyers, Owners and Architects" (promotional brochure). In the Roland Park Company Papers, 1921, Manuscript Collection, Olin Research Library, Cornell University.

Handlin, David P. *The American Home: Architecture and Society, 1815–1915.* Boston: Little, Brown and Company, 1979.

Harmon, W. H. "The Proper Handling of Subdivisions." *National Real Estate Journal,* August 15, 1914, 104.

Hindman, Albert H. "Old Mansions on Warwick Boulevard Recall Era of Spacious Hospitality." *Kansas City Times,* December 31, 1951.

Holt, Glen E., and Dominic A. Pacyga. *Chicago: A Historical Guide to the Neighborhoods.* Chicago: Chicago Historical Society, 1979.

"Home Building Operations of the Nichols Company." *National Real Estate Journal* 40:2 (February 1939): 60–63.

"A Home of Her Own Designing." *Kansas City Star,* July 10, 1908, 8A.

"Home with Glass Enclosed Bathtubs." *Kansas City Star,* December 21, 1913, 16B.

"Homes Around a Park." *Kansas City Star,* January 10, 1897, 1.

"The Homes Association Handbook—ULI Technical Bulletin no. 50—Highlights of the Findings and Recommendations." *Urban Land,* October 1964, 4.

"Houses Designed and Built by the J. C. Nichols Companies." *National Real Estate Journal* 40:2 (February 1939): 40–47.

Housing America. Edited by the Editors of *Fortune.* New York: Harcourt, Brace and Company, 1932.

Hoye's Kansas City Directory. On file in the Missouri Valley Room of the Kansas City, Missouri, Public Library.

Hoyt, Homer. *The Structure and Growth of Residential Neighborhoods in American Cities*. Washington, D.C.: Federal Housing Administration, 1939.

Hubbard, Henry V. "The Influence of Topography on the Layout of Land Subdivisions." *Landscape Architecture* 18:3 (April 1928): 188–99.

———. "Land Subdivision Restrictions." *Landscape Architecture* 16:2 (January 1926): 53–56.

Hubbard, Henry V., and Theodora Kimball. *An Introduction to the Study of Landscape Design*. 1917. Rev. ed. Boston: Hubbard Educational Trust, 1959.

———, and Theodora Kimball Hubbard. *Our Cities To-Day and To-Morrow: a Survey of Planning and Zoning Progress in the United States*. Cambridge: Harvard University Press, 1929.

Hubbard, Theodora Kimball. "Riverside, Illinois: A Residential Neighborhood Designed Over Sixty Years Ago." *Landscape Architecture* 21:4 (1931): 257–91.

Hurd, Richard M. *Principles of City Land Values*. New York: The Record and Guide Publishing Co., 1903; 4th ed., 1924.

Hyde, Henry M. "Roland Park–Guilford: An Appreciation." *Gardens, Houses and People*, October 1931, 9, 20.

"Important Realty Sales of the Week." *Kansas City Star*, April 26, 1908.

"Into 1926 Apts., 1 Million." *Kansas City Star*, August 2, 1925, 1D.

J. C. Nichols Company, 75 Years: A Commemorative Publication. Kansas City: J. C. Nichols Company, 1980.

Jackson, Kenneth T. *Crabgrass Frontier: The Suburbanization of the United States*. New York: Oxford University Press, 1985.

"Joins Beauty and Business." *Kansas City Star*, April 30, 1922, 12D.

Kansas City. Kansas City: Kansas City Chapter of the American Institute of Architects, 1981.

Kansas City: A Place in Time. Kansas City: Kansas City Landmarks Commission and Historic Kansas City Foundation, 1980.

"Kansas City Country Club District." *National Real Estate Journal*, January 1920, 17.

Kansas City Directory and Reference Book for 1867–68. Quincy, Ill.: Excelsior Book Co., 1868.

"Kansas City Realtors Build 2000 Homes." *National Real Estate Journal*, December 17, 1923, 33–37.

"King Developments." *National Real Estate Journal*, December 6, 1920, 19–21.

Kinkead, Paul. "This Is the Town That Jess Built." *Liberty Magazine*, April

16, 1927. In J. C. Nichols Clippings File, Missouri Valley Room, Kansas City Public Library.

Kintrea, Frank. "Tuxedo Park." *American Heritage* 29:5 (August-September 1978): 70–77.

Kissell, H. S. "Community Features for Subdivisions." In *Annals of Real Estate Practice*, 124–37. Chicago: National Association of Real Estate Boards, 1925.

"A Kitchen at the Front of the House." *Kansas City Star*, January 12, 1913, 9C.

"Lake Forest: The Beautiful Suburb of Chicago." *House and Garden* 5:6 (June 1904): 265–75.

Lefcoe, George. *Land Development Law: Cases and Materials*. Indianapolis: Bobbs-Merrill, 1966.

Lubove, Roy. "The Urbanization Process: An Approach to Historical Research." *Journal of the American Institute of Planners*, January 1967, 33–39. Rpt. in *American Urban History: An Interpretive Reader with Commentaries*, edited by Alexander B. Callow, Jr., 660–71. 2d ed. New York: Oxford University Press, 1973.

McMichael, Stanley. *Real Estate Subdivision*. New York: Prentice-Hall, 1949.

Mannheim, Ernest. *Kansas City and Its Neighborhoods: Facts and Figures*. Kansas City: Kansas City Council of Churches and Department of Sociology of the University of Kansas City, 1943.

Manon, Calvin. "Street Cars Have a Long and Varied History in Kansas City." *Kansas City Times*, June 18, 1957, 28.

Mayer, Harold M., and Richard C. Wade. *Chicago: Growth of a Metropolis*. Chicago: University of Chicago Press, 1969.

Mayer, Martin. *The Builders: Houses, People, Neighborhoods, Governments, Money*. New York: W. W. Norton and Co., 1978.

"Metropolitan Kansas City Living, Missouri and Kansas." Promotional pamphlet of the J. C. Nichols Company, n.d.

Miller, W. H. *The History of Kansas City, Together with a Sketch of the Commercial Resources of the Country with Which It Is Surrounded*. Kansas City: Birdsall and Miller, 1881.

"Millions in New Shops." *Kansas City Star*, April 30, 1922, 12D.

"Model Business Center." *National Real Estate Journal*, December 22, 1930, 35–36.

Monchow, Helen C. "Finding a Base-Year for the Study of Urban Problems." *Journal of Land and Public Utility Economics*, August 1929, 313.

———. *Seventy Years of Real Estate Subdividing in the Region of Chicago*. Evanston and Chicago: Northwestern University Press, 1939.

———. *The Use of Deed Restrictions in Subdivision Development*. Chicago: The Institute for Research in Land Economics and Public Utilities, 1928.

"More KATY Deeds Filed." *Kansas City Star,* December 10, 1905, 5.

"Nehemiah Holmes: Father of K. C. Street Car System." *Kansas City Journal,* April 16, 1922; found in Street Railways vertical file, Missouri Valley Room, Kansas City Public Library.

"New City . . . Planned for 1960 . . . and After: Palos Verdes Estates." *National Real Estate Journal,* April 15, 1929, 64– 65, 68.

"New Home of Charles Opel." *Kansas City Star,* December 6, 1914, 16A.

Nichols, J. C. "City Planning." *National Real Estate Journal,* May 15, 1916, 277–80.

———. "City Planning and Real Estate Development." *Landscape Architecture* 7:1 (October 1916): 27–35.

———. "Country Club District Upholds American Traditions." *Country Club District Bulletin,* April 1930, 1.

———. "A Developer's View of Deed Restrictions." *Journal of Land and Public Utility Economics* 5:2 (May 1929): 132–42.

———. "The Development of Outlying Shopping Centers." In *Planning Problems of Town, City and Rural Areas,* 23–24. Philadelphia: William Fell Co., 1929.

———. "Financial Effect of Good Planning in Land Subdivision." In *Proceedings of the Eighth Annual National Conference on City Planning* (Cleveland, Ohio, June 5–7, 1916), 91–106; discussion follows on 106–18. New York: National Conference on City Planning, 1916.

———. "Home Building and Subdividing Department." *National Real Estate Journal,* August 27, 1923, 28.

———. "Housing and the Real Estate Problem." *Annals of the American Academy of Political and Social Science* 51 (January 1914): 132–39.

———. "Mistakes We Have Made in Community Development." *ULI Technical Bulletin No. 1,* March 1945, 3.

———. "Mistakes We Have Made in Shopping Center Development." *ULI Technical Bulletin No. 4,* June 1945.

———. "The Planning and Control of Outlying Shopping Centers." *Journal of Land and Public Utility Economics* 2:1 (January 1926): 17–22.

———. *Real Estate Subdivisions: The Best Manner of Handling Them.* Washington, D.C.: American Civic Association, 1912.

———. "Realty as a Profession." *Kansas City Star,* January 29, 1937, 7.

———. "Suburban Subdivisions with Community Features." In *Annals of Real Estate Practice,* 10–20. Chicago: National Association of Real Estate Boards, 1924.

———. "When You Buy a Home Site, You Make an Investment; Try to

Make It a Safe One." *Good Housekeeping,* February 1923, 38–39, 172–76.

———. "Zoning." *National Real Estate Journal,* October 10, 1924, 38.

"The Nichols Organization and Its Activities." *National Real Estate Journal* 40:2 (February 1939): 70–72, 95.

"The Outlying Apartment Hotel as a New Development in Urban Housing." *National Real Estate Journal,* December 10, 1928, 32–36.

"Park Plans for South Side." *Kansas City Star,* January 16, 1910, 2A.

Peterson, Karl, Jr. "Color and Romance in History of Cable Cars." *Kansas City Star,* June 4, 1950, 2d section, 16.

"Planning and Management of Nichols Shopping Centers." *National Real Estate Journal* 40:2 (February 1939): 50–51.

"Portrait of a Salesman." *National Real Estate Journal* 40:2 (February 1939): 19–23, 76.

Price, Edward T. "The Matter of Housing: Notes on the Longevity of American Dwellings." *Landscape,* Winter 1955, 31–36.

"Problems in Designing Houses for Today's Buyers." *National Real Estate Journal* 40:2 (February 1939): 66.

Proceedings of the Eighth Annual National Conference on City Planning. Cleveland, Ohio, June 5–7, 1916. New York: National Conference on City Planning, 1916.

Proceedings of the 1923 Homebuilders' and Subdividers' Division Meeting. Chicago: National Association of Real Estate Boards, 1923.

Proceedings of the 1924 Homebuilders' and Subdividers' Division Meeting. Chicago: National Association of Real Estate Boards, 1924.

"Proposal for a Brush Creek Parkway." *Kansas City Star,* January 14, 1906, 1.

"Real Estate Transfers." *Kansas City Star,* August 9, 1908, 12A.

Reddig, William. *Tom's Town: Kansas City and the Pendergast Legend.* 1947. Reprint, with foreword by Charles N. Glaab. Columbia: University of Missouri Press, 1986.

Reed, Homer. *The Science of Real-Estate and Mortgage Investment.* Kansas City: Hudson-Kimberly Publishing Co., 1899.

Report of the Board of Commissioners of Parks and Boulevards. Kansas City: Board of Commissioners of Parks and Boulevards, 1893.

"Representative Real Estate Sales." *Kansas City Star,* July 16, 1905, 13.

"Restrictions Create Values in Country Club District." *National Real Estate Journal* 40:2 (February 1939): 37–39.

"Rich Chapter of the City's History in Evolution of the Street Car." *Kansas City Times,* June 8, 1937, page D, Microfilm Roll 59, NSA Collection, Missouri Valley Room, Kansas City Public Library.

Riddle, Don. "Homes to Last for All Time: The Story of Houston's River Oaks." *National Real Estate Journal,* March 4, 1929, 21, 24.

Robinson, Charles Mumford. *City Planning, with Special Reference to the Planning of Streets and Lots.* New York: G. P. Putnam's Sons, 1916.

"Rockhill District in Kansas City." *National Real Estate Journal,* March 29, 1920, 13–15.

Schauffler, E. R. "This Was Quality Hill in the Dollar Gold Piece Days." *Kansas City Star,* February 7, 1943, C1.

Schirmer, Sherry Lamb, and Richard D. McKinzie. *At the River's Bend: An Illustrated History of Kansas City, Independence and Jackson County.* Woodland Hills, Calif.: Windsor Publications, 1982.

Schmitt, Peter J. *Back to Nature: The Arcadian Myth in Urban America.* New York: Oxford University Press, 1969.

Scott, Mel. *American City Planning.* Berkeley: University of California Press, 1969.

Shoppell, R. W., et al. *Turn-of-the-Century Houses, Cottages, and Villas: Floor Plans and Illustrations of 118 Homes from Shoppell's Catalogs.* New York: Dover Publications, 1983.

Simmons, Fred. "Kansas City's Largest Home, a Fabulous Mansion, To Be Sold by Auction." *Kansas City Star,* January 31, 1951, 1A, 29A.

Social Prospectus of Kansas City, Missouri. Kansas City: Research Bureau of the Board of Public Welfare, 1913.

"Some Information About Your Homes Association." Pamphlet published by the Homes Associations of Country Club District Public Relations Committee, n.d.

"South Side Acres Sold." *Kansas City Star,* April 21, 1908, 1.

Spear, Allan H. *Black Chicago: The Making of a Negro Ghetto.* Chicago: University of Chicago Press, 1967.

Stern, Robert A. M. *Pride of Place: Building the American Dream.* Boston: Houghton Mifflin, 1986.

———, editor. *The Anglo-American Suburb.* London: Architectural Design, 1981.

Stoebuck, William B. "Running Covenants: An Analytical Primer." *Washington Law Review* 52 (1977): 861–921.

Streighthoff, Frank H. *The Distribution of Incomes in the United States.* New York: Columbia University Press, 1912.

Swift, Samuel. "Community Life in Tuxedo." *House and Garden* 8:2 (August 1905): 60–71.

———. "Llewellyn Park, West Orange, Essex Co., New Jersey: The First American Suburban Community." *House and Garden* 3:6 (June 1903): 327–35.

Timmons, Clark. "Why the Subdivider." *National Real Estate Journal*, January 18, 1929, 60.

Tunnard, Christopher. *The City of Man*. 2d ed. New York: Charles Scribner's Sons, 1970.

Twombley, Robert C. "Saving the Family: Middle Class Attraction to Wright's Prairie House, 1901–1909." *American Quarterly* 27:1 (March 1975): 57–72.

Tygiel, Jules. "Housing in Late Nineteenth-Century American Cities." *Historical Methods* 12:2 (Spring 1979): 84–97.

Van Brunt, Henry. "City Developed 'Courts' and 'Places' in the 1880s." *Kansas City Star*, April 4, 1955.

———. "Early Farm at Linwood and Troost Is Now 'Crossroads of Nation.'" *Kansas City Star*, November 2, 1947, real estate section.

———. "Elegance of Old Quality Hill Lives in Shadows of Progress." *Kansas City Star*, March 15, 1953, 4E, 9E.

"A Villa of Hollow Tile." *Kansas City Star*, June 7, 1914, 14B.

Wade, Richard C. "Urban Life in Western America, 1790–1830." *American Historical Review* 64:1 (October 1958): 14–30.

Walker, Lester. *American Shelter: An Illustrated Encyclopedia of the American Home*. Woodstock, N.Y.: Overlook Press, 1981.

Warner, Sam Bass, Jr. *The Private City: Philadelphia in Three Periods of Its Growth*. Philadelphia: University of Pennsylvania Press, 1968.

———. *Streetcar Suburbs: The Process of Growth in Boston, 1870–1900*. 1962. Rpt. New York: Atheneum, 1974.

———. *The Urban Wilderness: A History of the American City*. New York: Harper and Row, 1972.

Weiss, Marc A. *The Rise of the Community Builders: The American Real Estate Industry and Urban Land Planning*. New York: Columbia University Press, 1987.

Wenske, Paul. "Fulfilling a Vision: The J. C. Nichols Company; A Family's Vision Helps Shape a City." *Kansas City Times*, November 22, 1984, C1–C7.

Where These Rocky Bluffs Meet: Including the Story of the Kansas City Ten-Year Plan. Kansas City, Mo.: Chamber of Commerce, 1938.

White, Ann. "Old Hyde Park Was a Child's Wonderland." *Kansas City Star*, August 15, 1957.

Williamson, Joel, editor. *The Origins of Segregation*. Lexington, Mass.: D. C. Heath and Company, 1968.

Wilson, William H. *The City Beautiful Movement in Kansas City*. Columbia: University of Missouri Press, 1964.

Woodward, C. Vann. *The Strange Career of Jim Crow*. 3d rev. ed. New York: Oxford University Press, 1974.

Wright, Gwendolyn. *Building the Dream: A Social History of Housing in America*. New York: Pantheon Books, 1981.

———. *Moralism and the Model Home: Domestic Architecture and Cultural Conflict in Chicago: 1873–1913*. Chicago: University of Chicago Press, 1980.

Manuscript Sources, Public Records, and Dissertations

"Book of Restrictions." J. C. Nichols Investment Co., 1922, supplemented, October 1928, 37. Copy no. 0079 on file at Country Club Homes Associations offices, Kansas City, Missouri.

Coleman, Richard P. "The Kansas City Elite, 1914–1915." Unpublished memo to the Century of Leadership Project Staff, dated January 1, 1980.

———. "The Kansas City Elite, 1929–1930." Unpublished memo to the Century of Leadership Project Staff, dated early February 1980.

———. "The Kansas City Elite, 1974–1975." Unpublished memo to Century of Leadership Project Staff, dated September-October 1980.

———. Unpublished research on the history of the upper class in Kansas City from 1880 to 1980 in possession of the author.

"Declaration of Restrictions to Sagamore Hills." Filed October 19, 1937, Register of Deeds Office, Johnson County Courthouse, Olathe, Kansas, Book 22 Misc., 105.

Grantor lists for Jackson County for years 1865–1870. Microfilm, Property Records Division, Jackson County Courthouse, Kansas City, Missouri.

"History, Early (1876)." In Clippings File, Missouri Valley Room, Kansas City Public Library.

Jackson County Plat Books, Property Records Division, Jackson County Courthouse, Kansas City, Missouri. (Cited in Notes as "Plat Books.")

Landmarks Commission of Kansas City. "Nomination Form for the National Register of Historic Places." In Rockhill vertical file, Missouri Valley Room, Kansas City Public Library, n.d.

Naysmith, Clifford. "Quality Hill: The History of a Neighborhood." Missouri Valley Room Series, no. 1, Kansas City Public Library, 1962.

Nichols, J. C. General correspondence files, J. C. Nichols Collection, Western Historical Manuscript Collection, University of Missouri–Kansas City.

Nichols Company Scrapbooks. Held in the archives of the J. C. Nichols

Company, 310 Ward Parkway, Country Club Plaza, Kansas City, Missouri; microfilmed copies are available in the Western Historical Manuscript Collection, University of Missouri–Kansas City.

Nolen, John, Papers. Manuscripts and Archives Section, Olin Research Library, Cornell University, Ithaca, New York.

Proceedings of the First Annual Conference of Developers of High Class Residential Property. Meeting at Kansas City, Missouri, May 10–12, 1917. Microfilm of transcript, Manuscripts and Archives Section, Olin Research Library, Cornell University.

Proceedings of the Second Annual Conference of the Developers of High Class Residential Property. Meeting at Baltimore, Maryland, 1918. Microfilm of transcript at Olin Research Library.

Proceedings of the Third Annual Conference of Developers of High Class Residential Property. Meeting at the Tutwiler Hotel, Birmingham, Alabama, February 20–22, 1919. Microfilm of transcript at Olin Research Library.

Roland Park Company Papers. Collection no. 2828, Manuscripts and Archives Section, Olin Research Library, Cornell University.

Simon, Roger. "The Expansion of an Industrial City, Milwaukee, 1880–1910." Ph.D. diss., University of Wisconsin, 1971.

Treshadding, Ethel. "Genealogy of Jesse Clyde Nichols" (typescript). Available in J. C. Nichols Company archives.

U.S. Bureau of the Census. *1980 Census of Population and Housing: Census Tracts: Kansas City, Mo.-Kans. SMSA.* Washington, D.C., 1983.

Worley, William S. "J. C. Nichols and the Origins of the Planned Residential Community in the United States, 1903–1930." Ph.D. diss., University of Kansas, 1986. Available from University Microfilms.

Newspaper Advertisements

(Given in chronological order; all are found in the "For Sale–Real Estate" section unless otherwise noted.)

McKinney Highlands advertisement. *Kansas City Evening Star,* April 15, 1885, 4.

———. *Kansas City Journal,* June 6, 1886, classified display section.

"The Rockhill Neighborhood," display advertisement. *Kansas City Star,* February 6, 1904, 4.

Rockhill District advertisement. *Kansas City Star,* February 7, 1904, 14.

Reed, Nichols & Co. advertisements. *Kansas City Star,* April 2, 1905, 18, 2d section; April 9, 1905, 18; April 30, 1905, 19; June 5, 1905, 19;

May 28, 1905, 19; August 20, 1905, 17; March 4, 1906, 18; March 18, 1906, 15; May 18, 1906, 17. July 22, 1906, 15; October 21, 1906, 16; April 1, 1907, 11; July 14, 1907, 17B; April 26, 1908, 15C.

"Rockhill Park Home," advertisement. *Kansas City Star,* April 23, 1908, 13.

J. C. Nichols Co. display advertisements. *Kansas City Star,* April 30, 1908, 15C.

Commerce Trust advertisement. *Kansas City Star,* July 17, 1908, 14.

J. C. Nichols Co. advertisements. *Kansas City Star,* July 19, 1908, 13C; October 3, 1909, 19C; November 11, 1909, 17; March 6, 1910, 4A; April 10, 1910, 20B; April 17, 1910, 4A; October 23, 1910, 16B; January 1, 1911, 11A.

The Westmoreland Company advertisement. *Kansas City Star,* March 16, 1911, 11A.

J. C. Nichols Co. advertisements. *Kansas City Star,* March 26, 1911, 8A; April 2, 1911, 5C; April 23, 1911, 8A; July 24, 1911, 5A; July 30, 1911, 3A; September 24, 1911, 8A; October 1, 1911, 16B; October 8, 1911, 11A; October 29, 1911, 7A; March 17, 1912, 5A; September 15, 1912, 6A; April 20, 1913, 3A; June 8, 1913, 15B; June 22, 1913, 8A; July 11, 1915, 16B; July 16, 1916, 11A; September 17, 1916, 8A; October 8, 1916, 13A; July 27, 1919, 1A; May 1, 1921, 4B; June 18, 1921, 2B; May 28, 1922, 14D; May 13, 1923, 4F; August 3, 1924, 1D; April 12, 1925, 2D.

INDEX

Note: Numbers in bold refer to illustrations.

ciation, 260; residential area,
79, 84, 124, 129, 148–54;
sewers in, xvi, 108–10, 196–97
Country Club Heights subdivision, xvi, xxi, 133
Country Club Plaza, xvi, xx, xxi,
xxiii, 6, 7, 37, **119**, 209–10,
223–24, 234–35, **242**, 243–46;
architectural style, xx; Christmas lights, xxii, **38**; Merchants
Association, 260; parking,
254–55, **263**; planning and
development, 247–63; van-
dalism in, 113
Country Club Ridge subdivision,
xv, xxi, 129, 133, 173
Country Club streetcar line, 79,
268
Country Day School, xv
Country Side Extension subdivision, xiv, xxii, 127, 133
Country Side residential area, xiv,
xxii, 133
Cowherd Land Company, xiv, 181
Crestwood residential area, xix–
xxi, 113, 157, 171–72, 210
Crestwood shopping center, xx,
242, 252
Crowell, Frank, xiii, 69, 77
Curvilinear street planning, 97,
106
Cushing's Island subdivision, ME,
140

Deed restrictions, 7, 23, 28, 33–
34, 54, 70–72, **83**, 117–19,
124–26, 155; against Catholics,
148; against Jews, 148–53;
against Orientals, 149; review
and approval of architectural
plans in, 135–37
Delk, Edward Beuhler, 247, 254
Demarest, William, 149–52

Democratic party, xix, 76
Derr, Isla, xix, xx, 75
Developers of High Class Residen-
tial Property, ix, xix, 92, 148–
54, 169, 209, 232
Dickey, W. S., 198–99
Dodson "dummy" streetcar line,
xiv, 50–51, 78, 96, 164
Douglass, Harlan P., 27

E. C. White School, xv
Electrical House, 212–13, **212**
Epperson, U. S., 199

Fairway subdivision, xxv, 174, 227,
228
Fieldston residential area, xxii,
xxiii, xxv, 174
Filling stations (for autos), 232–33,
233
Fishman, Robert, 93, 137
Ford, George B., 89–90
Forest Hills Gardens residential
area, NY, 35, 123, 148–52,
205, 207, 278

Grammercy Park residential area,
New York, 158
Grant, Frank, xvii
Grasty, Charles, 29–32
Great Depression, effect on Nich-
ols, xxiii, 75, 85, 102, 114,
138–39, 153, 174, 178, 210,
224–25, 255–56, 285–86
Greenway Fields residential area,
xix
Gross, Samuel E., 13
Guy, Frank, xxii

Hall, Herbert F., xiii, 69, 74, 76–
77, 164, 198
Hampstead Gardens residential
area, xvii, xviii, 106

Hare & Hare, xvii, 94, 106
Harmon, W. E., 19–20
Harsch, Paul, 91, 151
Highland Park, TX, shopping center, 245
Hill, Dr. A. Ross, 114
Homebuilders' and Subdividers' Division of NAREB, 92, 94
Homebuilding boom of 1920s, 221–22
Homebuilding industry and financing, 4, 5, 11–12, 14, 18–21, 137, 190–91, 193–94, 203–4
Homes associations, xxi, 7, 35, 71, 156–77
Home warranties, 205–6
Howard, Ebenezer, 93
Hoyt, Homer, sector theory of urban growth, 67
Hyde Park residential area, Kansas City, 52–53, 59, 85, 156, 163, 241, 268

Indian Hills Country Club, xix, 112, 270
Indian Hills residential area, xxii, 174
Interior parks within blocks, 113–14

Janssen Place residential area, 57, 59
Jarvis & Conklin, 30–31, 52–53, 268
Jemison, Robert, ix, 91, 151, 279–80
Jobes, A. C., xvii, 81–82
Jones, A. R., xx, 210–11, **211**

Kansas City, KS, xiii
Kansas City, MO, banking crisis in, xxiv; early land subdivision in,

46–48, 95, 97; founding and growth to 1905, 39–62; parks and boulevards movement, 55–57, 80, 95–96; population, 42–43, 46, 49; racial segregation in, 147, 292–96; railroad development in, 45–46; real estate boom in, 29, 53–55, 111; real estate business in, 65–66; school board, xviii, xix; streetcar line development in, 49–51; ten-year plan bond election, xxiv, 91
Kansas City Board of Trade, xiv
Kansas City Country Club, xvii, xix, xxii, 6, 67–69, 74, 111–12, 114, 163–64, 268–71
Keith, C. S., residence, xvi, 199–200, **200**
Kemper, William T., 76–77, 101
Kessler, George, 31, 34, 53, 56, 70, 79–80, 93–94, 96, 187
King, A. J., 181
Kissell, Harry, 150, 175, 271, 278

Lake Forest, IL, residential area, 24–25, 271
Lake Hiwassee, xxiii, 113
Landscape architects, in residential area design, 22, 31–32, 70
Land subdivision process, 3–5, 11–14, 17–18
Law, George F., xvi
Leicester Square residential area, London, 158
Levittown, NY, residential area, 229–30, 261–62
Llewellyn Park, NJ, residential area, 6, 22–24, 53, 158–59
Long, R. A., 53–54
Loose Park, xxii, 114, 170
Louisburg Square, Boston, residential area, 53, 158–59